Thackray's 2010 Investor's Guide

THACKRAY'S
2010
INVESTOR'S
GUIDE

Brooke Thackray MBA, CIM, CFP

Published in 2009 by: MountAlpha Media:

alphamountain.com

ISBN13: 978-0-9782200-3-7

Printed and Bound by Webcom
10 9 8 7 6 5 4 3 2 1

To my wife Jane

Acknowledgements

This book is the product of many years of research and could not have been written without the help of many people. I would like to thank my wife, Jane Steer-Thackray, and my children Justin, Megan, Carly and Madeleine, for the help they have given me and their patience during the many hours that I have devoted to writing this book. I would also like to thank the proofreaders and editors, Amanda ODonnell and Jane Stiegler. Special mention goes to Jane for the countless hours she spent helping with writing, formatting and editing. This book could not have been written without her help. In addition I would like to thank Amanda Gorski, Nancy Gorski and Harsh Shah for their help with computer programming.

Special mention goes to Muhammed Faizan who put in countless hours writing and perfecting many of the computer programs that were used to develop the investment strategies in this book. He has a very strong ability to see the bigger picture and develop effecient code to meet the necessary investment requirements. He also played an active role in suggesting and developing creative solutions. Muhammed's belief that anything can be accomplished was greatly appreciated.

INTRODUCTION

THACKRAY'S 2010 INVESTOR'S GUIDE

You can choose great companies to invest in and still underperform the market. Unless you are in the market at the right time and in the best sectors, your investment expertise can be all for naught.

Successful investors know when they should be in the market. Very successful investors know when they should be in the market, and the best sectors in which to invest. *Thackray's 2010 Investor's Guide* is designed to provide investors with the knowledge of when and what to buy, and when to sell.

The goal of this book is to help investors capture extra profits by taking advantage of the seasonal trends in the markets. This book is straightforward. There are no complicated rules and there are no complex algorithms. The strategies put forward are intuitive and easy to understand.

It does not matter if you are a short-term or long-term investor, this book can be used to help establish entry and exit points. For the short-term investor, specific periods are identified that can provide profitable opportunities. For the long-term investor best buy dates are identified to launch new investments on a sound footing.

The stock market has its seasonal rhythms. Historically, the broad markets, such as the S&P 500, have a seasonal trend of outperforming during certain times of the year. Likewise, different sectors of the market have their own seasonal trends of outperformance. When oil stocks tend to do well in the springtime before "driving season," health care stocks tend to underperform the market. When utilities do well in the summertime, industrials do not. With different markets and different sectors having a tendency to outperform at different times of the year, there is always a place to invest.

Until recently, investors did not have access to the information necessary to analyze and create sector strategies. In recent years there have been a great number of sector Exchange Traded Funds (ETFs) and sector indexes introduced into the market. For the first time, investors are now able to easily implement a sector rotation strategy. This book provides a seasonal road map of what sectors tend to do well at different times of the year. It is a first of its kind, revealing new sector-based strategies that have never before been published.

In terms of market timing there are ample strategies in this book to help determine the times when equities should be over or underweight. During a favorable time for the market, investments can be purchased to overweight equities relative to their target weight in a portfolio (staying within risk tolerances). During an unfavorable time, investments can be sold to underweight equities relative to their target.

A large part of the book is devoted to sector seasonality – the underpinnings for a sector rotation strategy. The most practical rotation strategy is to create a core part of a portfolio that represents the broad market and then set aside an allocation to be rotated between favored sectors from one time period to the next.

It does not makes sense to apply any investment strategy only once with a large investment. Seasonal strategies are no exception. The best way to apply an investment strategy is to use a disciplined methodology that allows for diversification and a large enough number of investments to help remove the anomalies of the market. This reduces risk and increases the probability of a long term gain.

Following the specific buy and sell dates put forth in this book would have netted an investor large, above market returns. To "turbo-charge" gains, an investor can combine seasonality with technical analysis. As the seasonal periods are never exactly the same, technical analysis can help investors capture the extra gains when a sector turns up early, or momentum extends the trend.

IMPORTANT:
The beginning date of every strategy period in this book represents a full day in the market; therefore, investors should buy at the end of the preceding market day, i.e. The Biotech Summer Solstice June 23rd to September 13th, would require an investor to enter the market before the closing bell on June 22nd.

What is Seasonal Investing?

In order to properly understand seasonal investing in the stock market, it is important to look briefly at its evolution. It may surprise investors to know that seasonal investing at the broad market level, i.e. Dow Jones or S&P 500, has been around for a long time. The initial seasonal strategies were written by Fields (1931, 1934) and Watchel (1942), who focused on the *January Effect*. Coincidentally, this strategy is still bantered about in the press every year.

Yale Yirsch Senior has been largely responsible for the next stage in the evolution, producing the Stock Trader's Almanac over the last forty years. This publication focuses on broad market trends such as the best six months of the year and tendencies of the market to do well depending on the political party in power and holiday trades.

Recently, Brooke Thackray and Bruce Lindsay (1999) wrote, Time In Time Out: Outsmart the Market Using Calendar Investment Strategies. This work focused on a comprehensive analysis of the six month seasonal cycle and other shorter seasonal cycles in the broad markets such as the S&P 500.

Don Vialoux, considered the patriarch of seasonal investing in Canada, has written many articles on seasonal investing. His writings on this topic have developed a large following, via his free newsletter available at www.timingthemarket.ca.

Seasonal investing has changed over time. The focus has shifted from broad market strategies to taking advantage of sector rotation opportunities – investing in different sectors at different times of the year, depending on their seasonal strength. This has created a whole new set of investment opportunities. Rather than just being "in or out" of the market, investors can now always be invested by shifting between different sectors and asset classes, taking advantage of both up and down markets.

Definition – Seasonal investing is a method of investing in the market at the time of the year when it typically does well, or investing in a sector of the market when it typically outperforms the broad market such as the S&P 500.

The term seasonal investing is somewhat of a misnomer, and it is easy to see why some investors might believe that the discipline relates to investing based upon the seasons of the year – winter, spring, summer and autumn. Other than with agricultural commodities, generally, seasonal investment strategies only use the calendar as a reference for buy and sell dates. It is usually a specific event, i.e. Christmas sales, that occurs on a recurring annual basis that creates the opportunity.

The discipline of seasonal investing is not restricted to the stock market. It has been used successfully for a number of years in the commodities market. The opportunities in this market tend to be based upon changes in supply and/or demand that occur on a yearly basis. Most commodities, especially the agricultural commodities, tend to have cyclical supply cycles, i.e., crops are harvested only at certain times of the year. The supply bulge that occurs at the same time every year provides seasonal investors with profit opportunities. Recurring increased seasonal demand for commodities also plays a major part in providing opportunities for seasonal investors. This applies to most metals and many other commodities, whether the end-product is industrial or consumer based.

Seasonal investment strategies can be used with a lot of different types of investments. The premise is the same, outperformance during a certain period of the year based upon a repeating event in the markets or economy. In my past writings I have developed seasonal strategies that have been used successfully in the stock, commodity, bond and foreign exchange markets. Seasonal investing is still relatively new for most markets with a lot of new opportunities waiting to be discovered.

How Does Seasonal Investing Work?

Most stock market sector seasonal trends are the result of a recurring annual catalyst: an event that affects the sector positively. These events can range from a seasonal spike in demand, seasonal inventory lows, weather effects, conferences and other events. Mainstream investors very often anticipate a move in a sector and incorrectly try to take a position just before an event takes place that is supposed to drive a sector higher. A good example of this would be investors buying oil just before the cold weather sets in. Unfortunately, their efforts are usually unsuccessful as they are too late to the party and the opportunity has already passed.

By the time the anticipated event occurs, a substantial amount of investors have bought into the sector – fully pricing in the expected benefit. At this time there is little potential left in the short-term. Unless there is a strong positive surprise, the sector's outperformance tends to slowly roll over. If the event produces less than its desired result, the sector can be severely punished.

So how does the seasonal investor take advantage of this opportunity? "Be there" before the mainstream investors, and get out before they do. Seasonal investors usually enter a sector two or three months before an event is anticipated to have a positive effect on a sector and get out before the actual event takes place. In essence, seasonal investors are benefiting from the mainstream investor's tendency to "buy in" too late.

Seasonality in the markets occurs because of three major reasons: money flow, changing market analyst expectations and the *Anticipation-Realization Cycle*. First, money flows vary throughout the year and at different times of the month. Generally, money flows increase at the end of the year and into the start of the next year. This is a result of year end bonuses and tax related investments. In addition, money flows increase at month end from money managers "window dressing" their portfolios. As a result of these money flows, the months around the end of the year and the days around the end of the month, tend to have a stronger performance than the other times of the year.

Second, the analyst expectations cycle tends to push markets up at the end of the year and the beginning of the next year. Stock market analysts tend to be a positive bunch – the large investment houses pay them to be positive. They start the year with aggressive earnings for all of their favorite companies. As the year progresses, they generally back off their earnings forecast, which decreases their support for the market. After a lull in the summer and early autumn months, they start to focus on the next year with another rosy forecast. As a result, the stock market tends to rise once again at the end of the year.

Third, at the sector level, sectors of the market tend to be greatly influenced by the *Anticipation-Realization Cycle*. Although some investors may not be familiar with the term "anticipation-realization," they probably are familiar with the concept of "buy the rumor – sell the fact," or in the famous words of Lord Rothschild "Buy on the sound of the war-cannons; sell on the sound of the victory trumpets."

The *Anticipation-Realization Cycle* as it applies to human behavior has been much studied in psychology journals. In the investment world, the premise of this cycle rests on investors anticipating a positive event in the market to drive prices higher and buying in ahead of the event. When the event takes place, or is realized, upward pressure on prices decreases as there is very little impetus for further outperformance.

A good example of the *Anticipation-Realization Cycle* takes place with the "conference effect." Very often large industries have major conferences that occur at approximately the same time every year. Major companies in the industry often hold back positive announcements and product introductions to be released during the conference.

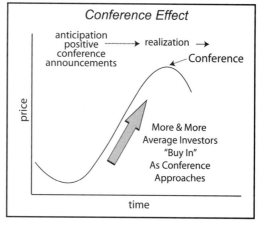

Two to three months prior to the conference, seasonal investors tend to buy into the sector. Shortly afterwards, the mainstream investors anticipate "good news" from the conference and start to buy in. As a result, prices are pushed up. Just before the conference starts, seasonal investors capture their profits by exiting their positions. As the conference unfolds, company announcements are made (realized), but as the potential good news has already been priced into the sector, there is little to push prices higher and the sector typically starts to rolls over.

The same *Anticipation-Realization Cycle* takes place with increased demand for oil to meet the "summer driving season", increased sales of goods at Christmas time, increased demand for gold jewellery to meet the autumn and winter demand, and many other events that tend to drive the outperformance of different sectors.

Does Seasonal Investing ALWAYS Work?

The simple answer to the above question is "No." There is not any investment system in the world that works all of the time. When following any investment system, it is probability of success that counts. It has often been said that "being correct in the markets 60% of the time will make you rich." Investors tend to forget this and become too emotionally attached to their losses. Just about every investment trading book states that investors typically fail to let their profits run and cut their losses quickly. I concur. In my many years in the investment industry, the biggest mistake that I have found with investors is not being able to cut their losses. Everyone wants to be right, that is how we have been raised. Investors feel that if they sell at a loss they have failed, and as a result, often suffer bigger losses by waiting for their position to trade at profit.

With any investment system, investors should let probability work for them. This means that investors should be able to enter and exit positions capturing both gains and losses without becoming emotionally attached to any positions. Emotional attachment clouds judgement, which leads to errors. When all of the trades are put together, the goal is for profits to be larger than losses in a way that minimizes risks and beats the market.

If we examine the winter oil stock trade, my favorite seasonal trade, we can see how probability has worked in an investor's favor. This trade is based upon the premise that at the tail end of winter, the refineries drive up demand for oil in order to produce enough gas for the approaching "driving season" that starts in the spring. As a result, oil stocks tend to increase and outperform the market (from February 25th to May 9th).

The oil stock sector, represented by the Amex Oil Index (XOI), has been very successful at this time of year, producing an average return of 8.6% and beating the S&P 500 by 6%, from 1984 to 2008. In addition it has been positive 92% of the time. Not all seasonal trades are created equal:

XOI / S&P 500 1984 to 2008			
Feb 25		positive	
to May 9	XOI	S&P 500	Diff
1984	5.6 %	1.7 %	3.9 %
1985	4.9	1.4	3.5
1986	7.7	6.0	1.7
1987	25.5	3.7	21.8
1988	5.6	-3.0	8.6
1989	8.1	6.3	1.8
1990	-0.6	5.8	-6.3
1991	6.8	4.8	2.0
1992	5.8	0.9	4.9
1993	6.3	0.3	6.0
1994	3.2	-4.7	7.9
1995	10.3	7.3	3.1
1996	2.2	-2.1	4.3
1997	4.7	1.8	2.9
1998	9.8	7.5	2.3
1999	35.4	7.3	28.1
2000	22.2	4.3	17.9
2001	10.2	0.8	9.4
2002	5.3	-1.5	6.9
2003	5.7	12.1	-6.4
2004	4.0	-3.5	7.5
2005	-1.0	-1.8	0.8
2006	9.4	2.8	6.6
2007	10.1	4.2	5.8
2008	7.6	2.6	5.0
Avg	8.6 %	2.6 %	6.0 %

this strategic sector trade is at the top of the list. Investors should always evaluate the strength of seasonal trades before applying them to their own portfolios. Above is a table of the results.

If an investor started using the seasonal investment discipline in 1984 and chose to invest in the winter-oil trade, they would have been very happy with the results. If they had chosen almost any other year in the last 25 years, they would have also been very pleased with the results. The exception to this occurs in the years 1990 and 2005. These years produced nominal losses of 0.6% and 1.0%, respectively.

Does this mean the system does not work? No. An investor can start any methodology of trading at the "wrong time," and be unsuccessful for a particular trade. In fact, if the investor started in 1990 and had given up in the same year, they would have missed the following successful twelve years. They would have also missed all of the other successful seasonal trades that took place in the year. Investors have to remember that it is the final score that counts, after all of the gains have been weighed against the losses.

In practical terms, investors should not put all of their investment strategies in one basket. If one or two large investments were made based upon seasonal strategies, it is possible that the seasonal methodology might be inappropriately evaluated and its use discontinued. A much more prudent strategy is to use a larger number of strategic seasonal investments with smaller investments. The end result will be to put the seasonal probability to work with a much greater chance of success.

Measuring Seasonal Performance

How do you determine if a seasonal strategy has been successful? Many people feel that ten years of data is a good sample size, others feel that fifteen years is better, and yet others feel that the more data the better. I tend to fall into the camp that, if possible, it is best to use fifteen or twenty years of data for sectors and more data for the broad markets, such as the S&P 500. Although the most recent data in almost any analytical framework is the most relevant, it is important to get enough data to reflect a sector's performance across different economic conditions. Given that historically the economy has performed on an eight year cycle, four years of expansion and then four years of contraction, using a short data set does not provide for enough exposure to different economic conditions.

A data set that is too long can run into the problem of older data having too much of an influence on the numbers when fundamental factors affecting a sector have changed. It is important to look at trends over time and assess if there has been a change that should be considered in determining the dates for a seasonal cycle. Each sector should be judged on its own merit. The analysis tables in this book illustrate the performance level for each year in order to provide the opportunity for readers to determine any relevant changes.

In order to determine if a seasonal strategy is effective there are two possible benchmarks, absolute and relative performance. Absolute performance measures if a profit is made and relative performance measures the performance of a sector in relationship to a major market. Both measurements have their merits and depending on your investment style, one measurement may be more valuable than another. This book provides both sets of measurement in tables and graphs.

It is not just the average percent gain of a sector over a certain time period that determines success. It is possible that one or two spectacular years of performance skew the results substantially (particularly with a small data set). The frequency of success is also very important: the higher the percentage of success the better. Also, the fewer large drawdowns the better. There is no magic number (percent success rate) per se of what constitutes a successful strategy. The success rate should be above fifty percent, otherwise it would be better to just invest in the broad market. Ideally speaking a strategy should have a high percentage success rate on both an absolute and relative basis. Some strategies are stronger than others, but that does not mean that the weaker strategies should not be used. Prudence should be used in determining the ideal portfolio allocation.

Illustrating the strength of a sector's seasonal performance can be accomplished through either an absolute yearly average performance graph, or a relative yearly average performance graph. The absolute graph shows the average yearly cumulative gain for a set number of years. It lets a reader visually identify the strong periods during the year. The relative graph shows the average yearly cumulative gain for the sector relative to the benchmark index.

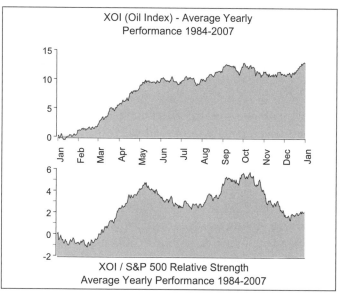

Both graphs are useful in determining the strength of a particular seasonal strategy. In the above diagram, the top graph illustrates the average year for the XOI (Oil Index) from 1984 to 2007. Essentially it illustrates the cumulative average gain if an investment were made in the index. The steep rising line starting in January/February shows the overall price rise that typically occurs in this sector at this time of year. In May the line flattens out and then rises very modestly starting in July.

The bottom graph is a ratio graph, illustrating the strength of the XOI Index relative to the S&P 500. It is derived by dividing the average year of the XOI by the average year of the S&P 500. When the line in the graph is rising, the XOI is outperforming the S&P 500, and vise versa when it is declining. This is an important graph and should be used in considering seasonal investments because the S&P 500 is a viable alternative to the energy sector. If both markets are increasing, but the S&P 500 is increasing at a faster rate, the S&P 500 represents a more attractive opportunity. This is particularly true when measuring the risk of a volatile sector relative to the broad market. If both investments were expected to produce the same rate of return, generally the broad market is a better investment because of its diversification.

Who Can Use Seasonal Investing?

Any investor from novice to expert, from short-term trader to long-term investor can benefit from using seasonal analysis. Seasonal investing is unique because it is an easy to understand system that can be used by itself or as a complement to another investment discipline. For the novice it provides an easy to follow strategy that makes intuitive sense. For the expert it can be used as a stand-alone system or as a complement to an existing system.

Behind the scenes money managers use seasonal analysis a lot more than they let on. I have talked to money managers who have extolled the virtues of making investments based upon seasonal trends. Because of its simplicity, they tend not to emphasize the methodology in public. They fear that the investing public will question why they are getting paid the "big bucks" if they are using such a simple system.

Seasonal investing is easily understood by all levels of investors, which allows investors to make rational decisions. This may seem obvious, but it is very common for investors to listen to a "guru of the market", be impressed and blindly follow his advice. When the advice works there is no problem. When the advice does not work investors wonder why they made the investment in the first place. When investors do not understand their investments it causes stress, bad decisions and a lack of "stick-to-it ness" with any investment discipline. Even expert investors realize the importance of understanding your investments. Michael Lynch of Fidelity Investments used to say "Never invest in any idea that you can't illustrate with a crayon." Investors do not need to go that far, but they should understand their investments.

Novice investors find seasonal strategies very easy to understand because they are intuitive. They do not have to be investing for years to understand why seasonal strategies work. They understand that an increase in demand for gold every year at the same time causes a ripple effect in the stock market pushing up gold stocks at the same time every year.

Most expert investors use information from a variety of sources in making their decisions. Even experts that primarily use fundamental analysis can benefit from using seasonal trends to get an edge in the market. Fundamental analysis is a very crude tool and provides very little in the way of timing an investment. Using seasonal trends can help with the timing of the buy and sell decisions and produce extra profit.

Seasonal investing can be used by both short-term and long-term investors, but in different ways. For short-term investors it provides a complete trade – buy and sell dates. For long-term investors it can provide a buy date for a sector of interest.

Combining Seasonal Analysis with other Investment Disciplines

Seasonal investing used by itself has historically produced above average market returns. Depending on an investor's particular style, it can be combined with one of the other three investment disciplines: fundamental, quantitative and technical analysis. There are two basic ways to combine seasonal analysis with other investment methodologies – as the primary or secondary method. If it is used as a primary method, seasonally strong time periods are established for a number of sectors and then appropriate sectors are chosen based upon fundamental, quantitative or technical screens. If it is used as a secondary method, sector selections are first made based upon one of three methods and then final sectors are chosen based upon which ones are in their seasonally strong period.

Technical analysis is an ideal mate for seasonal analysis. Unlike fundamental and quantitative analysis, which are very blunt timing tools at best, seasonal and technical analysis can provide specific trigger points to buy and sell. The combination can turbo-charge investment strategies, adding extra profits by fine-tuning entry and exit dates.

Seasonal analysis provides both buy and sell dates. Although a sector in the market can sometimes bottom on the exact seasonal buy date, it more often bottoms a bit early or a bit late. After all, the seasonal buy date is based upon an average of historical performance. Depending on the sector, buying opportunities start to develop approximately one month before and after the seasonal buy date. Using technical analysis gives an investor the advantage of buying into a sector when it turns up early or waiting when it turns up late. Likewise, technical analysis can be used to trigger a sell signal when the market turns down before or after the sell date.

The sell decision can be extended with the help of a trailing stop-loss order. If a sector has strong momentum and the technical tools do not provide a sell signal, it is possible to let the sector "run." When a trailing stop-loss is used, a profitable sell point is established. If the price continues to run, then the selling point is raised. If, on the other hand, the price falls through the stop-loss point, the position is sold.

Global Industry Classification Standard (GICS)

Source: www.standardandpoors.com

Energy Sector - The GICS Energy Sector comprises companies whose businesses are dominated by either of the following activities: the construction or provision of oil rigs, drilling equipment and other energy related services or equipment, including seismic data collection, companies engaged in the exploration, production, marketing, refining and/or transportation of oil and gas products, coal and other consumable fuels.

Materials Sector – The GICS Materials Sector encompasses a wide range of commodity-related manufacturing industries. Included in this sector are companies that manufacture chemicals, construction materials, glass, paper, forest products and related packaging products, and metals, minerals and mining companies, including producers of steel.

Industrials Sector – The GICS Industrials Sector includes companies whose businesses are dominated by one of the following activities: the manufacture and distribution of capital goods, including aerospace & defense, construction, engineering & building products, electrical equipment and industrial machinery; the provision of commercial services and supplies including printing, employment, environmental and office services; the provision of transportation services including airlines, couriers, marine, road & rail and transportation infrastructure.

Consumer Discretionary Sector – The GICS Consumer Discretionary Sector encompasses those industries that tend to be the most sensitive to economic cycles. Its manufacturing segment includes automotive, household durable goods, textiles & apparel and leisure equipment. The services segment includes hotels, restaurants and other leisure facilities, media production and services, and consumer retailing and services.

Consumer Staples Sector – The GICS Consumer Staples Sector comprises companies whose businesses are less sensitive to economic cycles. It includes manufacturers and distributors of food, beverages and tobacco and producers of nondurable household goods and personal products. It also includes food & drug retailing companies as well as hypermarkets and consumer super centers.

Health Care Sector - The GICS Health Care Sector encompasses two main industry groups. The first includes companies who manufacture health care equipment and supplies or provide health care related services, including distributors of health care products, providers of basic health care services, and owners and operators of health care facilities and organizations. The second regroups companies primarily involved in the research, development, production and marketing of pharmaceuticals and biotechnology products.

Financials Sector - The GICS Financial Sector contains companies involved in activities such as banking, mortgage finance, consumer finance, specialized finance, investment banking and brokerage, asset management and custody, corporate lending, insurance, and financial investment, and real estate, including REITs.

Information Technology Sector - The GICS Information Technology Sector covers the following general areas: firstly, Technology Software & Services, including companies that primarily develop software in various fields such as the Internet, applications, systems, database management and/or home entertainment, and companies that provide information technology consulting and services, as well as data processing and out sourced services; secondly, Technology Hardware & Equipment, including manufacturers and distributors of communications equipment, computers & peripherals, electronic equipment and related instruments; and thirdly, Semiconductors & Semiconductor Equipment Manufacturers.

Telecommunications Services Sector - The GICS Telecommunications Services Sector contains companies that provide communications services primarily through a fixed-line, cellular, wireless, high bandwidth and/or fiber optic cable network.

Utilities Sector - The GICS Utilities Sector encompasses those companies considered electric, gas or water utilities, or companies that operate as independent producers and/or distributors of power.

Sectors of the Market

Standard & Poor's has done an excellent job in categorizing the U.S. stock market into its different parts. Although the demand for this service initially came from institutional investors, many individual investors now seek the same information. Knowing the sector breakdown in the market allows investors to see how different their portfolio is relative to the market. As a result, they are able to make conscious decisions on what parts of the stock market to overweight based upon their beliefs of which sectors will outperform. It also helps control the amount of desired risk.

Standard & Poor's uses four levels of detail in its Global Industry Classification Standard (GICS©) to categorize stock markets around the world. From the most specific, it classifies companies into sub-industries, industries, industry groups and finally economic sectors. All companies in the Standard & Poor's global family of indices are classified according to the GICS structure.

This book focuses on the U.S. market, analyzing the trends of the venerable S&P 500 index and its economic sectors and industry groups. The following diagram illustrates the index classified according to its economic sectors.

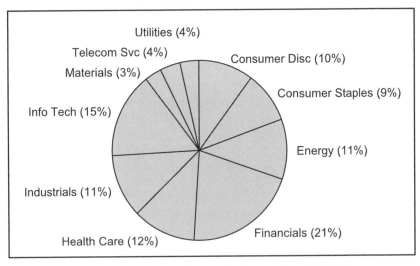

Standard and Poor's, Understanding Sectors, June 30, 2007

For more information on Standard and Poor's Global Industry Classification Standard (GICS©), refer to www.standardandpoors.com

Investment Products – Which One Is The Right One?

There are many ways to take advantage of the seasonal trends at the broad stock market and sector levels. Regardless of the investment products that you currently use, whether exchange traded funds, mutual funds, stocks or options, all can be used with the strategies in this book. Different investments offer different risk-reward relationships and return potential.

Exchange Traded Funds (ETFs)

Exchange Traded Funds (ETFs) offer the purest method of seasonal investment. The broad market ETFs are designed to track the major indices and the sector ETFs are designed to track specific sectors without using active management. Relatively new, ETFs are a great way to capture both market and sector trends. They were originally introduced into the Canadian market in 1993 to represent the Toronto stock market index. Shortly afterward they were introduced to the U.S. market and there are now hundreds of ETFs to represent almost every market, sector, style of investing and company capitalization. Originally ETFs were mainly of interest to institutional investors, but individual investors have fast realized the merits of ETF investing and have made some of the broad market ETFs the most heavily traded securities in the world.

An ETF is a single security that represents a market, such as the S&P 500; a sector of the market, such as the financial sector; or a commodity, such as gold. In the case of the S&P 500, an investor buying one security is buying all 500 stocks in the index. By investing into a financial ETF, an investor is buying the companies that make up the financial sector of the market. By investing into a gold commodity ETF, an investor is buying a security that represents the price of gold.

ETFs trade on the open market just like stocks. They have a bid and an ask, can be shorted and many are option eligible. They are a very low cost, tax efficient method of targeting specific parts of the market.

Mutual Funds

Mutual funds are a good way to combine market or sector investing with active management. In recent years, many mutual fund companies have added sector funds to accommodate an increasing appetite in this area.

As the seasonal strategies put forward in this book have a short-term nature, it is important to make sure that there are no fees (or a nominal charge) for getting into and out of a position in the market.

Stocks

Stocks provide an opportunity to make better returns than the market or sector. If the market increases during its seasonal period, some stocks will increase dramatically more than the index. Choosing one of the outperforming stocks will greatly enhance returns; choosing one of the underperforming stocks can create substantial loses. Using stocks requires increased attention to diversification and security selection.

Options

Disclaimer: Options involve risk and are not suitable for every investor. Because they are cash-settled, investors should be aware of the special risks associated with index options and should consult a tax advisor. Prior to buying or selling options, a person must receive a copy of Characteristics and Risks of Standardized Options and should thoroughly understand the risks involved in any use of options. Copies may be obtained from The Options Clearing Corporation, 440 S. LaSalle Street, Chicago, IL 60605.

Options, for more sophisticated investors, are a good tool to take advantage of both market and sector opportunities. An option position can be established with either stocks or ETFs. There are many different ways to use options for seasonal trends: establish a long position on the market during its seasonally strong period, establish a short position during its seasonally weak period, or create a spread trade to capture the superior gains of a sector over the market.

this page left intentionally blank

THACKRAY'S 2010 INVESTOR'S GUIDE

CONTENTS

JANUARY

	MONDAY	TUESDAY	WEDNESDAY
	28	**29**	**30**
WEEK 01	**4** 27	**5** 26	**6** 25
WEEK 02	**11** 20	**12** 19	**13** 18
WEEK 03	**18** 13 USA Market Closed- Martin Luther King Jr. Day	**19** 12	**20** 11
WEEK 04	**25** 6	**26** 5	**27** 4

THURSDAY	FRIDAY
31	**1** 30
7 24	**8** 23
14 17	**15** 16
21 10	**22** 9
28 3	**29** 2

FEBRUARY

M	T	W	T	F	S	S
1	2	3	4	5	6	7
8	9	10	11	12	13	14
15	16	17	18	19	20	21
22	23	24	25	26	27	28

MARCH

M	T	W	T	F	S	S
1	2	3	4	5	6	7
8	9	10	11	12	13	14
15	16	17	18	19	20	21
22	23	24	25	26	27	28
29	30	31				

APRIL

M	T	W	T	F	S	S
			1	2	3	4
5	6	7	8	9	10	11
12	13	14	15	16	17	18
19	20	21	22	23	24	25
26	27	28	29	30		

MAY

M	T	W	T	F	S	S
					1	2
3	4	5	6	7	8	9
10	11	12	13	14	15	16
17	18	19	20	21	22	23
24	25	26	27	28	29	30
31						

JANUARY SUMMARY

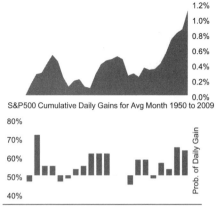

1.2%
1.0%
0.8%
0.6%
0.4%
0.2%
0.0%

S&P500 Cumulative Daily Gains for Avg Month 1950 to 2009

80%
70%
60%
50%
40%

Prob. of Daily Gain

BEST / WORST JANUARY BROAD MKTS. 2000-2009

BEST JANUARY MARKETS
♦ Nasdaq (2001) 12.2%
♦ Russell 2000 (2006) 8.9%
♦ Russell 3000 Gr (2001) 7.0%

WORST JANUARY MARKETS
♦ Russell 3000 Val (2009) -11.9%
♦ Russell 2000 (2009) -11.2%
♦ Nasdaq (2008) -9.9%

In the last decade the S&P 500 has been positive less than 50% of the time. ♦ In 2009 the markets fell hard in January as the outlook for the global economy deteriorated. ♦ The weak January correctly forecasted a negative rest of the year. ♦ Information Technology outperformed the S&P 500 during its seasonally strong period.

Index Values End of Month

	2000	2001	2002	2003	2004	2005	2006	2007	2008	2009
Dow	10,941	10,887	9,920	8,054	10,488	10,490	10,865	12,622	12,650	8,001
S&P 500	1,394	1,366	1,130	856	1,131	1,181	1,280	1,438	1,379	826
Nasdaq	3,940	2,773	1,934	1,321	2,066	2,062	2,306	2,464	2,390	1,476
TSX	8,481	9,322	7,648	6,569	8,521	9,204	11,946	13,034	13,155	8,695
Russell 1000	1,415	1,389	1,147	873	1,163	1,219	1,341	1,507	1,444	860
Russell 2000	1,235	1,263	1,201	925	1,443	1,551	1,822	1,989	1,773	1,102
Russell 3000 Growth	3,069	2,654	1,944	1,378	1,872	1,871	2,066	2,238	2,214	1,386
Russell 3000 Value	2,013	2,213	2,051	1,668	2,229	2,450	2,717	3,151	2,883	1,638

Percent Gain for January

	2000	2001	2002	2003	2004	2005	2006	2007	2008	2009
Dow	-4.8	0.9	-1.0	-3.5	0.3	-2.7	1.4	1.3	-4.6	-8.8
S&P 500	-5.1	3.5	-1.6	-2.7	1.7	-2.5	2.5	1.4	-6.1	-8.6
Nasdaq	-3.2	12.2	-0.8	-1.1	3.1	-5.2	4.6	2.0	-9.9	-6.4
TSX	0.8	4.3	-0.5	-0.7	3.7	-0.5	6.0	1.0	-4.9	-3.3
Russell 1000	-4.2	3.2	-1.4	-2.5	1.8	-2.6	2.7	1.8	-6.1	-8.3
Russell 2000	-1.7	5.1	-1.1	-2.9	4.3	-4.2	8.9	1.6	-6.9	-11.2
Russell 3000 Growth	-4.4	7.0	-1.9	-2.5	2.2	-3.5	2.4	2.5	-8.0	-5.1
Russell 3000 Value	-3.3	0.4	-0.8	-2.6	1.7	-2.1	4.1	1.1	-4.2	-11.9

January Market Avg. Performance 2000 to 2009 [1]

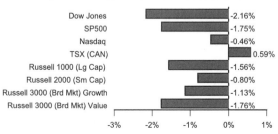

Dow Jones	-2.16%
SP500	-1.75%
Nasdaq	-0.46%
TSX (CAN)	0.59%
Russell 1000 (Lg Cap)	-1.56%
Russell 2000 (Sm Cap)	-0.80%
Russell 3000 (Brd Mkt) Growth	-1.13%
Russell 3000 (Brd Mkt) Value	-1.76%

-3% -2% -1% 0% 1%

Interest Corner Jan[2]

	Fed Funds % [3]	3 Mo. T-Bill % [4]	10 Yr % [5]	20 Yr % [6]
2009	0.25	0.24	2.87	3.86
2008	3.00	1.96	3.67	4.35
2007	5.25	5.12	4.83	5.02
2006	4.50	4.47	4.53	4.74
2005	2.25	2.51	4.14	4.64

(1) Russell Data provided by Russell (2) Federal Reserve Bank of St. Louis- end of month values (3) Target rate set by FOMC (4)(5)(6) Constant yield maturities.

JANUARY SECTOR PERFORMANCE

THACKRAY SECTOR THERMOMETER

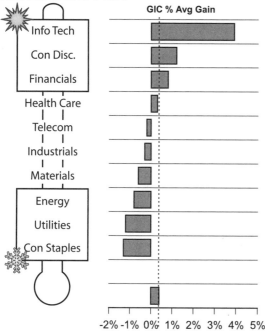

	GIC[2] % Avg Gain	Fq % Gain >S&P 500	
	SP GIC SECTOR 1990-2008[1]		
	3.9 %	79 %	Information Technology
	1.2	53	Consumer Discretionary
	0.8	63	Financials
	0.3	58	Health Care
	-0.2	53	Telecom
	-0.3	26	Industrials
	-0.6	42	Materials
	-0.8	37	Energy
	-1.2	32	Utilities
	-1.3	21	Consumer Staples
	0.4 %	N/A %	S&P 500

Hot Box - 3 Best Sectors
Info Tech ◆ Con Disc. ◆ Financials
January Portfolio

	Avg % Gain	Avg % Gain > S&P 500	Fq % Gain >S&P 500
1990-2008	2.0%	1.6%	79%
2008	-4.8%	1.3%	

Cold Box - 3 Worst Sectors
Energy ◆ Utilities ◆ Con Staples
January Portfolio

	Avg % Gain	Avg % Gain > S&P 500	Fq % Gain >S&P 500
1990-2008	-1.1%	-1.5%	32%
2008	-7.7%	-1.6%	

Commentary

◆ January has been the month for Information Technology, returning an average 3.9% and beating the S&P 500, 79% of the time from 1990 to 2008. ◆ Information Technology has been the best sector in November, the worst sector in December and then the best sector in January. Overall this has presented a good strategy for short-term investors willing to trade the volatility of the market. ◆ In 2008 the technology market dropped almost 13% in January, but the performance of the financial and consumer discretionary sectors helped the *Hot Box 3 Best Sectors* to outperform the S&P 500. ◆ The Consumer Discretionary sector is right in its seasonal sweet spot. ◆ With the major U.S. banks reporting their year-ends in January, the sector can perform well at this time of year.

(1) Sector data provided by Standard and Poors (2) GIC is short form for Global Industry Classification (3) Sub Sector data provided by Standard and Poors, except where marked by symbol.

THACKRAY SECTOR THERMOMETER PORTFOLIO (TSTP) BEATS MARKET BY (1990-2008)

14% /yr

Investing in the three sectors (S&P GIC) that have averaged the best monthly performance over the long-term, has significantly rewarded investors.

From a portfolio perspective, funds are divided up evenly amongst the three top sectors at the beginning of the starting month. At the end of the month the three sectors are sold and the proceeds are invested in the top three sectors for the next month. The process repeats itself with the accumulated funds being invested at the start of each month. Funds are accumulated month by month until the end of the time period.

For each month the same sectors are used from year to year, over the study period. For example the same three sectors would be used every January.

TSTP Avg. Gain of 21% vs. 6.9% for S&P 500

Following the Thackray Sector Thermometer Portfolio (TSTP) from 1990 to 2008 has produced an averge return of 21%, compared with the S&P 500 which produced an average return of 6.9% over the same period. To illustrate how much of an impact investing in different sectors of the market can have on a portfolio, I used the same sector selection process, for the three worst performing sectors. Investing in the three worst sectors from 1990 to 2008 has produced a surprisingly an average loss of 4% per year.

Most investors get caught up investing in a certain stock or company. There is a a lot of research proving that it is much more important to pick the appropriate asset class or even sector of the market compared to picking stocks. Comparing the best three sector performance (*Hot Box 3 Best Sectors*) to the worst three sector performance (*Cold Box 3 Worst Sectors*) shows the impact of sector selection.

> *Hot and Cold Box 3 Sector Portfolio results are posted on the monthly Sector Performance pages.*
>
> The TSTP is designed to illustrate the performance differential between the best and the worst sectors. Investors should consider their own personal risk profile in determining suitable investments.

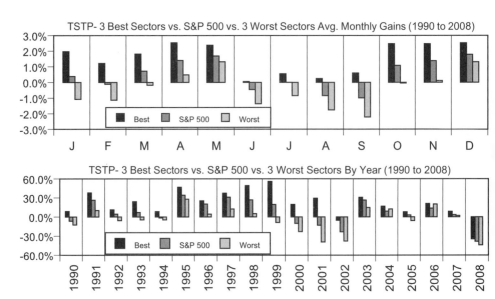

28 MONDAY

29 TUESDAY

30 WEDNESDAY

31 THURSDAY

JANUARY

M	T	W	T	F	S	S
				1	2	3
4	5	6	7	8	9	10
11	12	13	14	15	16	17
18	19	20	21	22	23	24
25	26	27	28	29	30	31

FEBRUARY

M	T	W	T	F	S	S
1	2	3	4	5	6	7
8	9	10	11	12	13	14
15	16	17	18	19	20	21
22	23	24	25	26	27	28

1 FRIDAY   001 / 364

MARCH

M	T	W	T	F	S	S
1	2	3	4	5	6	7
8	9	10	11	12	13	14
15	16	17	18	19	20	21
22	23	24	25	26	27	28
29	30	31				

30 day	Sunday January 31
60 day	Tuesday March 2
90 day	Thursday April 1
180 day	Wednesday June 30
1 year	Saturday January 1

Weekly avg closing values- except Fed Funds Rate & CAN overnight tgt rate which are weekly closing values.

PLATINUM RECORDS SOLID RESULTS
January 1st to May 31st

☑ 2009 Performance

Platinum bottomed at the beginning of its seasonal cycle and peaked at the end. It does not always happen so perfectly. In the last six months of 2008, platinum fell by more than 50%. At the beginning of this year investors realized that platinum was still in demand and bid up the price significantly over the next few months.

Most investors focus on gold in the precious metals sector, some look at silver, but few notice platinum. Platinum outperforms gold starting at the beginning of the year until the end of May.

A large portion of the platinum produced each year is consumed by catalytic converters, mainly used in the automotive sector to control exhaust emissions. Approximately 40% of platinum is used for jewellery, 37% for catalytic converters and the rest used for other industrial purposes.

7.9% extra and 83% of the time better than Gold

Platinum vs. Gold 1987 to 2009*

Jan 1 to May 31	Platinum	Gold	Positive Diff
1987 %	22.1 %	16.0 %	6.1 %
1988	13.8	-5.9	19.7
1989	-2.6	-11.8	9.2
1990	-0.9	-8.9	8.0
1991	-4.9	-6.7	1.8
1992	4.5	-4.4	9.0
1993	9.0	12.6	-3.6
1994	2.0	-1.1	3.1
1995	3.5	0.3	3.2
1996	-0.2	0.9	-1.2
1997	10.5	-6.4	16.9
1998	0.1	1.2	-1.0
1999	0.4	-6.7	7.1
2000	23.4	-6.2	29.6
2001	-0.6	-2.5	2.0
2002	14.8	18.1	-3.4
2003	7.6	4.1	3.5
2004	2.9	-5.5	8.4
2005	0.5	-4.9	5.3
2006	32.6	27.3	5.3
2007	13.7	4.3	9.4
2008	31.2	6.2	24.9
2009	29.4	12.2	17.3
Avg.	9.3 %	1.4 %	7.9 %

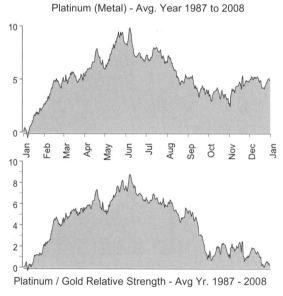

Platinum (Metal) - Avg. Year 1987 to 2008

Platinum / Gold Relative Strength - Avg Yr. 1987 - 2008

Platinum does well at the beginning of the year as it benefits from positive worldwide economic forecasts that dominate the market at the time. Strong economic forecasts translates into healthy worldwide auto production, which in turn translates into healthy platinum demand. Later in the year as economic forecasts are curtailed, platinum tends to lose its upwards momentum. In recent years, platinum has been in a strong bull market because of increasing inflation expectations, increasing jewellery usage, more stringent automotive emission requirements and supply problems in the South African mines.

Although palladium, a cheaper metal in the Platinum Group of Metals (PGM) can be substituted for platinum in auto catalyst usage, platinum is a more effective agent with diesel emissions. Currently, approximately 50% of Europe's automobiles are diesel powered. As higher fuel prices change North American driving patterns (a small fraction of autos are powered by diesel), it is expected that the automotive industry will respond by offering a greater selection of diesel powered autos. This should help increase overall platinum demand.

Platinum data based upon Bloomberg closing prices & Gold data based upon London PM price.

4 MONDAY	004 / 361		**5** TUESDAY	005 / 360

Market Indices & Rates
Weekly Values*

Stock Markets	2008	2009
Dow	13,041	8,741
S&P500	1,444	899
Nasdaq	2,592	1,568
TSX	13,879	8,922
FTSE	6,425	4,427
DAX	7,889	4,829
Nikkei	14,691	8,803
Hang Seng	27,445	14,499

Commodities	2008	2009
Oil	98.90	42.50
Gold	853.53	874.83

Bond Yields	2008	2009
USA 5 Yr Treasury	3.29	1.55
USA 10 Yr T	3.94	2.24
USA 20 Yr T	4.43	3.02
Moody's Aaa	5.35	4.73
Moody's Baa	6.49	8.07
CAN 5 Yr T	3.79	1.72
CAN 10 Yr T	3.94	2.70

30 day	Wednesday February 3
60 day	Friday March 5
90 day	Sunday April 4
180 day	Saturday July 3
1 year	Tuesday January 4

30 day	Thursday February 4
60 day	Saturday March 6
90 day	Monday April 5
180 day	Sunday July 4
1 year	Wednesday January 5

Money Market	2008	2009
USA Fed Funds	4.25	0.25
USA 3 Mo T-B	3.27	0.09
CAN tgt overnight rate	4.25	1.50
CAN 3 Mo T-B	3.78	0.84

6 WEDNESDAY	006 / 359		**7** THURSDAY	007 / 358

Foreign Exchange	2008	2009
USD/EUR	1.47	1.41
USD/GBP	1.99	1.46
CAN/USD	0.99	1.22
JPY/USD	110.64	90.50

JANUARY

M	T	W	T	F	S	S
				1	2	3
4	5	6	7	8	9	10
11	12	13	14	15	16	17
18	19	20	21	22	23	24
25	26	27	28	29	30	31

30 day	Friday February 5
60 day	Sunday March 7
90 day	Tuesday April 6
180 day	Monday July 5
1 year	Thursday January 6

30 day	Saturday February 6
60 day	Monday March 8
90 day	Wednesday April 7
180 day	Tuesday July 6
1 year	Friday January 7

FEBRUARY

M	T	W	T	F	S	S
1	2	3	4	5	6	7
8	9	10	11	12	13	14
15	16	17	18	19	20	21
22	23	24	25	26	27	28

8 FRIDAY	008 / 357

MARCH

M	T	W	T	F	S	S
1	2	3	4	5	6	7
8	9	10	11	12	13	14
15	16	17	18	19	20	21
22	23	24	25	26	27	28
29	30	31				

30 day	Sunday February 7
60 day	Tuesday March 9
90 day	Thursday April 8
180 day	Wednesday July 7
1 year	Saturday January 8

* Weekly avg closing values- except Fed Funds Rate & CAN overnight tgt rate which are weekly closing values.

RETAIL – POST HOLIDAY BARGAIN
Ist of II Retail Strategies for the Year
SHOP Jan 21st and RETURN Your Investment Apr 12th

☑ **2009 Performance**

The retail sector responded like it typically does, correcting at the beginning of January and then rebounding into April. Even before the March low, the retail sector was outperforming the broad market. At the end of its seasonal cycle the retail sector beat the S&P 500 by a significant amount.

A few weeks after the Christmas holidays retail stocks go on sale, representing a good buying opportunity in mid to late January. The opportunity coincides with the earnings season.

Historically, the retail sector has outperformed from January 21st until April 12th - the start of the next earnings season. During these two and a half months the retail sector has averaged 8.5%, compared with the S&P 500 which has averaged 1.8%. Not only has the retail sector had greater gains than the broad market, but it has also outperformed it on a fairly regular basis: 80% of the time.

S&P Retail Sector vs. S&P 500 1990 to 2009

Jan 21 to Apr 12	Retail	Positive S&P 500	Diff
1990	9.7 %	1.5 %	8.1 %
1991	29.9	14.5	15.4
1992	-2.7	-2.9	0.2
1993	-0.6	3.5	-4.0
1994	2.0	-5.8	7.8
1995	7.4	9.1	-1.8
1996	19.7	4.1	15.7
1997	6.0	-5.0	11.0
1998	20.1	13.5	6.6
1999	23.4	8.1	15.2
2000	5.8	1.5	4.3
2001	-0.5	-11.8	11.3
2002	6.7	-1.5	8.2
2003	6.5	-3.7	10.3
2004	6.7	0.6	6.1
2005	-1.6	1.1	-2.7
2006	3.4	2.1	1.3
2007	-0.7	1.2	-1.9
2008	3.5	0.6	3.0
2009	25.1	6.4	18.7
Avg.	8.5 %	1.8 %	6.6 %

*6.6% extra & 80% of the time
better than the S&P 500*

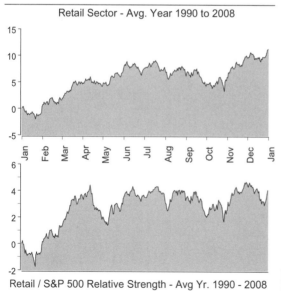

Retail Sector - Avg. Year 1990 to 2008

Retail / S&P 500 Relative Strength - Avg Yr. 1990 - 2008

Most investors think the best time to invest in retail stocks is before Black Friday in November. Yes,

there is a positive seasonal cycle at this time, but it is not nearly as strong as the cycle from January to April.

The January retail bounce coincides with the "rosy" stock market analysts' forecasts that tend to occur at the beginning of the year. These forecasts generally rely on healthy consumer spending as it makes up approximately 2/3 of the GDP. The retail sector benefits from the optimistic forecasts and tends to outperform.

Surprisingly, there have only been minimal drawdowns over the last twenty years during the retail seasonal period. The worst loss was 2.7% in 1992, and even in this year the retail sector beat the S&P 500.

ⓘ *Retail SP GIC Sector # 2550:
An index designed to represent a cross section of retail companies*
For more information on the retail sector, see www.standardandpoors.com.

11 MONDAY	011 / 354

12 TUESDAY	012 / 353

Market Indices & Rates
Weekly Values*

Stock Markets	2008	2009
Dow	12,722	8,816
S&P500	1,407	914
Nasdaq	2,469	1,614
TSX	13,603	9,237
FTSE	6,278	4,536
DAX	7,776	4,922
Nikkei	14,425	9,015
Hang Seng	27,201	14,971

Commodities	2008	2009
Oil	94.70	44.51
Gold	877.88	850.65

Bond Yields	2008	2009
USA 5 Yr Treasury	3.13	1.62
USA 10 Yr T	3.85	2.48
USA 20 Yr T	4.40	3.40
Moody's Aaa	5.36	5.04
Moody's Baa	6.53	8.23
CAN 5 Yr T	3.62	1.83
CAN 10 Yr T	3.86	2.88

30 day	Wednesday February 10
60 day	Friday March 12
90 day	Sunday April 11
180 day	Saturday July 10
1 year	Tuesday January 11

30 day	Thursday February 11
60 day	Saturday March 13
90 day	Monday April 12
180 day	Sunday July 11
1 year	Wednesday January 12

Money Market	2008	2009
USA Fed Funds	4.25	0.25
USA 3 Mo T-B	3.21	0.11
CAN tgt overnight rate	4.25	1.50
CAN 3 Mo T-B	3.71	0.84

13 WEDNESDAY	013 / 352

14 THURSDAY	014 / 351

Foreign Exchange	2008	2009
USD/EUR	1.47	1.36
USD/GBP	1.97	1.49
CAN/USD	1.01	1.20
JPY/USD	109.44	92.54

JANUARY

M	T	W	T	F	S	S
				1	2	3
4	5	6	7	8	9	10
11	12	13	14	15	16	17
18	19	20	21	22	23	24
25	26	27	28	29	30	31

30 day	Friday February 12
60 day	Sunday March 14
90 day	Tuesday April 13
180 day	Monday July 12
1 year	Thursday January 13

30 day	Saturday February 13
60 day	Monday March 15
90 day	Wednesday April 14
180 day	Tuesday July 13
1 year	Friday January 14

FEBRUARY

M	T	W	T	F	S	S
1	2	3	4	5	6	7
8	9	10	11	12	13	14
15	16	17	18	19	20	21
22	23	24	25	26	27	28

15 FRIDAY	015 / 350

MARCH

M	T	W	T	F	S	S
1	2	3	4	5	6	7
8	9	10	11	12	13	14
15	16	17	18	19	20	21
22	23	24	25	26	27	28
29	30	31				

30 day	Sunday February 14
60 day	Tuesday March 16
90 day	Thursday April 15
180 day	Wednesday July 14
1 year	Saturday January 15

* Weekly avg closing values- except Fed Funds Rate & CAN overnight tgt rate which are weekly closing values.

MATERIAL STOCKS (Rocks, Paper, Trees, Steel & Chemicals)
MATERIAL GAINS – Jan 29 to May 6

☑ 2009 Performance

At the start of their seasonal cycle, material stocks kept on par with the S&P 500. When the market turned around at the beginning of March, material stocks accelerated. The end result was a significant outperformance of 14% versus the S&P 500.

The materials sector of the market was shunned during the 90s as being too "old economy." The general belief was that there were minimal, if any, return possibilities for companies that worked with "stuff" that came out of the ground.

Even though this sector underperformed the broad market on an average yearly basis during the 1990s, it still managed to outperform from January 29th to May 6th. Over the last few years the materials sector has produced very good results.

4.5% extra & 14 out of 20 years better than the S&P 500

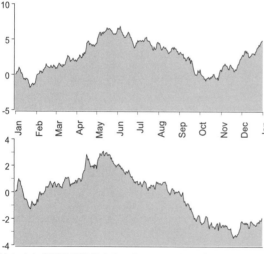

Materials Sector - Avg. Year 1990 to 2008

Materials / S&P 500 Relative Strength - Avg Yr. 1990-2008

In 1999 the materials sector beat the overall market by 28.1%, in 2001 by 21.2% and in 2002 by 14.5%. The 1999 outperformance was the result of the world bouncing back from the affect of the Asian Financial Flu, when several Asian currencies plummeted and economies crumbled. At the time, investors drove the price of commodities down because of the fear that Asian demand for commodities would dry up.

Materials Sector vs. S&P500 1990 to 2009

Jan 29 to May 6	Materials	Positive S&P 500	Diff
1990 %	-1.4 %	3.9 %	-5.3 %
1991	12.2	13.1	-0.9
1992	4.7	0.4	4.2
1993	2.4	1.0	1.3
1994	-6.2	-6.5	0.2
1995	10.7	10.6	0.1
1996	10.5	3.1	7.4
1997	5.0	8.2	-3.2
1998	15.5	13.0	2.4
1999	33.4	5.3	28.1
2000	-2.3	5.3	-7.6
2001	14.7	-6.5	21.2
2002	7.4	-7.1	14.5
2003	6.4	8.8	-2.5
2004	-2.1	-1.3	-0.8
2005	0.6	0.0	0.6
2006	9.4	3.3	6.1
2007	8.6	5.9	2.7
2008	11.3	4.7	6.5
2009	19.2	5.2	14.0
Avg.	8.0 %	3.5 %	4.5 %

Today, the commodities market is largely influenced by the Chinese economy. China consumes a large percentage of the world's commodities every year and as a result, "as the Chinese economy goes up or down, so does the price of commodities." Over the last decade, China has had a high GDP growth rate, between six and thirteen percent. In 2007 and 2008 China was able to mitigate the effects of the global slowdown by introducing a massive construction stimulus package.

Managing a high growth economy is difficult and as a result, there are fears of the Chinese economy imploding. Although this phenomenon is difficult to predict, focusing on material sector investments in the strong seasonal period will reduce the risk in the rest of the year.

> ⓘ *The SP GICS Materials Sector # 15 encompasses a wide range of commodity-related manufacturing industries, including companies that manufacture chemicals, construction materials, glass, paper, forest products and related packaging products and metals, minerals and mining companies, including producers of steel.*
> *For more information on the materials sector, see www.standardandpoors.com*

18 MONDAY 018 / 347

19 TUESDAY 019 / 346

WEEK 03

Market Indices & Rates
Weekly Values*

Stock Markets	2008	2009
Dow	12,401	8,323
S&P500	1,366	856
Nasdaq	2,395	1,523
TSX	13,125	8,849
FTSE	5,998	4,255
DAX	7,500	4,496
Nikkei	13,780	8,276
Hang Seng	25,415	13,568

Commodities	2008	2009
Oil	91.53	36.91
Gold	895.00	823.75

Bond Yields	2008	2009
USA 5 Yr Treasury	2.97	1.42
USA 10 Yr T	3.72	2.30
USA 20 Yr T	4.32	3.23
Moody's Aaa	5.29	4.89
Moody's Baa	6.52	7.97
CAN 5 Yr T	3.49	1.62
CAN 10 Yr T	3.80	2.65

Money Market	2008	2009
USA Fed Funds	4.25	0.25
USA 3 Mo T-B	3.09	0.12
CAN tgt overnight rate	4.25	1.50
CAN 3 Mo T-B	3.57	0.73

Foreign Exchange	2008	2009
USD/EUR	1.48	1.33
USD/GBP	1.96	1.47
CAN/USD	1.02	1.22
JPY/USD	107.24	89.66

18 MONDAY
- 30 day Wednesday February 17
- 60 day Friday March 19
- 90 day Sunday April 18
- 180 day Saturday July 17
- 1 year Tuesday January 18

19 TUESDAY
- 30 day Thursday February 18
- 60 day Saturday March 20
- 90 day Monday April 19
- 180 day Sunday July 18
- 1 year Wednesday January 19

20 WEDNESDAY 020 / 345

21 THURSDAY 021 / 344

20 WEDNESDAY
- 30 day Friday February 19
- 60 day Sunday March 21
- 90 day Tuesday April 20
- 180 day Monday July 19
- 1 year Thursday January 20

21 THURSDAY
- 30 day Saturday February 20
- 60 day Monday March 22
- 90 day Wednesday April 21
- 180 day Tuesday July 20
- 1 year Friday January 21

22 FRIDAY 022 / 343

22 FRIDAY
- 30 day Sunday February 21
- 60 day Tuesday March 23
- 90 day Thursday April 22
- 180 day Wednesday July 21
- 1 year Saturday January 22

JANUARY

M	T	W	T	F	S	S
				1	2	3
4	5	6	7	8	9	10
11	12	13	14	15	16	17
18	19	20	21	22	23	24
25	26	27	28	29	30	31

FEBRUARY

M	T	W	T	F	S	S
1	2	3	4	5	6	7
8	9	10	11	12	13	14
15	16	17	18	19	20	21
22	23	24	25	26	27	28

MARCH

M	T	W	T	F	S	S
1	2	3	4	5	6	7
8	9	10	11	12	13	14
15	16	17	18	19	20	21
22	23	24	25	26	27	28
29	30	31				

* Weekly avg closing values- except Fed Funds Rate & CAN overnight tgt rate which are weekly closing values.

JANUARY PREDICTOR
Predicting the Rest of the Year

☑ 2008 Performance

January, usually a strong month, was down 6.1% (S&P 500), forecasting a negative return for the rest of the year. From the end of January to the end of the year the market continued its decline, putting in a further loss of 34.4%.

January has an uncanny trait of predicting the rest of the year. "As January goes, the rest of the year goes." In other words, if January is positive, the rest of the year tends to be positive, and if January is negative, the rest of the year tends to be negative.

75% accuracy predicting S&P 500 direction 1950 to 2008

There have been quite a few different theories as to why January is a good predictor for the rest of the year. Generally speaking, the explanation that makes the most sense is that investors and money managers are setting up their expectations for the rest of the year. If money managers are expecting a good year, they are more inclined to move more money into the market in January, boosting the performance of January and the rest of the year. If money managers are expecting a sub-performance year, they are more inclined to hold back on funds in January, producing a negative January and rest of the year.

In the past there have been different pundits that have included January's performance with the full year performance, which overstates the success of January's predictive ability. Nevertheless, January has predicted the rest of the year with an accuracy rate of 75% (45 times out of 60) for the S&P 500 from 1950 to 2008.

⚠ *Basing a yearly investment decision on one month's returns is not considered to be a reasonable portfolio investment strategy and large returns can be missed. For example, in 2003 the barometer predicted a negative rest of year return. The market returned an astonishing 30%.*

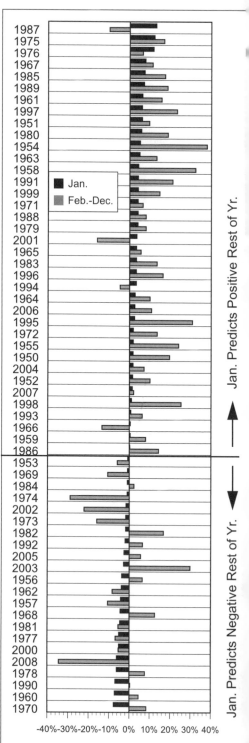

25 MONDAY   025 / 340   **26** TUESDAY   026 / 339

	WEEK 04

Market Indices & Rates
Weekly Values*

Stock Markets	2008	2009
Dow	12,207	8,094
S&P500	1,333	826
Nasdaq	2,324	1,473
TSX	12,647	8,644
FTSE	5,734	4,073
DAX	6,727	4,243
Nikkei	13,090	8,004
Hang Seng	23,666	12,824

Commodities	2008	2009
Oil	89.49	42.18
Gold	892.40	854.25

Bond Yields	2008	2009
USA 5 Yr Treasury	2.74	1.58
USA 10 Yr T	3.58	2.56
USA 20 Yr T	4.28	3.52
Moody's Aaa	5.30	5.10
Moody's Baa	6.54	8.15
CAN 5 Yr T	3.46	1.71
CAN 10 Yr T	3.84	2.74

Money Market	2008	2009
USA Fed Funds	3.50	0.25
USA 3 Mo T-B	2.31	0.11
CAN tgt overnight rate	4.00	1.00
CAN 3 Mo T-B	3.43	0.80

Foreign Exchange	2008	2009
USD/EUR	1.46	1.30
USD/GBP	1.96	1.40
CAN/USD	1.02	1.26
JPY/USD	106.45	89.63

30 day	Wednesday February 24
60 day	Friday March 26
90 day	Sunday April 25
180 day	Saturday July 24
1 year	Tuesday January 25

30 day	Thursday February 25
60 day	Saturday March 27
90 day	Monday April 26
180 day	Sunday July 25
1 year	Wednesday January 26

27 WEDNESDAY   027 / 338   **28** THURSDAY   028 / 337

JANUARY

M	T	W	T	F	S	S
				1	2	3
4	5	6	7	8	9	10
11	12	13	14	15	16	17
18	19	20	21	22	23	24
25	26	27	28	29	30	31

FEBRUARY

M	T	W	T	F	S	S
1	2	3	4	5	6	7
8	9	10	11	12	13	14
15	16	17	18	19	20	21
22	23	24	25	26	27	28

MARCH

M	T	W	T	F	S	S
1	2	3	4	5	6	7
8	9	10	11	12	13	14
15	16	17	18	19	20	21
22	23	24	25	26	27	28
29	30	31				

30 day	Friday February 26
60 day	Sunday March 28
90 day	Tuesday April 27
180 day	Monday July 26
1 year	Thursday January 27

30 day	Saturday February 27
60 day	Monday March 29
90 day	Wednesday April 28
180 day	Tuesday July 27
1 year	Friday January 28

29 FRIDAY   029 / 336

30 day	Sunday February 28
60 day	Tuesday March 30
90 day	Thursday April 29
180 day	Wednesday July 28
1 year	Saturday January 29

* Weekly avg closing values- except Fed Funds Rate & CAN overnight tgt rate which are weekly closing values.

FEBRUARY

	MONDAY	TUESDAY	WEDNESDAY
WEEK 05	**1** 27	**2** 26	**3** 25
WEEK 06	**8** 20	**9** 19	**10** 18
WEEK 07	**15** 13 CAN Market Closed - Family Day USA Market Closed - President's Day	**16** 12	**17** 11
WEEK 08	**22** 6	**23** 5	**24** 4
WEEK 09	1	2	3

THURSDAY		FRIDAY	
4	24	**5**	23
11	17	**12**	16
18	10	**19**	9
25	3	**26**	2
4		5	

MARCH

M	T	W	T	F	S	S
1	2	3	4	5	6	7
8	9	10	11	12	13	14
15	16	17	18	19	20	21
22	23	24	25	26	27	28
29	30	31				

APRIL

M	T	W	T	F	S	S
			1	2	3	4
5	6	7	8	9	10	11
12	13	14	15	16	17	18
19	20	21	22	23	24	25
26	27	28	29	30		

MAY

M	T	W	T	F	S	S
					1	2
3	4	5	6	7	8	9
10	11	12	13	14	15	16
17	18	19	20	21	22	23
24	25	26	27	28	29	30
31						

JUNE

M	T	W	T	F	S	S
	1	2	3	4	5	6
7	8	9	10	11	12	13
14	15	16	17	18	19	20
21	22	23	24	25	26	27
28	29	30				

FEBRUARY
S U M M A R Y

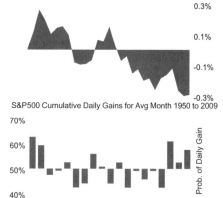

S&P500 Cumulative Daily Gains for Avg Month 1950 to 2009

STRATEGIES	PAGE

STRATEGIES STARTING
Oil– Winter/Spring Strategy I of II   21
Presidents' Day Negative Trio (Bearish)   23

STRATEGIES FINISHING
Presidents' Day Negative Trio (Bearish)   23

♦ On average, February has been a fairly flat month. But underneath the average number there have been some large ups and downs – February 2009 being no exception, as it produced a loss of 11% (S&P 500). ♦ The beginning of February tends to be stronger than the rest of the month. In 2009 the first few days were positive and then the rest of the month was downhill. ♦ Oil stocks tend to either do well in February or bottom towards the end of the month for a strong move into May. In 2009 oil stocks started their rise at the beginning of February.

BEST / WORST FEBRUARY BROAD MKTS. 2000-2009

BEST FEBRUARY MARKETS
♦ Nasdaq (2000) 19.2%
♦ Russell 2000 (2000) 16.4%
♦ TSX (2000) 7.6%

WORST FEBRUARY MARKETS
♦ Nasdaq (2001) -22.4%
♦ Russell 3000 Gr (2001) -16.8%
♦ Russell 3000 Val (2009) -13.8%

Index Values End of Month

	2000	2001	2002	2003	2004	2005	2006	2007	2008	2009
Dow	10,128	10,495	10,106	7,891	10,584	10,766	10,993	12,269	12,266	7,063
S&P 500	1,366	1,240	1,107	841	1,145	1,204	1,281	1,407	1,331	735
Nasdaq	4,697	2,152	1,731	1,338	2,030	2,052	2,281	2,416	2,271	1,378
TSX	9,129	8,079	7,638	6,555	8,788	9,668	11,688	13,045	13,583	8,123
Russell 1000	1,410	1,258	1,122	858	1,178	1,244	1,341	1,478	1,396	768
Russell 2000	1,438	1,179	1,166	896	1,455	1,576	1,816	1,972	1,705	967
Russell 3000 Growth	3,259	2,208	1,858	1,367	1,880	1,889	2,059	2,195	2,165	1,276
Russell 3000 Value	1,877	2,152	2,051	1,619	2,272	2,522	2,725	3,094	2,755	1,412

Percent Gain for February

	2000	2001	2002	2003	2004	2005	2006	2007	2008	2009
Dow	-7.4	-3.6	1.9	-2.0	0.9	2.6	1.2	-2.8	-3.0	-11.7
S&P 500	-2.0	-9.2	-2.1	-1.7	1.2	1.9	0.0	-2.2	-3.5	-11.0
Nasdaq	19.2	-22.4	-10.5	1.3	-1.8	-0.5	-1.1	-1.9	-5.0	-6.7
TSX	7.6	-13.3	-0.1	-0.2	3.1	5.0	-2.2	0.1	3.3	-6.6
Russell 1000	-0.4	-9.4	-2.1	-1.7	1.2	2.0	0.0	-1.9	-3.3	-10.7
Russell 2000	16.4	-6.7	-2.8	-3.1	0.8	1.6	-0.3	-0.9	-3.8	-12.3
Russell 3000 Growth	6.2	-16.8	-4.4	-0.7	0.5	1.0	-0.3	-1.9	-2.2	-7.9
Russell 3000 Value	-6.7	-2.8	0.0	-3.0	1.9	2.9	0.3	-1.8	-4.5	-13.8

February Market Avg. Performance 2000 to 2009[1]

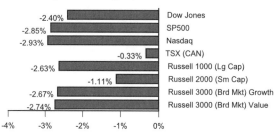

Dow Jones -2.40%
SP500 -2.85%
Nasdaq -2.93%
TSX (CAN) -0.33%
Russell 1000 (Lg Cap) -2.63%
Russell 2000 (Sm Cap) -1.11%
Russell 3000 (Brd Mkt) Growth -2.67%
Russell 3000 (Brd Mkt) Value -2.74%

Interest Corner Feb[2]

	Fed Funds % [3]	3 Mo. T-Bill % [4]	10 Yr % [5]	20 Yr % [6]
2009	0.25	0.26	3.02	3.98
2008	3.00	1.85	3.53	4.37
2007	5.25	5.16	4.56	4.78
2006	4.50	4.62	4.55	4.70
2005	2.50	2.76	4.36	4.79

(1) Russell Data provided by Russell (2) Federal Reserve Bank of St. Louis- end of month values (3) Target rate set by FOMC (4)(5)(6) Constant yield maturities.

- 17 -

THACKRAY SECTOR THERMOMETER

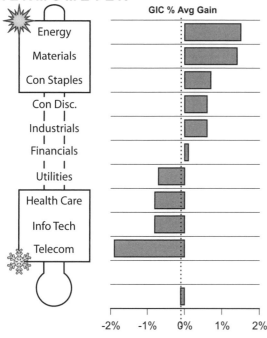

	GIC[2] % Avg Gain	Fq % Gain >S&P 500	SP GIC SECTOR 1990-2008[1]
Energy	1.5 %	53 %	Energy
Materials	1.4	63	Materials
Con Staples	0.7	53	Consumer Staples
Con Disc.	0.6	68	Consumer Discretionary
Industrials	0.6	58	Industrials
Financials	0.1	68	Financials
Utilities	-0.7	26	Utilities
Health Care	-0.8	42	Health Care
Info Tech	-0.8	47	Information Technology
Telecom	-1.9	37	Telecom
	-0.1 %	N/A %	S&P 500

-2%   -1%   0%   1%   2%

Hot Box - 3 Best Sectors
Energy ♦ Materials. ♦ Con Staples
February Portfolio

	Avg % Gain	Avg % Gain > S&P 500	Fq % Gain >S&P 500
1990-2008	1.2 %	1.3 %	68 %
2008	2.8 %	6.2 %	

Cold Box - 3 Worst Sectors
Health Care ♦ Info Tech ♦ Telecom
February Portfolio

	Avg % Gain	Avg % Gain > S&P 500	Fq % Gain >S&P 500
1990-2008	-1.1 %	-1.0 %	16 %
2008	-5.4 %	-2.0 %	

Commentary

♦ Although February is a mediocre month, there are six sectors that have produced positive results from 1990 to 2008. The big winners are the Energy Sector, up 1.5%, and the Materials Sector, up 1.4%. ♦ Information Technology has produced a negative number, along with the three defensive sectors: Health Care, Utilities and Telecom. ♦ Information Technology drops from a solid #1 in January to the bottom half of the ranks, producing a negative average return. ♦ In 2008 the *Hot Box 3 Best Sectors* were at the top of the sector ranks and as a trio outperformed the S&P 500 by over 6%. There was a very wide 18% range in performance between the top sector (Energy) and the worst sector (Financials).

(1) Sector data provided by Standard and Poors (2) GIC is short form for Global Industry Classification (3) Sub Sector data provided by Standard and Poors, except where marked by symbol.

CHANGE YOUR OIL SECTOR
Exploration & Production (E&P) Jan 30 to Apr 13
Equipment and Services (E&S) Apr 14 to May 17

☑ 2009 Performance

The two sub-sector approach to this strategy paid off in 2009. The exploration and production sector slightly underperformed the S&P 500, but the equipment and services sector more than made up for it with strong outperformance.

Periodically, drivers change their oil to extend the life of their car. Investors that have changed their oil sectors at the right time have extended their profits. The energy seasonal cycle has taken place from February 25th to May 9th (see *Oil-Winter/Spring Effect* strategy). This cycle has been extended on both sides by investing in exploration and production stocks at the end of January (January 30), and then switching to equipment and services stocks in mid-April (April 13) and holding until mid-May (May 17).

14.9% extra & 18 out of 20 times better than the S&P 500

Very often when a sector seasonally outperforms, such as energy, it is the more speculative sub-sector, such as exploration and production, that starts the outperformance and the more conservative sub-sector, such as equipment and services that outperforms at the end of the cycle.

ⓘ *Exploration and Production - S&P GIC sector Equipment and Services 10102020 & S&P GIC Oil Integrated sector 10102010. For more information please see www.standardandpoors.com*

Ⓨ *Alternate Strategy - The cumulative gain graph for the three major sub-sectors of the energy market has been included to illustrate a possible strategy for money managers to maintain an equity position in the energy sector throughout the year. The Oil Integrated companies (major oil companies involved in all aspects of oil production and sales), provide a good alternative to the Oil E&P sector during less favorable times for oil stocks.*

Oil E&P and E&S Sector Switch 1990 to 2009*   Positive ☐

	E&P Jan 30 to Apr 13	E&S Apr 14 to May 17	E&P & E&S Jan 30 to May 17**	S&P 500 Jan 30 to May 17	Diff
1990	12.7%	10.8%	24.9%	9.0%	15.9
1991	11.2	2.0	13.5	10.9	2.6
1992	4.8	10.4	15.8	-0.1	15.8
1993	27.0	3.7	31.7	0.4	31.4
1994	-11.4	8.3	-4.1	-6.1	2.0
1995	14.3	9.7	25.3	12.0	13.2
1996	7.7	-0.7	7.0	7.2	-0.2
1997	-16.3	13.9	-4.6	7.4	-12.1
1998	9.0	7.9	17.5	12.5	5.0
1999	35.7	9.7	48.8	4.7	44.1
2000	17.9	22.2	44.0	6.4	37.6
2001	5.4	17.8	24.2	-5.5	29.8
2002	14.3	4.1	19.0	0.5	18.5
2003	1.2	15.3	16.7	9.2	7.4
2004	8.9	-5.1	3.3	-4.4	7.7
2005	14.6	-3.8	10.3	0.2	10.1
2006	-4.0	4.0	-0.2	-1.0	0.9
2007	12.4	7.3	20.6	6.5	14.1
2008	29.9	16.8	51.7	4.6	47.1
2009	-3.3	15.4	11.6	4.5	7.1
Avg.	9.6%	8.5%	18.8%	3.9%	14.9%

* Buy date uses close value from day before
** Cumulative Gain - E&P Jan 30 to Apr 13 and E&S Apr 14 to May 17

Oil E&P / Oil E&S - Relative Strength
Avg. Jan 30 to Jun 1 - 1990 - 2009

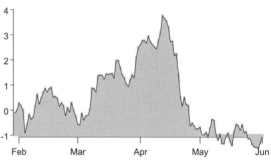

Oil E&P & Oil E&S & Oil Integrated
Avg. Cumulative Gain 1990 - 2008

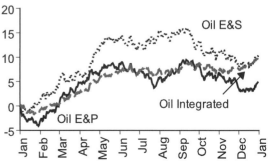

1 MONDAY 032 / 333

2 TUESDAY 033 / 332

30 day Wednesday March 3
60 day Friday April 2
90 day Sunday May 2
180 day Saturday July 31
1 year Tuesday February 1

30 day Thursday March 4
60 day Saturday April 3
90 day Monday May 3
180 day Sunday August 1
1 year Wednesday February 2

3 WEDNESDAY 034 / 331

4 THURSDAY 035 / 330

30 day Friday March 5
60 day Sunday April 4
90 day Tuesday May 4
180 day Monday August 2
1 year Thursday February 3

30 day Saturday March 6
60 day Monday April 5
90 day Wednesday May 5
180 day Tuesday August 3
1 year Friday February 4

5 FRIDAY 036 / 329

30 day Sunday March 7
60 day Tuesday April 6
90 day Thursday May 6
180 day Wednesday August 4
1 year Saturday February 5

WEEK 05

Market Indices & Rates
Weekly Values*

Stock Markets	2008	2009
Dow	12,540	8,163
S&P500	1,369	845
Nasdaq	2,372	1,507
TSX	13,101	8,756
FTSE	5,884	4,208
DAX	6,882	4,387
Nikkei	13,400	8,019
Hang Seng	23,916	13,216

Commodities	2008	2009
Oil	91.13	42.52
Gold	920.65	902.95

Bond Yields	2008	2009
USA 5 Yr Treasury	2.84	1.74
USA 10 Yr T	3.67	2.75
USA 20 Yr T	4.35	3.74
Moody's Aaa	5.38	5.23
Moody's Baa	6.63	8.22
CAN 5 Yr T	3.50	2.02
CAN 10 Yr T	3.87	2.98

Money Market	2008	2009
USA Fed Funds	3.00	0.25
USA 3 Mo T-B	2.18	0.19
CAN tgt overnight rate	4.00	1.00
CAN 3 Mo T-B	3.39	0.82

Foreign Exchange	2008	2009
USD/EUR	1.48	1.31
USD/GBP	1.99	1.42
CAN/USD	1.00	1.22
JPY/USD	106.58	89.44

FEBRUARY

M	T	W	T	F	S	S
1	2	3	4	5	6	7
8	9	10	11	12	13	14
15	16	17	18	19	20	21
22	23	24	25	26	27	28

MARCH

M	T	W	T	F	S	S
1	2	3	4	5	6	7
8	9	10	11	12	13	14
15	16	17	18	19	20	21
22	23	24	25	26	27	28
29	30	31				

APRIL

M	T	W	T	F	S	S
			1	2	3	4
5	6	7	8	9	10	11
12	13	14	15	16	17	18
19	20	21	22	23	24	25
26	27	28	29	30		

* Weekly avg closing values- except Fed Funds Rate & CAN overnight tgt rate which are weekly closing values.

OIL – WINTER/SPRING STRATEGY

Ist of II Oil Stock Strategies for the Year

(Stocks) February 25th to May 9th

☒ 2009 Performance

It is hard to count this strategy as producing a loss when it was up 15.8%. Just after the start of this strategy the S&P 500 rallied hard as investors anticipated the end of "bad times." Although oil stocks benefited, investors were more interested in rewarding other sectors of the market such as financials that had been beaten up badly.

The *Oil- Winter/Spring Strategy* is one of the strongest seasonal outperformance trends. From 1984 to 2009, for the two and half months starting on February 25th and ending May 9th, the energy sector (XOI) has outperformed the S&P 500 by an average 5.6%. What is even more impressive are the positive returns 24 out of 26 times, and the outperformance of the S&P 500, 23 out of 26 times.

5.6% extra and 24 out of 26 times positive, in just over two months

XOI / S&P 500 1984 to 2009

Feb 25 to May 9	XOI	positive S&P 500	Diff
1984	5.6 %	1.7 %	3.9 %
1985	4.9	1.4	3.5
1986	7.7	6.0	1.7
1987	25.5	3.7	21.8
1988	5.6	-3.0	8.6
1989	8.1	6.3	1.8
1990	-0.6	5.8	-6.3
1991	6.8	4.8	2.0
1992	5.8	0.9	4.9
1993	6.3	0.3	6.0
1994	3.2	-4.7	7.9
1995	10.3	7.3	3.1
1996	2.2	-2.1	4.3
1997	4.7	1.8	2.9
1998	9.8	7.5	2.3
1999	35.4	7.3	28.1
2000	22.2	4.3	17.9
2001	10.2	0.8	9.4
2002	5.3	-1.5	6.9
2003	5.7	12.1	-6.4
2004	4.0	-3.5	7.5
2005	-1.0	-1.8	0.8
2006	9.4	2.8	6.6
2007	10.1	4.2	5.8
2008	7.6	2.6	5.0
2009	15.8	20.2	-4.4
Avg	8.9 %	3.3 %	5.6 %

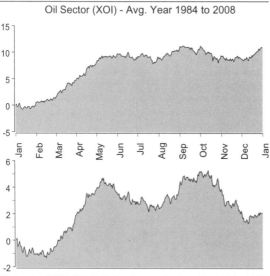

Oil Sector (XOI) - Avg. Year 1984 to 2008

Oil Sector / S&P 500 Relative Strength - Avg Yr. 1984 - 2008

Refineries have a choice: they can produce either gasoline or heating oil. As the winter progresses, refineries start to convert their operations from heating oil to gasoline. During this switch-over time, low inventory levels of both heating oil and gasoline can drive up the price of a barrel of oil and oil stocks. In early May, before the kick-off of the driving season (Memorial Day in May), the refineries have finished their conversion to gasoline. The price of oil and oil stocks tend to decline.

A lot of investors assume that the time to buy oil stocks is just before the winter cold sets in. The rationale is that oil will climb in price as the temperature drops. The results in the market have not supported this assumption. The dynamic of the price for a barrel of oil has more to do with oil inventory.

ⓘ *Amex Oil Index (XOI):*
An index designed to represent a cross section of widely held oil corporations involved in various phases of the oil industry.
For more information on the XOI index, see www.cboe.com

8 MONDAY 039 / 326

9 TUESDAY 040 / 325

30 day Wednesday March 10
60 day Friday April 9
90 day Sunday May 9
180 day Saturday August 7
1 year Tuesday February 8

30 day Thursday March 11
60 day Saturday April 10
90 day Monday May 10
180 day Sunday August 8
1 year Wednesday February 9

10 WEDNESDAY 041 / 324

11 THURSDAY 042 / 323

30 day Friday March 12
60 day Sunday April 11
90 day Tuesday May 11
180 day Monday August 9
1 year Thursday February 10

30 day Saturday March 13
60 day Monday April 12
90 day Wednesday May 12
180 day Tuesday August 10
1 year Friday February 11

12 FRIDAY 043 / 322

30 day Sunday March 14
60 day Tuesday April 13
90 day Thursday May 13
180 day Wednesday August 11
1 year Saturday February 12

WEEK 06
Market Indices & Rates
Weekly Values*

Stock Markets	2008	2009
Dow	12,306	8,063
S&P500	1,342	842
Nasdaq	2,314	1,533
TSX	12,994	8,763
FTSE	5,856	4,198
DAX	6,823	4,459
Nikkei	13,386	7,953
Hang Seng	24,437	13,107

Commodities	2008	2009
Oil	89.09	40.50
Gold	900.05	912.15

Bond Yields	2008	2009
USA 5 Yr Treasury	2.72	1.88
USA 10 Yr T	3.66	2.92
USA 20 Yr T	4.39	3.86
Moody's Aaa	5.40	5.29
Moody's Baa	6.69	8.18
CAN 5 Yr T	3.40	2.03
CAN 10 Yr T	3.82	3.05

Money Market	2008	2009
USA Fed Funds	3.00	0.25
USA 3 Mo T-B	2.19	0.29
CAN tgt overnight rate	4.00	1.00
CAN 3 Mo T-B	3.31	0.83

Foreign Exchange	2008	2009
USD/EUR	1.46	1.28
USD/GBP	1.96	1.44
CAN/USD	1.00	1.24
JPY/USD	106.95	89.65

FEBRUARY
M	T	W	T	F	S	S
1	2	3	4	5	6	7
8	9	10	11	12	13	14
15	16	17	18	19	20	21
22	23	24	25	26	27	28

MARCH
M	T	W	T	F	S	S
1	2	3	4	5	6	7
8	9	10	11	12	13	14
15	16	17	18	19	20	21
22	23	24	25	26	27	28
29	30	31				

APRIL
M	T	W	T	F	S	S
		1	2	3	4
5	6	7	8	9	10	11
12	13	14	15	16	17	18
19	20	21	22	23	24	25
26	27	28	29	30		

* Weekly avg closing values- except Fed Funds Rate & CAN overnight tgt rate which are weekly closing values.

PRESIDENTS' DAY NEGATIVE TRIO
Markets Not Very Patriotic
2 Days Before and 1 Day After

☑ 2009 Performance

The trio was strongly negative this year with the day before President's Day down 1% and the day after down almost 5%. This was the strongest performance of the trio over the last 60 years.

You may like the current President, but that does not mean that you have to invest on either side of Presidents' Day. Two days before and one day after Presidents' Day, have produced results that are less than formidable and have often been back to back negative days. These three days are aptly called the Presidents' Day Negative Trio.

The day before Presidents' Day is typically the worst day of the Trio- an average negative return and down 67% of the time

From 1971 to 2009, all three days of the trio have produced an average negative return. The two days before have been negative most of the time. The day after has just scraped by with an even chance at being positive or negative.

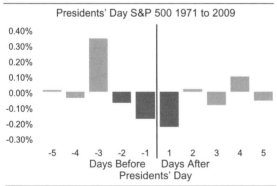

Presidents' Day S&P 500 1971 to 2009

The average negative returns may have more to do with the part of the month the holiday falls on rather than the holiday itself. Presidents' Day often occurs right after the third Friday, which tends to be the most negative day of the month. This Friday is the day that the options and futures contracts expire and is commonly referred to as Witching Day. The Friday and the day after, tend to be volatile and produce negative returns (see *Witches' Hangover* strategy). If Presidents' Day occurs after the third Friday, then it tends to be surrounded by poor performance.

S&P500	2 Days Before	1 Day Before	1 Day After
			Negative
1971	0.53	0.53 %	0.23 %
1972	-0.03	-0.29	0.01
1973	-0.56	0.46	0.37
1974	-0.03	1.45	-0.16
1975	1.36	0.60	-0.70
1976	-0.52	-0.58	-0.62
1977	-0.57	-0.43	0.00
1978	-0.84	-0.14	-0.42
1979	-0.14	-0.06	0.76
1980	-1.45	-1.12	-0.70
1981	-0.59	-0.39	0.65
1982	-0.20	-0.04	-0.28
1983	0.01	0.38	-1.70
1984	-0.08	-0.25	-0.71
1985	-0.51	-0.44	-0.15
1986	0.66	1.09	1.22
1987	-0.69	1.48	2.07
1988	-0.28	0.66	0.85
1989	0.19	0.66	-0.26
1990	0.87	-0.65	-1.42
1991	-1.30	1.33	0.09
1992	-0.82	-0.29	-1.24
1993	0.32	-0.69	-2.40
1994	-0.52	-0.56	0.81
1995	0.14	-0.67	0.16
1996	-0.65	-0.51	-1.13
1997	1.13	-0.41	0.97
1998	0.40	-0.40	0.26
1999	2.49	-1.91	0.95
2000	0.04	-3.04	0.45
2001	0.81	-1.89	-1.74
2002	-0.18	-1.10	-1.89
2003	-0.16	2.14	1.95
2004	-0.49	-0.55	0.98
2005	-0.79	0.07	-1.45
2006	0.73	-0.17	-0.33
2007	0.10	-0.09	0.28
2008	-1.34	0.08	-0.09
2009	0.17	-1.00	-4.56
Avg	-0.07	-0.17 %	-0.23 %
Fq > 0	41.03 %	33.33 %	46.15 %

ⓘ *Presidents' Day was originally set aside to honor George Washington's birthday, and later incorporated Abraham Lincoln's birthday which also fell in February. To stem the confusion about which day to celebrate, legislation was enacted in 1971, setting the date to the third Monday in February. The day is now commonly used to celebrate all past American Presidents.*

FEBRUARY

15 MONDAY　　　　046 / 319　　**16** TUESDAY　　　　047 / 318

WEEK 07

Market Indices & Rates
Weekly Values*

Stock Markets	2008	2009
Dow	12,378	7,976
S&P500	1,351	839
Nasdaq	2,334	1,545
TSX	13,187	8,812
FTSE	5,833	4,229
DAX	6,896	4,505
Nikkei	13,335	7,850
Hang Seng	23,375	13,594

Commodities	2008	2009
Oil	94.12	36.91
Gold	910.50	924.30

Bond Yields	2008	2009
USA 5 Yr Treasury	2.73	1.83
USA 10 Yr T	3.72	2.88
USA 20 Yr T	4.49	3.80
Moody's Aaa	5.54	5.21
Moody's Baa	6.83	8.01
CAN 5 Yr T	3.39	2.09
CAN 10 Yr T	3.84	2.97

Money Market	2008	2009
USA Fed Funds	3.00	0.25
USA 3 Mo T-B	2.28	0.30
CAN tgt overnight rate	4.00	1.00
CAN 3 Mo T-B	3.26	0.72

Foreign Exchange	2008	2009
USD/EUR	1.46	1.29
USD/GBP	1.96	1.45
CAN/USD	1.00	1.24
JPY/USD	107.49	90.84

15 MONDAY 30 day Wednesday March 17 / 60 day Friday April 16 / 90 day Sunday May 16 / 180 day Saturday August 14 / 1 year Tuesday February 15

16 TUESDAY 30 day Thursday March 18 / 60 day Saturday April 17 / 90 day Monday May 17 / 180 day Sunday August 15 / 1 year Wednesday February 16

17 WEDNESDAY　　048 / 317　　**18** THURSDAY　　049 / 316

17 WEDNESDAY 30 day Friday March 19 / 60 day Sunday April 18 / 90 day Tuesday May 18 / 180 day Monday August 16 / 1 year Thursday February 17

18 THURSDAY 30 day Saturday March 20 / 60 day Monday April 19 / 90 day Wednesday May 19 / 180 day Tuesday August 17 / 1 year Friday February 18

19 FRIDAY　　050 / 315

19 FRIDAY 30 day Sunday March 21 / 60 day Tuesday April 20 / 90 day Thursday May 20 / 180 day Wednesday August 18 / 1 year Saturday February 19

FEBRUARY
M	T	W	T	F	S	S
1	2	3	4	5	6	7
8	9	10	11	12	13	14
15	16	17	18	19	20	21
22	23	24	25	26	27	28

MARCH
M	T	W	T	F	S	S
1	2	3	4	5	6	7
8	9	10	11	12	13	14
15	16	17	18	19	20	21
22	23	24	25	26	27	28
29	30	31				

APRIL
M	T	W	T	F	S	S
			1	2	3	4
5	6	7	8	9	10	11
12	13	14	15	16	17	18
19	20	21	22	23	24	25
26	27	28	29	30		

* Weekly avg closing values- except Fed Funds Rate & CAN overnight tgt rate which are weekly closing values.

PRESIDENTIAL ELECTION CYCLE
2nd Year – Worst Year

Avg. 2nd Year Presidential Term vs.
1st, 3rd, 4th Years S&P 500 1901 to 2008

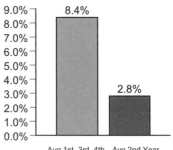

As 2010 is the second year for the new President, it is important to note that the second year of the presidential election cycle tends to be the weakest year of the four year cycle. The theory is built upon the tenet that the President makes tough decisions to bring the economy back on track in the first and second years of his term. In the third and fourth years, the President creates policies that help get him re-elected.

2nd worst year of Presidential Cycle

The second year of the cycle has produced some large up and down years. Overall, it has produced an average return of 2.8% from 1901 to 2008. This is in comparison to the average of the other years of the election cycle where the S&P 500 has returned an average of 5.0% in the first year, 12.6% in the third year and 7.5% in the fourth year.

Not only has the second year had mediocre performance, it has only been positive 54% of the time.

Given the weak state of the economy, large government deficits and the economic crisis, the current President will have his work cut out for him. The situation is particularly difficult as the government does not have a lot of ammunition left to thwart off another decline in the economy. The printing presses have been running over time and the government has been spending an unprecedented amount of money.

4 Year President Cycle- Dow Jones

President	1st Year	2nd Year	3rd Year	4th Year
1901 McKinley (R)	-8.7 %	-0.4 %	-23.6 %	41.7 %
1905 T. Roosevelt (R)	38.2	-1.9	-37.7	46.6
1909 Taft (R)	15.0	-17.9	0.4	7.6
1913 Wilson (D)	-10.3	-30.7	81.7	-4.2
1917 Wilson (D)	-21.7	10.5	30.5	-32.9
1921 Harding (R)	12.7	21.7	-3.3	26.2
1925 Coolidge (R)	30.0	0.3	28.8	48.2
1929 Hoover (R)	-17.2	-33.8	-52.7	-23.1
1933 Roosevelt (R)	66.8	4.1	38.6	24.8
1937 Roosevelt (R)	-32.8	28.0	-3.0	-12.7
1941 Roosevelt (R)	-15.3	7.6	13.8	12.1
1945 Roosevelt (R)	26.7	-8.1	2.3	-2.2
1949 Truman (D)	12.9	17.6	14.4	8.4
1953 Eisenhower (R)	-3.8	44.0	20.8	2.3
1957 Eisenhower (R)	-12.8	34.0	16.4	-9.3
1961 Kennedy (D)	18.7	-10.8	17.0	14.6
1965 Johnson (D)	10.9	-18.9	15.2	4.3
1969 Nixon (R)	-15.2	4.8	6.1	14.6
1973 Nixon (R)	-16.6	-27.6	38.3	17.9
1977 Carter (D)	-17.3	-3.2	4.2	14.9
1981 Reagan (R)	-9.2	19.6	20.3	-3.7
1985 Reagan (R)	27.7	22.6	2.3	11.9
1989 G. H. Bush (R)	27.0	-4.3	20.3	4.2
1993 Clinton (D)	13.7	2.1	33.5	26.0
1997 Clinton (D)	22.6	16.1	25.2	-6.2
2001 G.W. Bush (R)	-7.1	-16.8	25.3	3.1
2005 G.W. Bush (R)	-0.6	16.3	6.4	-33.8
Average Return	5.0	2.8	12.6	7.5
% Positive Year	48 %	56 %	82 %	67 %

> ⓘ *The Presidential Cycle is closely aligned with the well known and closely followed 4 Year Cycle. In this cycle the market tends to bottom approximately every four years. The bottom is typically predicted to occur towards the end of the 2nd year in the Presidential Cycle at the time of mid-term elections.*

22 MONDAY   053 / 312

---

30 day	Wednesday March 24
60 day	Friday April 23
90 day	Sunday May 23
180 day	Saturday August 21
1 year	Tuesday February 22

24 WEDNESDAY   055 / 310

---

30 day	Friday March 26
60 day	Sunday April 25
90 day	Tuesday May 25
180 day	Monday August 23
1 year	Thursday February 24

26 FRIDAY   057 / 308

---

30 day	Sunday March 28
60 day	Tuesday April 27
90 day	Thursday May 27
180 day	Wednesday August 25
1 year	Saturday February 26

23 TUESDAY   054 / 311

---

30 day	Thursday March 25
60 day	Saturday April 24
90 day	Monday May 24
180 day	Sunday August 22
1 year	Wednesday February 23

25 THURSDAY   056 / 309

---

30 day	Saturday March 27
60 day	Monday April 26
90 day	Wednesday May 26
180 day	Tuesday August 24
1 year	Friday February 25

WEEK 08

Market Indices & Rates
Weekly Values*

Stock Markets	2008	2009
Dow	12,357	7,485
S&P500	1,351	782
Nasdaq	2,309	1,456
TSX	13,524	8,172
FTSE	5,926	4,017
DAX	6,916	4,204
Nikkei	13,578	7,581
Hang Seng	23,680	13,028

Commodities	2008	2009
Oil	99.56	37.12
Gold	927.05	968.80

Bond Yields	2008	2009
USA 5 Yr Treasury	2.89	1.79
USA 10 Yr T	3.85	2.75
USA 20 Yr T	4.58	3.80
Moody's Aaa	5.62	5.25
Moody's Baa	6.93	8.01
CAN 5 Yr T	3.45	2.07
CAN 10 Yr T	3.89	2.88

Money Market	2008	2009
USA Fed Funds	3.00	0.25
USA 3 Mo T-B	2.23	0.30
CAN tgt overnight rate	4.00	1.00
CAN 3 Mo T-B	3.25	0.69

Foreign Exchange	2008	2009
USD/EUR	1.47	1.27
USD/GBP	1.95	1.43
CAN/USD	1.01	1.26
JPY/USD	107.70	92.73

FEBRUARY

M	T	W	T	F	S	S
1	2	3	4	5	6	7
8	9	10	11	12	13	14
15	16	17	18	19	20	21
22	23	24	25	26	27	28

MARCH

M	T	W	T	F	S	S
1	2	3	4	5	6	7
8	9	10	11	12	13	14
15	16	17	18	19	20	21
22	23	24	25	26	27	28
29	30	31				

APRIL

M	T	W	T	F	S	S
			1	2	3	4
5	6	7	8	9	10	11
12	13	14	15	16	17	18
19	20	21	22	23	24	25
26	27	28	29	30		

* Weekly avg closing values- except Fed Funds Rate & CAN overnight tgt rate which are weekly closing values.

MARCH

	MONDAY	TUESDAY	WEDNESDAY
WEEK 09	**1** 30	**2** 29	**3** 28
WEEK 10	**8** 23	**9** 22	**10** 21
WEEK 11	**15** 16	**16** 15	**17** 14
WEEK 12	**22** 9	**23** 8	**24** 7
WEEK 13	**29** 2	**30** 1	**31**

THURSDAY		FRIDAY	
4	27	**5**	26
11	20	**12**	19
18	13	**19**	12
25	6	**26**	5
1		2	

APRIL

M	T	W	T	F	S	S
		1	2	3	4	
5	6	7	8	9	10	11
12	13	14	15	16	17	18
19	20	21	22	23	24	25
26	27	28	29	30		

MAY

M	T	W	T	F	S	S
					1	2
3	4	5	6	7	8	9
10	11	12	13	14	15	16
17	18	19	20	21	22	23
24	25	26	27	28	29	30
31						

JUNE

M	T	W	T	F	S	S
	1	2	3	4	5	6
7	8	9	10	11	12	13
14	15	16	17	18	19	20
21	22	23	24	25	26	27
28	29	30				

JULY

M	T	W	T	F	S	S
			1	2	3	4
5	6	7	8	9	10	11
12	13	14	15	16	17	18
19	20	21	22	23	24	25
26	27	28	29	30	31	

MARCH
S U M M A R Y

1.5%
1.0%
0.5%
0.0%
S&P500 Cumulative Daily Gains for Avg Month 1950 to 2009

STRATEGIES	PAGE
STRATEGIES STARTING	
STRATEGIES FINISHING	
Small Cap (Small Company) Effect	153

70%
60%
50%
40%

Prob. of Daily Gain

♦ March has been a turning point month before – remember 2000 when the market topped early in the month? In 2009 the turning point was once again the beginning of March – this time the market bottomed and set up for a strong rally. ♦ The financial sector was the top performing sector, followed by materials and then the consumer discretionary. The financials sector usually does well until the middle of April. The materials and consumer discretionary sectors are also typically strong candidates for top sectors.

BEST / WORST MARCH BROAD MKTS. 2000-2009

BEST MARCH MARKETS
♦ Russell 3000 Val (2000) 11.1%
♦ Nasdaq (2009) 10.9%
♦ S&P500 (2000) 9.7%

WORST MARCH MARKETS
♦ Nasdaq (2001) -14.5%
♦ Russell 3000 Gr (2001) -10.8%
♦ Russell 1000 (2001) -6.7%

Index Values End of Month

	2000	2001	2002	2003	2004	2005	2006	2007	2008	2009
Dow	10,922	9,879	10,404	7,992	10,358	10,504	11,109	12,354	12,263	7,609
S&P 500	1,499	1,160	1,147	848	1,126	1,181	1,295	1,421	1,323	798
Nasdaq	4,573	1,840	1,845	1,341	1,994	1,999	2,340	2,422	2,279	1,529
TSX	9,462	7,608	7,851	6,343	8,586	9,612	12,111	13,166	13,350	8,720
Russell 1000	1,536	1,173	1,167	866	1,160	1,222	1,359	1,492	1,385	834
Russell 2000	1,341	1,120	1,259	906	1,467	1,529	1,902	1,990	1,710	1,051
Russell 3000 Growth	3,441	1,970	1,928	1,391	1,847	1,850	2,094	2,206	2,149	1,387
Russell 3000 Value	2,086	2,076	2,150	1,620	2,252	2,481	2,765	3,137	2,733	1,529

Percent Gain for March

	2000	2001	2002	2003	2004	2005	2006	2007	2008	2009
Dow	7.8	-5.9	2.9	1.3	-2.1	-2.4	1.1	0.7	0.0	7.7
S&P 500	9.7	-6.4	3.7	0.8	-1.6	-1.9	1.1	1.0	-0.6	8.5
Nasdaq	-2.6	-14.5	6.6	0.3	-1.8	-2.6	2.6	0.2	0.3	10.9
TSX	3.7	-5.8	2.8	-3.2	-2.3	-0.6	3.6	0.9	-1.7	7.4
Russell 1000	9.0	-6.7	4.0	0.9	-1.5	-1.7	1.3	0.9	-0.8	8.5
Russell 2000	-6.7	-5.0	7.9	1.1	0.8	-3.0	4.7	0.9	0.3	8.7
Russell 3000 Growth	5.6	-10.8	3.7	1.7	-1.8	-2.1	1.7	0.5	-0.7	8.7
Russell 3000 Value	11.1	-3.5	4.8	0.0	-0.9	-1.6	1.5	1.4	-0.8	8.3

March Market Avg. Performance 2000 to 2009 [1]

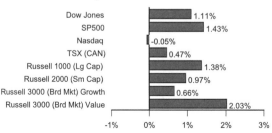

Dow Jones 1.11%
SP500 1.43%
Nasdaq -0.05%
TSX (CAN) 0.47%
Russell 1000 (Lg Cap) 1.38%
Russell 2000 (Sm Cap) 0.97%
Russell 3000 (Brd Mkt) Growth 0.66%
Russell 3000 (Brd Mkt) Value 2.03%

-1% 0% 1% 2% 3%

Interest Corner Mar[2]

	Fed Funds % [3]	3 Mo. T-Bill % [4]	10 Yr % [5]	20 Yr % [6]
2009	0.25	0.21	2.71	3.61
2008	2.25	1.38	3.45	4.30
2007	5.25	5.04	4.65	4.92
2006	4.75	4.63	4.86	5.07
2005	2.75	2.79	4.50	4.88

(1) Russell Data provided by Russell (2) Federal Reserve Bank of St. Louis- end of month values (3) Target rate set by FOMC (4)(5)(6) Constant yield maturities.

THACKRAY SECTOR THERMOMETER

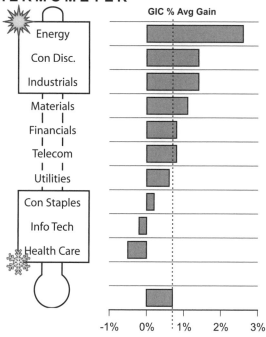

	GIC(2) % Avg Gain	Fq % Gain >S&P 500	SP GIC SECTOR 1990-2008(1)
	2.6 %	68 %	Energy
	1.4	74	Consumer Discretionary
	1.4	68	Industrials
	1.1	47	Materials
	0.8	63	Telecom
	0.8	53	Financials
	0.6	53	Utilities
	0.2	53	Consumer Staples
	-0.2	37	Information Technology
	-0.5	26	Health Care
	0.7 %	N/A %	S&P 500

Thermometer labels (top to bottom): Energy, Con Disc., Industrials, Materials, Financials, Telecom, Utilities, Con Staples, Info Tech, Health Care

---

Hot Box - 3 Best Sectors
Energy ♦ Con Disc. ♦ Industrials
March Portfolio

	Avg % Gain	Avg % Gain > S&P 500	Fq % Gain >S&P 500
1990-2008	1.8 %	1.1 %	79 %
2008	-0.2 %	0.4 %	

Cold Box - 3 Worst Sectors
Con Staples ♦ Info Tech ♦ Health Care
March Portfolio

	Avg % Gain	Avg % Gain > S&P 500	Fq % Gain >S&P 500
1990-2008	-0.2 %	-0.9 %	26 %
2008	0.4 %	0.2 %	

Commentary

♦ In March, it is the Energy sector that is on top again. This is the seasonal sweet spot for the sector (see *Oil- Winter/Spring Effect*). ♦ Consumer Discretionary is once again close to the top as the positive beginning of the year forecasts for consumer spending still have an uplifting affect. ♦ Industrials, which usually track the market closely are for the second month in a row a solid performing sector. ♦ Although Materials has fallen down the list, its performance is still solid. ♦ In 2008 both the average Hot Box and Cold Box 3 Sectors marginally outperformed the S&P 500. The *Hot Box 3 Sector* portfolio was helped by the strong performance of the industrial sector.

(1) Sector data provided by Standard and Poors (2) GIC is short form for Global Industry Classification (3) Sub Sector data provided by Standard and Poors, except where marked by symbol.

VALUE FOR FIRST 4 MONTHS OF THE YR.
GROWTH FOR LAST 3 MONTHS

☑ 2008 Performance

The *Value-Growth* strategy produced an extra 1/2% in 2008. Not a lot, but every bit helps.

There are many ways to invest in the markets. Investing in value or growth stocks is an investment style that is becoming more popular with investors.

Value stocks generally have low prices relative to their book values and/or low price to earnings ratios.

Growth stocks generally have high prices relative to their book values and/or high price to earnings ratios.

There have been many studies over time about which style of investing, value or growth, produces better returns with less risk, and in which type of economic environment. The scope of this book is concerned with the annual cycle of out-performance. On an annual basis, growth tends to outperform value during the last three months of the year. Value stocks tend to outperform for the first four months. In the middle of the year, June is an anomaly as growth stocks tend to outperform value.

Compared with value stocks, growth stocks tend to be better known companies with greater earnings stability. As a result, investors are willing to pay a higher premium for growth stocks. In the beginning of the year, almost every analyst on Wall Street calls for a market return between 8% and 12%. In this positive environment value stocks tend to outperform. In the summer months there is not a clear trend between growth and value investment styles, except for the month of June when growth stocks outperform.

ⓘ *Russell 1000 Growth: Growth companies from the Russell 1000 index. Russell 1000 Value: Value companies from the Russell 1000 index.*
For more information on the Russell indexes, see www.russell.com.

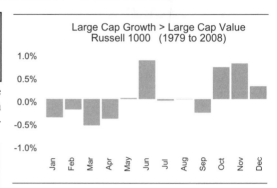

Large Cap Growth > Large Cap Value
Russell 1000 (1979 to 2008)

Large Cap Growth (Russell 1000 Growth) vs.
Large Cap Value (Russell 1000 Value)

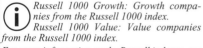

Jan. to Apr. (Value > Growth)

Oct. to Dec. (Growth > Value)

Year	Jan to Apr % Gain			Oct to Dec % Gain		
	Value	- Growth	= Diff	Growth	- Value	= Diff
1979	7.9	6.0	1.9	3.7	-4.2	7.9
1980	-2.8	-2.2	-0.7	10.6	4.7	5.9
1981	2.9	-6.6	9.5	8.0	4.1	4.0
1982	-5.1	-7.0	2.0	20.3	14.2	6.1
1983	17.7	15.6	2.1	-3.3	0.1	-3.4
1984	-1.7	-8.2	6.6	0.4	1.1	-0.7
1985	8.8	7.6	1.2	18.4	13.3	5.1
1986	9.6	15.0	-5.4	4.4	2.6	1.8
1987	13.6	20.9	-7.3	-23.9	-22.5	-1.4
1988	10.0	2.5	7.5	2.2	1.1	1.1
1989	10.3	12.6	-2.3	2.1	-1.4	3.4
1990	-7.9	-5.6	-2.3	10.2	6.7	3.4
1991	12.4	16.6	-4.2	12.3	3.4	8.9
1992	4.3	-4.9	9.1	6.4	4.9	1.5
1993	7.2	-5.4	12.6	3.4	-1.1	4.4
1994	-2.7	-4.5	1.8	0.3	-2.6	2.9
1995	11.6	11.4	0.3	4.2	5.8	-1.6
1996	5.1	7.7	-2.6	5.7	9.2	-3.5
1997	6.0	6.8	-0.8	1.3	3.9	-2.6
1998	11.6	16.4	-4.8	26.5	16.0	10.5
1999	10.2	6.2	4.0	25.0	4.9	20.1
2000	-1.4	1.9	-3.2	-21.4	3.1	-24.5
2001	-1.8	-11.0	9.2	14.9	6.8	8.1
2002	-0.1	-10.7	10.6	6.8	8.4	-1.6
2003	2.6	5.9	-3.2	10.1	13.4	-3.4
2004	-0.2	-0.7	0.4	8.9	9.7	0.8
2005	-2.5	-6.2	3.8	2.7	0.6	2.1
2006	7.8	2.6	5.2	5.6	7.3	-1.7
2007	4.2	5.6	-1.4	-1.1	-6.5	5.4
2008	-5.1	-5.8	0.7	-23.2	-23.0	-0.2
Avg.	4.4	2.7	1.7	4.7	2.8	1.9

1 MONDAY	060 / 305	**2** TUESDAY	061 / 304

Market Indices & Rates
Weekly Values*

Stock Markets	2008	2009
Dow	12,560	7,196
S&P500	1,366	754
Nasdaq	2,326	1,405
TSX	13,746	7,950
FTSE	6,003	3,852
DAX	6,895	3,893
Nikkei	13,860	7,426
Hang Seng	24,078	12,937

Commodities	2008	2009
Oil	100.89	41.67
Gold	953.10	967.40

Bond Yields	2008	2009
USA 5 Yr Treasury	2.80	1.97
USA 10 Yr T	3.78	2.91
USA 20 Yr T	4.56	3.87
Moody's Aaa	5.60	5.31
Moody's Baa	6.91	8.13
CAN 5 Yr T	3.35	2.07
CAN 10 Yr T	3.79	2.99

Money Market	2008	2009
USA Fed Funds	3.00	0.25
USA 3 Mo T-B	2.01	0.29
CAN tgt overnight rate	4.00	1.00
CAN 3 Mo T-B	3.18	0.65

Foreign Exchange	2008	2009
USD/EUR	1.50	1.28
USD/GBP	1.98	1.44
CAN/USD	0.99	1.25
JPY/USD	106.60	96.57

Monday March 1:
30 day	Wednesday March 31
60 day	Friday April 30
90 day	Sunday May 30
180 day	Saturday August 28
1 year	Tuesday March 1

Tuesday March 2:
30 day	Thursday April 1
60 day	Saturday May 1
90 day	Monday May 31
180 day	Sunday August 29
1 year	Wednesday March 2

3 WEDNESDAY	062 / 303	**4** THURSDAY	063 / 302

Wednesday March 3:
30 day	Friday April 2
60 day	Sunday May 2
90 day	Tuesday June 1
180 day	Monday August 30
1 year	Thursday March 3

Thursday March 4:
30 day	Saturday April 3
60 day	Monday May 3
90 day	Wednesday June 2
180 day	Tuesday August 31
1 year	Friday March 4

5 FRIDAY	064 / 301

Friday March 5:
30 day	Sunday April 4
60 day	Tuesday May 4
90 day	Thursday June 3
180 day	Wednesday September 1
1 year	Saturday March 5

MARCH

M	T	W	T	F	S	S
1	2	3	4	5	6	7
8	9	10	11	12	13	14
15	16	17	18	19	20	21
22	23	24	25	26	27	28
29	30	31				

APRIL

M	T	W	T	F	S	S
			1	2	3	4
5	6	7	8	9	10	11
12	13	14	15	16	17	18
19	20	21	22	23	24	25
26	27	28	29	30		

MAY

M	T	W	T	F	S	S
					1	2
3	4	5	6	7	8	9
10	11	12	13	14	15	16
17	18	19	20	21	22	23
24	25	26	27	28	29	30
31						

* Weekly avg closing values- except Fed Funds Rate & CAN overnight tgt rate which are weekly closing values.

WITCHES' HANGOVER
Day After Witching Day – Worst Day of the Month

Double, double toil and trouble;
Fire burn and cauldron bubble.
(Shakespeare, *Macbeth*, Act IV, Scene 1)

☒ **2008 Performance**

In 2008, Witching Day and the day after (Witches Hangover) proved to be positive. Other than very strong performances in October and November, Witches' Hangover was negative. Investors should always use caution in using a short-term bearish strategy during times when the market often rises.

Looking for a negative day to establish a long position, or even short the market? In our book <u>Time In Time Out, Outsmart the Market Using Calendar Investment Strategies</u>, Bruce Lindsay and I coined the term "Witches' Hangover" (WH) to describe the most negative day of the month. It is aptly coined because it is the trading day after Witching Day (WD).

WH avg. gain -0.1% & negative 64% of the time

Witches' Hangover (WH)
Days Before & After Avg. 1974 to 2008

Days Before Witches' Hangover   Days After Witches' Hangover

Witching Day (WD), the third Friday of every month, has a track record of volatility and negative performance. This is the day that stock options and futures expire.

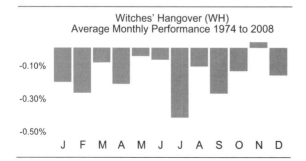

Witches' Hangover (WH)
Average Monthly Performance 1974 to 2008

	Daily Avg. Gains for WD & WH 1974 to 2008 Negative	
	WD	WH
1974	-0.54 %	-0.64 %
1975	-0.13	-0.23
1976	-0.01	0.03
1977	-0.07	-0.26
1978	-0.35	-0.04
1979	-0.16	0.03
1980	-0.14	-0.13
1981	0.16	-0.19
1982	0.32	0.24
1983	-0.09	-0.07
1984	-0.33	-0.20
1985	0.04	0.27
1986	0.23	0.07
1987	-0.02	-1.81
1988	0.62	-0.27
1989	0.22	-0.56
1990	0.02	-0.69
1991	-0.11	-0.33
1992	0.15	-0.24
1993	-0.13	-0.12
1994	-0.19	-0.34
1995	-0.02	0.08
1996	0.27	0.09
1997	-0.46	0.10
1998	0.37	0.55
1999	0.06	0.07
2000	-0.81	-0.44
2001	-0.72	0.45
2002	-0.26	-0.55
2003	0.30	-0.86
2004	-0.03	-0.12
2005	-0.05	-0.08
2006	-0.13	-0.02
2007	0.28	0.00
2008	1.03	0.36
Avg.	-0.02 %	-0.17 %

Although investors have been led to believe that Witching Day is the worst day of the month, Witches' Hangover has produced a bigger negative performance. This may be a result of investors, after a Friday of volatility and poor performance, suffering a stock market hangover and selling into the market on the Monday. In the graph "Witches' Hangover (WH) - Days Before & After Avg" the average daily performance of Witches' Hangover is marked WH and is the darker column. Witching Day (WD) is the previous day. WH is clearly the worst day. Together they make a wicked pair.

8 MONDAY	067 / 298		**9** TUESDAY	068 / 297

Market Indices & Rates
Weekly Values*

Stock Markets	2008	2009
Dow	12,132	6,717
S&P500	1,318	695
Nasdaq	2,245	1,318
TSX	13,453	7,671
FTSE	5,781	3,569
DAX	6,605	3,731
Nikkei	12,991	7,281
Hang Seng	23,133	12,163

Commodities	2008	2009
Oil	103.42	43.26
Gold	979.35	921.70

Bond Yields	2008	2009
USA 5 Yr Treasury	2.51	1.87
USA 10 Yr T	3.61	2.90
USA 20 Yr T	4.48	3.85
Moody's Aaa	5.54	5.40
Moody's Baa	6.89	8.23
CAN 5 Yr T	3.03	1.87
CAN 10 Yr T	3.60	2.98

Money Market	2008	2009
USA Fed Funds	3.00	0.25
USA 3 Mo T-B	1.55	0.24
CAN tgt overnight rate	3.50	0.50
CAN 3 Mo T-B	2.73	0.45

Foreign Exchange	2008	2009
USD/EUR	1.53	1.26
USD/GBP	1.99	1.41
CAN/USD	0.99	1.29
JPY/USD	103.00	98.08

Monday 8:
30 day	Wednesday April 7
60 day	Friday May 7
90 day	Sunday June 6
180 day	Saturday September 4
1 year	Tuesday March 8

Tuesday 9:
30 day	Thursday April 8
60 day	Saturday May 8
90 day	Monday June 7
180 day	Sunday September 5
1 year	Wednesday March 9

10 WEDNESDAY	069 / 296		**11** THURSDAY	070 / 295

Wednesday 10:
30 day	Friday April 9
60 day	Sunday May 9
90 day	Tuesday June 8
180 day	Monday September 6
1 year	Thursday March 10

Thursday 11:
30 day	Saturday April 10
60 day	Monday May 10
90 day	Wednesday June 9
180 day	Tuesday September 7
1 year	Friday March 11

12 FRIDAY	071 / 294

Friday 12:
30 day	Sunday April 11
60 day	Tuesday May 11
90 day	Thursday June 10
180 day	Wednesday September 8
1 year	Saturday March 12

MARCH
M	T	W	T	F	S	S
1	2	3	4	5	6	7
8	9	10	11	12	13	14
15	16	17	18	19	20	21
22	23	24	25	26	27	28
29	30	31				

APRIL
M	T	W	T	F	S	S
			1	2	3	4
5	6	7	8	9	10	11
12	13	14	15	16	17	18
19	20	21	22	23	24	25
26	27	28	29	30		

MAY
M	T	W	T	F	S	S
					1	2
3	4	5	6	7	8	9
10	11	12	13	14	15	16
17	18	19	20	21	22	23
24	25	26	27	28	29	30
31						

* Weekly avg closing values- except Fed Funds Rate & CAN overnight tgt rate which are weekly closing values.

SUPER SEVEN DAYS
7 Best Days of the Month

☑ **2008 Performance**

Although two-thirds of 2008 the Super Seven was negative, the last third of the year produced extraordinarily large gains. The net gain for the year was 13.7%.

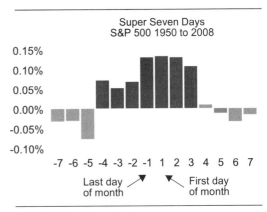

Super Seven Days
S&P 500 1950 to 2008

From 1950 to 2008
All 7 days better
than market average

The end of the month tends to be an excellent time to invest: portfolio managers "window dress" (adjust their portfolios to look good for month end reports), investors stop procrastinating and invest their extra cash, and brokers try to increase their commissions by investing their client's extra cash. All of these factors tend to produce above average returns for the market.

The above diagram illustrates the strength of the Super Seven days. The Super Seven days are the last four days of the month and the first three of the next month represented by the dark columns from day -4 to day 3. All of the Super Seven days have daily average gains above 0.03% which is the daily market average gain for the entire year.

% Gain Super Seven Day Period From 1998 to 2008

	1999	2000	2001	2002	2003	2004	2005	2006	2007	2008	Avg.
Jan	3.1 %	1.1 %	-0.2 %	-3.8 %	-1.1 %	-2.5 %	1.8 %	-0.1 %	1.6 %	-4.5	-0.5 %
Feb	-3.5	3.6	-0.9	5.2	-0.3	0.9	2.2	-0.4	-5.6	-2.8	-0.2
Mar	2.2	-2.4	-4.3	-2.0	0.2	3.7	0.9	0.8	0.1	1.2	0.0
Apr	-0.9	-1.0	3.2	-1.8	1.7	-1.2	1.2	0.0	1.5	1.3	0.4
May	-0.5	4.9	-0.7	-3.1	5.7	1.9	0.2	0.5	1.6	0.1	1.0
Jun	5.5	0.1	0.1	-3.6	0.2	-2.1	0.3	1.9	1.8	-3.9	0.0
Jul	-3.1	-1.5	2.0	-0.5	-3.3	1.3	1.3	0.9	-5.6	2.2	-0.6
Aug	-1.8	-0.9	-6.2	-7.3	3.4	0.8	1.7	0.4	0.8	-2.4	-1.1
Sep	1.9	-0.3	6.9	0.0	2.0	2.9	-1.6	1.8	1.4	-7.3	0.8
Oct	4.7	4.5	0.2	2.0	2.0	4.4	2.0	-1.3	-0.8	12.2	3.0
Nov	2.0	2.6	1.1	-2.6	2.8	1.2	-0.3	1.0	5.5	8.8	2.2
Dec	-3.8	2.1	2.4	4.1	2.7	-1.8	0.4	-0.1	-5.7	7.7	0.8
Avg.	0.5	1.1	0.3	-1.1	1.3	0.8	0.8	0.0	0.0	1.1	0.5

⚠ *Historically it has been best not to use the Super Seven for July and August. Both of these months have negative average performances and have been negative more often than positive over the last ten years.*

Although the Super Seven has done extremely well, there have been two trouble spots of negative performance. First, in 1998 when the Asian Financial Flu currency crisis struck the market, the market had three separate declines of more than 10%, which in turn resulted in three negative performances of the Super Seven greater than 5% at month ends. The months affected were July, August and September. Second, 2002 was a disastrous year for the market. The first major decline started on March 12 and pushed the market down more than 30%. The second major decline started on August 22 and pushed the market down more than 15%. Both of these declines had a large affect on the results of the Super Seven for the year. Despite these negative periods, the Super Seven has outperformed the broad market over the last ten years.

15 MONDAY · 074 / 291

_____
_____
_____
_____
_____
_____
_____
_____
_____
_____
_____
_____
_____
_____
_____

30 day	Wednesday April 14
60 day	Friday May 14
90 day	Sunday June 13
180 day	Saturday September 11
1 year	Tuesday March 15

16 TUESDAY · 075 / 290

_____
_____
_____
_____
_____
_____
_____
_____
_____
_____
_____
_____
_____
_____
_____

30 day	Thursday April 15
60 day	Saturday May 15
90 day	Monday June 14
180 day	Sunday September 12
1 year	Wednesday March 16

17 WEDNESDAY · 076 / 289

_____
_____
_____
_____
_____
_____
_____
_____
_____
_____
_____
_____
_____
_____

30 day	Friday April 16
60 day	Sunday May 16
90 day	Tuesday June 15
180 day	Monday September 13
1 year	Thursday March 17

18 THURSDAY · 077 / 288

_____
_____
_____
_____
_____
_____
_____
_____
_____
_____
_____
_____
_____
_____

30 day	Saturday April 17
60 day	Monday May 17
90 day	Wednesday June 16
180 day	Tuesday September 14
1 year	Friday March 18

19 FRIDAY · 078 / 287

_____
_____
_____

30 day	Sunday April 18
60 day	Tuesday May 18
90 day	Thursday June 17
180 day	Wednesday September 15
1 year	Saturday March 19

* Weekly avg closing values- except Fed Funds Rate & CAN overnight tgt rate which are weekly closing values.

WEEK 11

Market Indices & Rates
Weekly Values*

Stock Markets	2008	2009
Dow	12,021	6,960
S&P500	1,301	725
Nasdaq	2,229	1,371
TSX	13,269	8,009
FTSE	5,684	3,683
DAX	6,505	3,881
Nikkei	12,545	7,257
Hang Seng	22,732	11,899

Commodities	2008	2009
Oil	109.42	45.68
Gold	982.65	915.60

Bond Yields	2008	2009
USA 5 Yr Treasury	2.47	1.93
USA 10 Yr T	3.51	2.92
USA 20 Yr T	4.39	3.86
Moody's Aaa	5.53	5.49
Moody's Baa	6.91	8.40
CAN 5 Yr T	2.95	1.89
CAN 10 Yr T	3.53	2.93

Money Market	2008	2009
USA Fed Funds	3.00	0.25
USA 3 Mo T-B	1.37	0.22
CAN tgt overnight rate	3.50	0.50
CAN 3 Mo T-B	2.30	0.42

Foreign Exchange	2008	2009
USD/EUR	1.55	1.27
USD/GBP	2.02	1.39
CAN/USD	0.99	1.29
JPY/USD	101.56	98.07

MARCH

M	T	W	T	F	S	S
1	2	3	4	5	6	7
8	9	10	11	12	13	14
15	16	17	18	19	20	21
22	23	24	25	26	27	28
29	30	31				

APRIL

M	T	W	T	F	S	S
			1	2	3	4
5	6	7	8	9	10	11
12	13	14	15	16	17	18
19	20	21	22	23	24	25
26	27	28	29	30		

MAY

M	T	W	T	F	S	S
					1	2
3	4	5	6	7	8	9
10	11	12	13	14	15	16
17	18	19	20	21	22	23
24	25	26	27	28	29	30
31						

CANADIANS GIVE 3 CHEERS FOR AMERICAN HOLIDAYS

☑ 2008 Performance

The compound gain from Memorial Day, Independence Day and Thanksgiving in 2008 was just over 1/2%. The weakest holiday, Independence Day pulled the trio down. In the end Thanksgiving pulled the compound gain into positive territory.

1% average gain from 1977 to 2008 and 97% of the time positive

How the trade works

For the three big holidays in the United States that do not exist in Canada (Memorial, Independence and Thanksgiving Days), buy at the end of the market day before the holiday (TSX Composite) and sell at the end of the U.S. holiday when the U.S markets are closed.

For U.S. investors to take advantage of this trade they must have access to the TSX Composite.

When I used to work on the retail side of the investment business I was always amazed at how often the Canadian market increased on American holidays, when the Canadian stock market was open and the American market was closed. The holiday always had light volume, tended not to have large increases or decreases, but nevertheless usually ended the day with a gain.

Generally, markets perform well around most major American holidays, hence the trading strategies for American holidays included in this book. The main reason for the strong performance around these holidays is a lack of institutional involvement in the markets, allowing bullish retail investors to push up the markets.

On the actual holidays, there are no economic news releases in America and very seldom is there anything released in Canada of significance. During market hours, without any influences the market tends to float, preferring to wait until the next day before making any significant moves.

Despite this laxidasical action during the day, the TSX Comp tends to end the day on a gain. This is true for the three major holidays that are covered in this book: Memorial, Independence and Thanksgiving Day.

From a theoretical perspective a lot of the gain that is captured on the U.S. holiday is realized on the next day that the markets are open in the United States. This does not invalidate the Canadian trade – it presents more alternatives for the astute investor.

For example, an investor can allocate a portion of money to a standard American holiday trade and another portion to the Canadian version. By spreading out the exit days the overall risk in the trade is reduced.

TSX Comp
Gain 1977-2008   Positive ☐

	Memorial	Independence	Thanksgiving	Compound Growth
1977	0.10 %	-0.08 %	0.61 %	0.63 %
1978	-0.05	-0.16	0.57	0.36
1979	1.11	0.23	0.58	1.93
1980	1.64	0.76	0.89	3.32
1981	0.51	-0.15	1.03	1.40
1982	-0.18	-0.01	0.35	0.17
1983	0.29	0.53	0.15	0.97
1984	0.86	-0.11	0.73	1.48
1985	0.61	0.31	0.31	1.24
1986	0.23	-0.02	0.22	0.44
1987	-0.11	1.08	1.57	2.55
1988	0.44	0.08	0.58	1.11
1989	0.10	-0.12	-0.11	-0.13
1990	0.11	0.43	0.02	0.57
1991	0.02	0.18	-0.09	0.11
1992	-0.06	0.35	0.36	0.65
1993	0.42	-0.18	0.14	0.38
1994	-0.19	0.70	0.91	1.43
1995	0.14	0.25	0.29	0.68
1996	0.11	0.25	0.54	0.90
1997	1.08	-0.04	-0.85	0.18
1998	0.56	0.18	0.51	1.25
1999	0.57	1.63	1.14	3.39
2000	0.43	1.04	0.91	2.40
2001	-0.02	-0.23	0.70	0.45
2002	-0.01	0.08	0.38	0.45
2003	0.03	0.03	0.26	0.31
2004	0.84	-0.02	0.55	1.39
2005	0.56	0.39	1.48	2.45
2006	0.70	1.04	0.70	2.46
2007	0.35	-0.03	0.76	1.08
2008	0.24	-0.94	1.28	0.56
Avg	0.36 %	0.23 %	0.55 %	1.14 %
Fq > 0	78 %	59 %	90 %	97 %

22 MONDAY 081 / 284

23 TUESDAY 082 / 283

30 day	Wednesday April 21
60 day	Friday May 21
90 day	Sunday June 20
180 day	Saturday September 18
1 year	Tuesday March 22

30 day	Thursday April 22
60 day	Saturday May 22
90 day	Monday June 21
180 day	Sunday September 19
1 year	Wednesday March 23

24 WEDNESDAY 083 / 282

25 THURSDAY 084 / 281

30 day	Friday April 23
60 day	Sunday May 23
90 day	Tuesday June 22
180 day	Monday September 20
1 year	Thursday March 24

30 day	Saturday April 24
60 day	Monday May 24
90 day	Wednesday June 23
180 day	Tuesday September 21
1 year	Friday March 25

26 FRIDAY 085 / 280

30 day	Sunday April 25
60 day	Tuesday May 25
90 day	Thursday June 24
180 day	Wednesday September 22
1 year	Saturday March 26

* Weekly avg closing values- except Fed Funds Rate & CAN overnight tgt rate which are weekly closing values.

WEEK 12

Market Indices & Rates
Weekly Values*

Stock Markets	2008	2009
Dow	12,206	7,356
S&P500	1,309	776
Nasdaq	2,228	1,460
TSX	12,893	8,554
FTSE	5,515	3,837
DAX	6,314	4,028
Nikkei	12,124	7,893
Hang Seng	21,361	12,987

Commodities	2008	2009
Oil	105.59	49.46
Gold	975.56	927.75

Bond Yields	2008	2009
USA 5 Yr Treasury	2.34	1.75
USA 10 Yr T	3.39	2.75
USA 20 Yr T	4.22	3.78
Moody's Aaa	5.44	5.62
Moody's Baa	6.82	8.50
CAN 5 Yr T	2.87	1.79
CAN 10 Yr T	3.45	2.79

Money Market	2008	2009
USA Fed Funds	2.25	0.25
USA 3 Mo T-B	0.82	0.22
CAN tgt overnight rate	3.50	0.50
CAN 3 Mo T-B	1.83	0.40

Foreign Exchange	2008	2009
USD/EUR	1.56	1.32
USD/GBP	2.00	1.42
CAN/USD	1.00	1.26
JPY/USD	98.30	97.29

MARCH

M	T	W	T	F	S	S
1	2	3	4	5	6	7
8	9	10	11	12	13	14
15	16	17	18	19	20	21
22	23	24	25	26	27	28
29	30	31				

APRIL

M	T	W	T	F	S	S
			1	2	3	4
5	6	7	8	9	10	11
12	13	14	15	16	17	18
19	20	21	22	23	24	25
26	27	28	29	30		

MAY

M	T	W	T	F	S	S
					1	2
3	4	5	6	7	8	9
10	11	12	13	14	15	16
17	18	19	20	21	22	23
24	25	26	27	28	29	30
31						

18 DAY EARNINGS MONTH EFFECT
Markets Outperform 1st 18 Calendar Days of Earnings Months

☑ **2008 Performance**

Despite a large loss in January, the 18 Day Earnings Strategy produced a very large gain in 2008. The 19% gain in October definitely had an impact.

Earnings season occurs the first month of every quarter. At this time, public companies report their financials for the previous quarter and often give guidance on future expectations. As a result investors tend to bid up stocks anticipating good earnings.

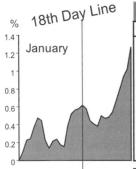

1st to 18th Day 1950-2008

Avg Gain 0.64%	Fq Pos 63%

The first month of the year generally has a good start. Investors and money managers generally push the market upward as they try to lock in their new positions for the year. The result is that the market tends to increase for the first eighteen days, pause, and then accelerate through the end of the month.

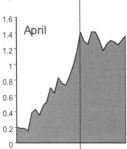

Avg Gain 1.4%	Fq Pos 72%

This month has a reputation of being a strong month. If you look at the graph you can see that almost all of the gains have come in the first half of the month. It is interesting to note that the month returns tend to peak just after the last day to file tax returns.

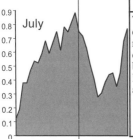

Avg Gain 0.72%	Fq Pos 63%

This is the month in which the market can peak in strong bull markets. The returns in the first half of the month can be positive, but investors should be cautious, as the time period following in August and September has a tendency towards negative returns.

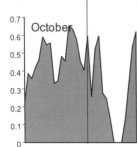

Avg Gain 0.6%	Fq Pos 63%

This is the month with a bad reputation. Once again, the first part of the month tends to do well. It is the middle segment, centered around the notorious Black Monday, that brings down the results. Toward the end of the month investors realize that the world has not ended and start to buy stocks again, providing a strong finish.

1st to 18th Day Gain S&P500

	Jan	Apr	Jul	Oct
1950	0.54 %	4.28 %	-3.56 %	2.88 %
1951	4.85	3.41	4.39	1.76
1952	2.02	-3.57	-0.44	-1.39
1953	-2.07	-2.65	0.87	3.38
1954	2.50	3.71	2.91	-1.49
1955	-3.28	4.62	3.24	-4.63
1956	-2.88	-1.53	4.96	2.18
1957	-4.35	2.95	2.45	-4.93
1958	2.78	1.45	1.17	2.80
1959	1.09	4.47	1.23	0.79
1960	-3.34	2.26	-2.14	1.55
1961	2.70	1.75	-0.36	2.22
1962	-4.42	-1.84	2.65	0.12
1963	3.30	3.49	-1.27	2.26
1964	2.05	1.99	2.84	0.77
1965	2.05	2.31	1.87	1.91
1966	1.64	2.63	2.66	2.77
1967	6.80	1.84	3.16	-1.51
1968	-0.94	7.63	1.87	2.09
1969	-1.76	-0.27	-2.82	3.37
1970	-1.24	-4.42	6.83	-0.02
1971	1.37	3.17	0.42	-1.01
1972	1.92	2.40	-1.22	-2.13
1973	0.68	0.02	2.00	1.46
1974	-2.04	0.85	-2.58	13.76
1975	3.50	3.53	-2.09	5.95
1976	7.55	-2.04	0.38	-3.58
1977	-3.85	2.15	0.47	-3.18
1978	-4.77	4.73	1.40	-2.00
1979	3.76	0.11	-1.19	-5.22
1980	2.90	-1.51	6.83	4.83
1981	-0.73	-0.96	-0.34	2.59
1982	-4.35	4.33	1.33	13.54
1983	4.10	4.43	-2.20	1.05
1984	1.59	-0.80	-1.16	1.20
1985	2.44	0.10	1.32	2.72
1986	-1.35	1.46	-5.77	3.25
1987	9.96	-1.64	3.48	-12.16
1988	1.94	0.12	-1.09	2.75
1989	3.17	3.78	4.20	-2.12
1990	-4.30	0.23	1.73	-0.10
1991	0.61	3.53	3.83	1.20
1992	0.42	3.06	1.83	-1.45
1993	0.26	-0.60	-1.06	2.07
1994	1.67	-0.74	2.46	1.07
1995	2.27	0.93	2.52	0.52
1996	-1.25	-0.29	-4.04	3.42
1997	4.78	1.22	3.41	-0.33
1998	-0.92	1.90	4.67	3.88
1999	1.14	2.54	3.36	-2.23
2000	-0.96	-3.80	2.69	-6.57
2001	2.10	6.71	-1.36	2.66
2002	-1.79	-2.00	-10.94	8.48
2003	2.50	5.35	1.93	4.35
2004	2.51	0.75	-3.46	-0.05
2005	-1.32	-2.93	2.50	-4.12
2006	2.55	1.22	0.51	3.15
2007	1.41	4.33	-3.20	1.48
2008	-9.75	5.11	-1.51	19.36
Avg	0.64 %	1.42 %	0.72 %	0.62 %

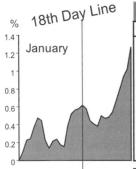

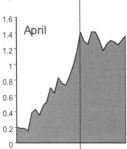

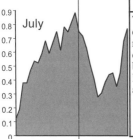

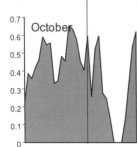

29 MONDAY   088 / 277 | **30** TUESDAY   089 / 276

Market Indices & Rates
Weekly Values*

Stock Markets	2008	2009
Dow	12,405	7,777
S&P500	1,337	818
Nasdaq	2,307	1,547
TSX	13,275	8,884
FTSE	5,690	3,918
DAX	6,538	4,210
Nikkei	12,671	8,489
Hang Seng	22,758	13,842

Commodities	2008	2009
Oil	104.26	53.07
Gold	938.63	932.85

Bond Yields	2008	2009
USA 5 Yr Treasury	2.58	1.76
USA 10 Yr T	3.52	2.74
USA 20 Yr T	4.32	3.69
Moody's Aaa	5.51	5.51
Moody's Baa	6.93	8.53
CAN 5 Yr T	2.96	1.88
CAN 10 Yr T	3.48	2.89

Money Market	2008	2009
USA Fed Funds	2.25	0.25
USA 3 Mo T-B	1.29	0.18
CAN tgt overnight rate	3.50	0.50
CAN 3 Mo T-B	1.76	0.38

Foreign Exchange	2008	2009
USD/EUR	1.57	1.35
USD/GBP	2.00	1.45
CAN/USD	1.02	1.23
JPY/USD	99.79	97.76

30 day Wednesday April 28
60 day Friday May 28
90 day Sunday June 27
180 day Saturday September 25
1 year Tuesday March 29

30 day Thursday April 29
60 day Saturday May 29
90 day Monday June 28
180 day Sunday September 26
1 year Wednesday March 30

31 WEDNESDAY   090 / 275 | **1** THURSDAY   091 / 274

30 day Friday April 30
60 day Sunday May 30
90 day Tuesday June 29
180 day Monday September 27
1 year Thursday March 31

30 day Saturday May 1
60 day Monday May 31
90 day Wednesday June 30
180 day Tuesday September 28
1 year Friday April 1

2 FRIDAY   092 / 273

30 day Sunday May 2
60 day Tuesday June 1
90 day Thursday July 1
180 day Wednesday September 29
1 year Saturday April 2

APRIL
M	T	W	T	F	S	S
			1	2	3	4
5	6	7	8	9	10	11
12	13	14	15	16	17	18
19	20	21	22	23	24	25
26	27	28	29	30		

MAY
M	T	W	T	F	S	S
					1	2
3	4	5	6	7	8	9
10	11	12	13	14	15	16
17	18	19	20	21	22	23
24	25	26	27	28	29	30
31						

JUNE
M	T	W	T	F	S	S
	1	2	3	4	5	6
7	8	9	10	11	12	13
14	15	16	17	18	19	20
21	22	23	24	25	26	27
28	29	30				

* Weekly avg closing values - except Fed Funds Rate & CAN overnight tgt rate which are weekly closing values.

APRIL

	MONDAY	TUESDAY	WEDNESDAY
WEEK 13	29	30	31
WEEK 14	5 25	6 24	7 23
WEEK 15	12 18	13 17	14 16
WEEK 16	19 11	20 10	21 9
WEEK 17	26 4	27 3	28 2

THURSDAY		FRIDAY	
1	29	**2**	28
		USA Market Closed- Good Friday CAN Market Closed- Good Friday	
8	22	**9**	21
15	15	**16**	14
22	8	**23**	7
29	1	**30**	

MAY

M	T	W	T	F	S	S
					1	2
3	4	5	6	7	8	9
10	11	12	13	14	15	16
17	18	19	20	21	22	23
24	25	26	27	28	29	30
31						

JUNE

M	T	W	T	F	S	S
	1	2	3	4	5	6
7	8	9	10	11	12	13
14	15	16	17	18	19	20
21	22	23	24	25	26	27
28	29	30				

JULY

M	T	W	T	F	S	S
			1	2	3	4
5	6	7	8	9	10	11
12	13	14	15	16	17	18
19	20	21	22	23	24	25
26	27	28	29	30	31	

AUGUST

M	T	W	T	F	S	S
						1
2	3	4	5	6	7	8
9	10	11	12	13	14	15
16	17	18	19	20	21	22
23	24	25	26	27	28	29
30	31					

APRIL
S U M M A R Y

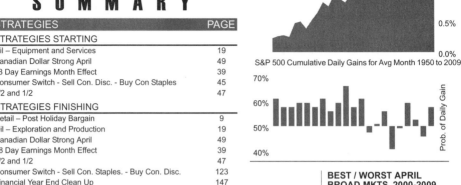

S&P 500 Cumulative Daily Gains for Avg Month 1950 to 2009

◆ April is always an interesting time in the markets, as the dynamics within the month present interesting opportunities. ◆ Historically, mid-month (last date to file taxes) tends to be an inflection point with a lot of sectors of the market reversing their trends. ◆ First, the broad market tends to peak. ◆ Second, short-term T-Bill rates tend to bottom. ◆ Third, technology stocks tend to bottom before a short-term up-trend. ◆ Fourth, financial stocks tend to do well in the first half of the month and poorly in the second half.

BEST / WORST APRIL BROAD MKTS. 2000-2009

BEST APRIL MARKETS
◆ Russell 2000 (2009) 15.3%
◆ Nasdaq (2001) 15.0%
◆ Russell 3000 Gr (2001) 12.6%

WORST APRIL MARKETS
◆ Nasdaq (2000) -15.6%
◆ Nasdaq (2002) -8.5%
◆ Russell 3000 Gr (2002) -7.8%

Index Values End of Month

	2000	2001	2002	2003	2004	2005	2006	2007	2008	2009
Dow	10,734	10,735	9,946	8,480	10,226	10,193	11,367	13,063	12,820	8,168
S&P 500	1,452	1,249	1,077	917	1,107	1,157	1,311	1,482	1,386	873
Nasdaq	3,861	2,116	1,688	1,464	1,920	1,922	2,323	2,525	2,413	1,717
TSX	9,348	7,947	7,663	6,586	8,244	9,369	12,204	13,417	13,937	9,325
Russell 1000	1,484	1,266	1,100	934	1,138	1,198	1,373	1,553	1,453	917
Russell 2000	1,260	1,206	1,269	991	1,391	1,440	1,900	2,024	1,780	1,212
Russell 3000 Growth	3,263	2,218	1,778	1,495	1,820	1,807	2,090	2,305	2,261	1,524
Russell 3000 Value	2,061	2,174	2,084	1,759	2,188	2,426	2,825	3,241	2,858	1,696

Percent Gain for April

	2000	2001	2002	2003	2004	2005	2006	2007	2008	2009
Dow	-1.7	8.7	-4.4	6.1	-1.3	-3.0	2.3	5.7	4.5	7.3
S&P 500	-3.1	7.7	-6.1	8.1	-1.7	-2.0	1.2	4.3	4.8	9.4
Nasdaq	-15.6	15.0	-8.5	9.2	-3.7	-3.9	-0.7	4.3	5.9	12.3
TSX	-1.2	4.5	-2.4	3.8	-4.0	-2.5	0.8	1.9	4.4	6.9
Russell 1000	-3.4	7.9	-5.8	7.9	-1.9	-2.0	1.1	4.1	5.0	10.0
Russell 2000	-6.1	7.7	0.8	9.4	-5.2	-5.8	-0.1	1.7	4.1	15.3
Russell 3000 Growth	-5.2	12.6	-7.8	7.5	-1.5	-2.3	-0.2	4.5	5.2	9.9
Russell 3000 Value	-1.2	4.7	-3.0	8.6	-2.8	-2.2	2.1	3.3	4.6	10.9

April Market Avg. Performance 2000 to 2009[1]

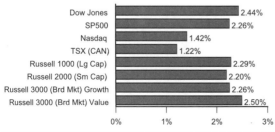

	Dow Jones	2.44%
	SP500	2.26%
	Nasdaq	1.42%
	TSX (CAN)	1.22%
	Russell 1000 (Lg Cap)	2.29%
	Russell 2000 (Sm Cap)	2.20%
	Russell 3000 (Brd Mkt) Growth	2.26%
	Russell 3000 (Brd Mkt) Value	2.50%

Interest Corner Apr[2]

	Fed Funds % [3]	3 Mo. T-Bill % [4]	10 Yr % [5]	20 Yr % [6]
2009	0.25	0.14	3.16	4.10
2008	2.00	1.43	3.77	4.49
2007	5.25	4.91	4.63	4.88
2006	4.75	4.77	5.07	5.31
2005	2.75	2.90	4.21	4.61

(1) Russell Data provided by Russell (2) Federal Reserve Bank of St. Louis- end of month values (3) Target rate set by FOMC (4)(5)(6) Constant yield maturities.

THACKRAY SECTOR THERMOMETER

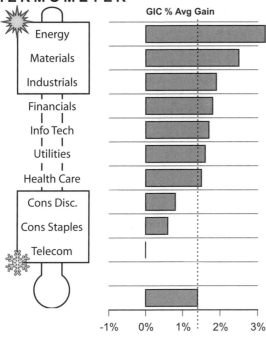

	GIC[2] % Avg Gain	Fq % Gain >S&P 500	SP GIC SECTOR 1990-2008[1]
Energy	3.2 %	74 %	Energy
Materials	2.5	53	Materials
Industrials	1.9	63	Industrials
Financials	1.8	47	Information Technology
Info Tech	1.7	58	Financials
Utilities	1.6	42	Utilities
Health Care	1.5	47	Health Care
Cons Disc.	0.8	47	Consumer Discretionary
Cons Staples	0.6	42	Consumer Staples
Telecom	0.0	32	Telecom
	1.4 %	N/A %	S&P 500

Hot Box - 3 Best Sectors
Energy ♦ Materials ♦ Industrials
April Portfolio

	Avg % Gain	Avg % Gain > S&P 500	Fq % Gain >S&P 500
1990-2008	2.5%	1.1%	58%
2008	5.8%	1.1%	

Cold Box - 3 Worst Sectors
Con Disc ♦ Con Staples ♦ Telecom
April Portfolio

	Avg % Gain	Avg % Gain > S&P 500	Fq % Gain >S&P 500
1990-2008	0.5%	-0.9%	37%
2008	2.6%	-2.2%	

Commentary

♦ Energy is still at the top of the thermometer. ♦ In the strong month of April, Information Technology makes a resurgence. ♦ Telecom is at the bottom of the ranking, producing an average return of 0.0% and only beating the S&P 500, 32% of the time. ♦ In 2008 Energy was the top sector with an almost 11% gain. Information Technology was the next best performing sector producing a gain of almost 7%. ♦ The *Hot Box 3 Best Sectors* outperformed the S&P 500 by 1.1%. ♦ *The Cold Box - 3 Worst Sectors* produced a combined gain of 2.6% and once again underperformed the market. The combination of the Consumer Discretionary, Consumer Staples and Telecom sectors has only outperformed the S&P 500 approximately one-third of the time since 1990.

(1) Sector data provided by Standard and Poors (2) GIC is short form for Global Industry Classification (3) Sub Sector data provided by Standard and Poors, except where marked by symbol.

CONSUMER SWITCH
SELL CONSUMER DISCRETIONARY
BUY CONSUMER STAPLES
Consumer Staples Outperform Apr 23 to Oct 27

☑ 2008 Performance

The consumer staples and discretionary sectors each outperformed during their seasonal strong periods – discretionary outperformed staples from October to April and staples ouperformed discretionary from April to October.

The *Consumer Switch* strategy has allowed investors to use a set portion of their account to switch between the two related consumer sectors. The end result has been outperformance compared with buying and holding both consumer sectors, or buying and holding the broad market.

1,096% total aggregate gain compared with 157% in the S&P 500

The basic premise of the strategy is that the Consumer Discretionary sector tends to outperform during the favorable six months when more money flows into the market, pushing up stock prices. On the other hand, the Consumer Staples sector tends to outperform when investors are looking for safety and stability of earnings in the six months when the market tends to move into a defensive mode.

Consumer Staples & Discretionary Switch Strategy*

Investment Period		Buy @ Beginning of Period	% Gain @ End of Period	% Gain Cumulative
90 Apr23 - 90 Oct29	Staples	7.7%	8%
90 Oct29 - 91 Apr23	Discretionary	41.7	53
91 Apr23 - 91 Oct28	Staples	2.1	56
91 Oct28 - 92 Apr23	Discretionary	15.9	81
92 Apr23 - 92 Oct27	Staples	6.3	92
92 Oct27 - 93 Apr23	Discretionary	6.3	104
93 Apr23 - 93 Oct27	Staples	5.8	116
93 Oct27 - 94 Apr25	Discretionary	-3.7	108
94 Apr25 - 94 Oct27	Staples	10.2	129
94 Oct27 - 95 Apr24	Discretionary	4.4	139
95 Apr24 - 95 Oct27	Staples	15.3	176
95 Oct27 - 96 Apr23	Discretionary	17.3	227
96 Apr23 - 96 Oct27	Staples	12.6	265
96 Oct27 - 97 Apr23	Discretionary	5.1	283
97 Apr23 - 97 Oct27	Staples	2.5	293
97 Oct27 - 98 Apr23	Discretionary	35.9	434
98 Apr23 - 98 Oct27	Staples	-0.7	423
98 Oct27 - 99 Apr23	Discretionary	41.8	651
99 Apr23 - 99 Oct27	Staples	-9.7	578
99 Oct27 - 00 Apr24	Discretionary	11.9	659
00 Apr24 - 00 Oct27	Staples	16.5	785
00 Oct27 - 01 Apr23	Discretionary	9.8	872
01 Apr23 - 01 Oct29	Staples	4.0	910
01 Oct29 - 02 Apr23	Discretionary	16.1	1073
02 Apr23 - 02 Oct28	Staples	-13.9	910
02 Oct28 - 03 Apr23	Discretionary	3.0	941
03 Apr23 - 03 Oct27	Staples	8.4	1028
03 Oct27 - 04 Apr23	Discretionary	9.6	1137
04 Apr23 - 04 Oct27	Staples	-7.4	1045
04 Oct27 - 05 Apr25	Discretionary	-2.0	1021
05 Apr25 - 05 Oct27	Staples	-0.5	1016
05 Oct27 - 06 Apr24	Discretionary	9.2	1119
06 Apr24 - 06 Oct27	Staples	10.6	1249
06 Oct27 - 07 Apr23	Discretionary	6.3	1334
07 Apr23 - 07 Oct29	Staples	4.6	1400
07 Oct29 - 08 Apr23	Discretionary	-13.7	1194
08 Apr23 - 08 Oct27	Staples	-21.5	916
08 Oct27 - 09 Apr23	Discretionary	17.7	1096

* If buy date lands on weekend or holiday, then date used is next trading date

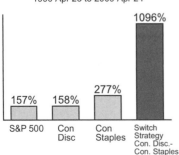

Total Gains From
1990 Apr 23 to 2009 Apr 24

S&P 500 157% | Con Disc 158% | Con Staples 277% | Switch Strategy Con. Disc.-Con. Staples 1096%

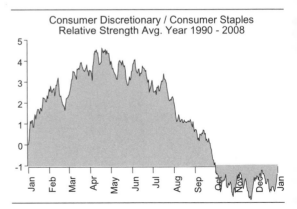

Consumer Discretionary / Consumer Staples
Relative Strength Avg. Year 1990 - 2008

5 MONDAY — 095 / 270

6 TUESDAY — 096 / 269

WEEK 14

Market Indices & Rates
Weekly Values*

Stock Markets	2008	2009
Dow	12,552	7,778
S&P500	1,360	815
Nasdaq	2,348	1,561
TSX	13,505	8,879
FTSE	5,862	3,960
DAX	6,708	4,194
Nikkei	13,011	8,433
Hang Seng	23,531	13,924

Commodities	2008	2009
Oil	103.49	50.32
Gold	902.65	914.35

Bond Yields	2008	2009
USA 5 Yr Treasury	2.64	1.73
USA 10 Yr T	3.55	2.76
USA 20 Yr T	4.37	3.64
Moody's Aaa	5.53	5.41
Moody's Baa	6.96	8.47
CAN 5 Yr T	3.06	1.80
CAN 10 Yr T	3.55	2.83

Money Market	2008	2009
USA Fed Funds	2.25	0.25
USA 3 Mo T-B	1.39	0.21
CAN tgt overnight rate	3.50	0.50
CAN 3 Mo T-B	1.98	0.39

Foreign Exchange	2008	2009
USD/EUR	1.57	1.33
USD/GBP	1.99	1.45
CAN/USD	1.02	1.25
JPY/USD	101.47	98.76

30 day Wednesday May 5
60 day Friday June 4
90 day Sunday July 4
180 day Saturday October 2
1 year Tuesday April 5

30 day Thursday May 6
60 day Saturday June 5
90 day Monday July 5
180 day Sunday October 3
1 year Wednesday April 6

7 WEDNESDAY — 097 / 268

8 THURSDAY — 098 / 267

30 day Friday May 7
60 day Sunday June 6
90 day Tuesday July 6
180 day Monday October 4
1 year Thursday April 7

30 day Saturday May 8
60 day Monday June 7
90 day Wednesday July 7
180 day Tuesday October 5
1 year Friday April 8

9 FRIDAY — 099 / 266

30 day Sunday May 9
60 day Tuesday June 8
90 day Thursday July 8
180 day Wednesday October 6
1 year Saturday April 9

APRIL

M	T	W	T	F	S	S
			1	2	3	4
5	6	7	8	9	10	11
12	13	14	15	16	17	18
19	20	21	22	23	24	25
26	27	28	29	30		

MAY

M	T	W	T	F	S	S
					1	2
3	4	5	6	7	8	9
10	11	12	13	14	15	16
17	18	19	20	21	22	23
24	25	26	27	28	29	30
31						

JUNE

M	T	W	T	F	S	S
	1	2	3	4	5	6
7	8	9	10	11	12	13
14	15	16	17	18	19	20
21	22	23	24	25	26	27
28	29	30				

* Weekly avg closing values- except Fed Funds Rate & CAN overnight tgt rate which are weekly closing values.

1/2 and 1/2
First 1/2 of April – Financial Stocks
Second 1/2 of April – Information Technology Stocks

☑ 2009 Performance

The main benefactor from the bounce off the March lows was the financial sector. The sector continued its rally into April and gained 23% in the first two weeks. Technology stocks also increased on que and outperformed the S&P 500.

The half and half is a short-term switch combination that takes advantage of the superior performance of the financial stocks in the first part of April and information technology stocks in the second half. The opportunity exists because technology stocks tend to increase at the same time financial stocks tend to decrease, creating an ideal switch opportunity.

> **3.5% extra & better than the S&P 500, 15 times out of 20**

Why do financial stocks tend to start their decline relative to the broad market at mid-month? Is it a coincidence that the rate on the three month T-Bill tends to bottom out at the same time? The common denominator that affects both of these markets is liquidity. Basically, investors sell-off their money market positions to cover their taxes, decreasing short-term money market rates.

Decreasing short-term yields are good for financial stocks, particularly banks. Banks tend to make more money with a steeper yield curve. They borrow short-term money (your meagre savings account) and lend out long-term (mortgages). The steeper the curve, the more money banks make. The end result is that financial stocks benefit from this trend in the first half of April.

On the flip side, investors stop selling their money market positions to cover taxes by mid-month. At this time, yields tend to increase and financial stocks decrease.

Financial & Info Tech & 1/2 & 1/2 > S&P 500

Year	April 1st to April 15th		April 16th to April 30th		April Compound Growth	
	S&P 500	Finan cials	S&P 500	Info Tech	S&P 500	1/2 & 1/2
1990	1.3 %	1.3 %	-3.9 %	-1.9 %	-2.7 %	-0.7 %
1991	1.6	2.3	-1.5	-3.1	0.0	-0.9
1992	3.1	1.0	-0.3	-1.3	2.8	-0.3
1993	-0.7	3.5	-1.8	-2.2	-2.5	1.3
1994	0.1	4.9	1.1	3.5	1.2	8.6
1995	1.7	2.9	1.1	5.8	2.8	8.8
1996	-0.5	-2.3	1.8	8.2	1.3	5.8
1997	-0.3	0.3	6.2	11.3	5.8	11.6
1998	1.6	5.5	-0.7	4.3	0.9	10.0
1999	2.8	5.0	0.9	1.3	3.8	6.4
2000	-9.5	-7.0	7.1	14.8	-3.1	6.8
2001	2.0	0.2	5.6	8.3	7.7	8.5
2002	-3.9	-1.6	-2.3	-3.5	-6.1	-5.1
2003	5.0	9.3	2.9	5.3	8.1	15.1
2004	0.2	-3.0	-1.9	-5.0	-1.7	-7.8
2005	-3.2	-2.6	1.2	2.3	-2.0	-0.4
2006	-0.4	-0.3	1.7	-1.3	1.2	-1.6
2007	2.3	0.5	2.0	2.7	4.3	3.2
2008	0.9	-0.6	3.8	6.8	4.8	6.2
2009	6.8	23.0	2.4	5.8	9.4	30.1
Avg.	0.5 %	2.1 %	1.3 %	3.1 %	1.8 %	5.3 %

Fortunately, information technology stocks tend to present a good opportunity at this time. By mid-April, technology stocks tend to become oversold for two reasons. First, technology stocks typically start to correct after a strong December and January (see *Information Technology - Use It or Lose It* strategy). The correction becomes exacerbated by investors selling off their holdings to pay their tax bill in mid-April. Investors typically sell off information technology stocks rather than the staid blue chip companies.

Ⓨ *Alternate Strategy—*
The first few days in May tend to produce gains. An alternate strategy is to hold the information technology position for the first three trading days in May.

ⓘ *The SP GICS Financial Sector # 40 encompasses a wide range financial based companies.*
The SP GICS Information Technology Sector # 45 encompasses a wide range technology based companies. For more information on the information technology sector, see www.standardandpoors.com

APRIL

12 MONDAY	102 / 263

30 day Wednesday May 12
60 day Friday June 11
90 day Sunday July 11
180 day Saturday October 9
1 year Tuesday April 12

13 TUESDAY	103 / 262

30 day Thursday May 13
60 day Saturday June 12
90 day Monday July 12
180 day Sunday October 10
1 year Wednesday April 13

14 WEDNESDAY	104 / 261

30 day Friday May 14
60 day Sunday June 13
90 day Tuesday July 13
180 day Monday October 11
1 year Thursday April 14

15 THURSDAY	105 / 260

30 day Saturday May 15
60 day Monday June 14
90 day Wednesday July 14
180 day Tuesday October 12
1 year Friday April 15

16 FRIDAY	106 / 259

30 day Sunday May 16
60 day Tuesday June 15
90 day Thursday July 15
180 day Wednesday October 13
1 year Saturday April 16

WEEK 15

Market Indices & Rates
Weekly Values*

Stock Markets	2008	2009
Dow	12,525	7,921
S&P500	1,357	833
Nasdaq	2,336	1,603
TSX	13,763	8,999
FTSE	5,970	3,958
DAX	6,724	4,380
Nikkei	13,216	8,833
Hang Seng	24,346	14,826

Commodities	2008	2009
Oil	109.74	50.46
Gold	922.85	877.63

Bond Yields	2008	2009
USA 5 Yr Treasury	2.66	1.88
USA 10 Yr T	3.54	2.93
USA 20 Yr T	4.33	3.80
Moody's Aaa	5.47	5.47
Moody's Baa	6.91	8.58
CAN 5 Yr T	3.07	1.87
CAN 10 Yr T	3.59	2.94

Money Market	2008	2009
USA Fed Funds	2.25	0.25
USA 3 Mo T-B	1.33	0.19
CAN tgt overnight rate	3.50	0.50
CAN 3 Mo T-B	2.23	0.39

Foreign Exchange	2008	2009
USD/EUR	1.58	1.33
USD/GBP	1.98	1.47
CAN/USD	1.01	1.23
JPY/USD	101.85	100.31

APRIL

M	T	W	T	F	S	S
		1	2	3	4
5	6	7	8	9	10	11
12	13	14	15	16	17	18
19	20	21	22	23	24	25
26	27	28	29	30

MAY

M	T	W	T	F	S	S
					1	2
3	4	5	6	7	8	9
10	11	12	13	14	15	16
17	18	19	20	21	22	23
24	25	26	27	28	29	30
31

JUNE

M	T	W	T	F	S	S
	1	2	3	4	5	6
7	8	9	10	11	12	13
14	15	16	17	18	19	20
21	22	23	24	25	26	27
28	29	30

Weekly avg closing values- except Fed Funds Rate & CAN overnight tgt rate which are weekly closing values.

- 48 -

CANADIAN DOLLAR STRONG APRIL

☑ 2009 Performance

The Canadian dollar rocketed upwards in April of 2009. There were predominately two factors pushing up the Canadian dollar, or should I say pushing the U.S. dollar down. First, oil was increasing in price. Second, risk appetite in the market was increasing and as a result investors were unloading their "safe-haven" U.S. dollars.

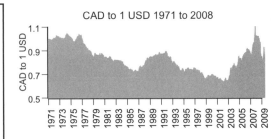

CAD to 1 USD 1971 to 2008

Since the year 2000 when oil started its ascent, the Canadian dollar has been labelled as a petro currency by foreign investors. All other things being equal, if oil increases in price, investors favor the Canadian dollar over the U.S. dollar. They do so with good reason, as Canada is a net exporter of oil and benefits from its rising price.

Oil tends to do well in the month of April as this is the heart of one of the strongest seasonal strategies – oil and oil stocks outperform from February 25th to May 9th (see *Oil Winter/Spring Strategy*). With the rising price of oil in April the Canadian dollar gets a free ride upwards.

April has been a strong month for the Canadian dollar relative to the U.S. dollar. All of the largest losses occurred in years when the Fed Reserve was aggressively hiking their target rate. At some point during the years 1987, 2000, 2004 and 2005, the Fed increased their target rate by a total of at least 1%. Since 1971 these years were the four biggest losers

for the Canadian dollar in the month of April. The Canadian dollar has been strong in April regardless of the long-term trend of the dollar. It started at approximately par in 1971 and reached a low in 2002 of $0.62 and a high of $1.09 in 2007. In both the ups and the downs in the economy, the Canadian dollar has outperformed the U.S. dollar in April.

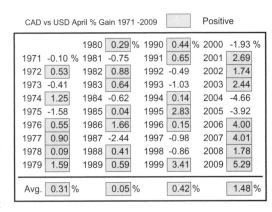

CAD vs USD April % Gain 1971 -2009 [   ] Positive

		1980	0.29 %	1990	0.44 %	2000	-1.93 %
1971	-0.10 %	1981	-0.75	1991	0.65	2001	2.69
1972	0.53	1982	0.88	1992	-0.49	2002	1.74
1973	-0.41	1983	0.64	1993	-1.03	2003	2.44
1974	1.25	1984	-0.62	1994	0.14	2004	-4.66
1975	-1.58	1985	0.04	1995	2.83	2005	-3.92
1976	0.55	1986	1.66	1996	0.15	2006	4.00
1977	0.90	1987	-2.44	1997	-0.98	2007	4.01
1978	0.09	1988	0.41	1998	-0.86	2008	1.78
1979	1.59	1989	0.59	1999	3.41	2009	5.29
Avg.	0.31 %		0.05 %		0.42 %		1.48 %

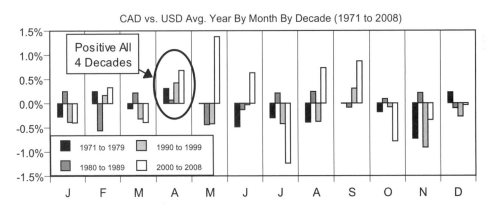

CAD vs. USD Avg. Year By Month By Decade (1971 to 2008)

Positive All 4 Decades

■ 1971 to 1979   ☐ 1990 to 1999
■ 1980 to 1989   ☐ 2000 to 2008

J F M A M J J A S O N D

19 MONDAY — 109 / 256

20 TUESDAY — 110 / 255

WEEK 16

Market Indices & Rates
Weekly Values*

Stock Markets	2008	2009
Dow	12,551	8,053
S&P500	1,357	857
Nasdaq	2,331	1,650
TSX	14,008	9,309
FTSE	5,964	4,026
DAX	6,673	4,598
Nikkei	13,186	8,835
Hang Seng	24,010	15,609

Commodities	2008	2009
Oil	114.41	49.80
Gold	931.20	882.38

Bond Yields	2008	2009
USA 5 Yr Treasury	2.79	1.79
USA 10 Yr T	3.67	2.87
USA 20 Yr T	4.44	3.80
Moody's Aaa	5.60	5.32
Moody's Baa	7.03	8.40
CAN 5 Yr T	3.11	1.89
CAN 10 Yr T	3.65	2.95

Money Market	2008	2009
USA Fed Funds	2.25	0.25
USA 3 Mo T-B	1.18	0.15
CAN tgt overnight rate	3.50	0.50
CAN 3 Mo T-B	2.50	0.39

Foreign Exchange	2008	2009
USD/EUR	1.59	1.32
USD/GBP	1.98	1.49
CAN/USD	1.01	1.21
JPY/USD	101.71	99.53

19 MONDAY:
- 30 day Wednesday May 19
- 60 day Friday June 18
- 90 day Sunday July 18
- 180 day Saturday October 16
- 1 year Tuesday April 19

20 TUESDAY:
- 30 day Thursday May 20
- 60 day Saturday June 19
- 90 day Monday July 19
- 180 day Sunday October 17
- 1 year Wednesday April 20

21 WEDNESDAY — 111 / 254

22 THURSDAY — 112 / 253

21 WEDNESDAY:
- 30 day Friday May 21
- 60 day Sunday June 20
- 90 day Tuesday July 20
- 180 day Monday October 18
- 1 year Thursday April 21

22 THURSDAY:
- 30 day Saturday May 22
- 60 day Monday June 21
- 90 day Wednesday July 21
- 180 day Tuesday October 19
- 1 year Friday April 22

23 FRIDAY — 113 / 252

23 FRIDAY:
- 30 day Sunday May 23
- 60 day Tuesday June 22
- 90 day Thursday July 22
- 180 day Wednesday October 20
- 1 year Saturday April 23

APRIL

M	T	W	T	F	S	S
		1	2	3	4	
5	6	7	8	9	10	11
12	13	14	15	16	17	18
19	20	21	22	23	24	25
26	27	28	29	30		

MAY

M	T	W	T	F	S	S
					1	2
3	4	5	6	7	8	9
10	11	12	13	14	15	16
17	18	19	20	21	22	23
24	25	26	27	28	29	30
31						

JUNE

M	T	W	T	F	S	S
	1	2	3	4	5	6
7	8	9	10	11	12	13
14	15	16	17	18	19	20
21	22	23	24	25	26	27
28	29	30				

* Weekly avg closing values- except Fed Funds Rate & CAN overnight tgt rate which are weekly closing values.

FIRST 3 MARKET DAYS IN MAY
The 1/2% Difference

☑ **2009 Performance**

The first three days in May of 2009 once again produced a positive gain. This strategy highlights how much of a difference a few critical days can make.

A lot of investors have profited by using the *6'N'6 Strategy* (the six favorable months strategy from the beginning of November to the end of April). Although they have done well, they could have increased their profits by making two small adjustments: investing four trading days before the end of October and selling at the end of the first three trading days in May. Investing at the end of October is discussed later in the book.

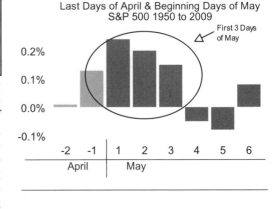

Last Days of April & Beginning Days of May
S&P 500 1950 to 2009

*1/2% extra gain &
positive 70% of the time*

For those investors that use the *6'N'6 Strategy*, selling just three trading days later has increased returns by an average of 1/2% from 1950 to 2009 (S&P 500). Using this strategy has produced positive returns 70% of the time.

The rationale for this is quite simple. The beginning of most months tends to be positive and May is no exception. The the first three trading days tend to be very strong. On average, they have had much better gains than the rest of the days in May, and the average trading day for the entire year.

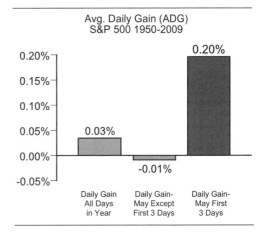

Avg. Daily Gain (ADG)
S&P 500 1950-2009

First 3 Days in May % Gain S&P 500 -1950 to 2009   ☐ Positive

1950	1.1 %	1960	1.2 %	1970	-3.6 %	1980	0.1 %	1990	1.4 %	2000	-2.6 %
1951	1.7	1961	1.3	1971	-0.2	1981	-1.9	1991	1.5	2001	-0.1
1952	1.2	1962	2.0	1972	-1.6	1982	1.1	1992	0.5	2002	-0.3
1953	1.7	1963	0.3	1973	3.0	1983	-0.7	1993	1.0	2003	1.1
1954	0.1	1964	1.8	1974	1.1	1984	0.7	1994	0.2	2004	1.3
1955	-0.8	1965	0.7	1975	3.2	1985	0.1	1995	1.1	2005	1.6
1956	-0.1	1966	-1.8	1976	-0.7	1986	0.9	1996	-1.9	2006	-0.2
1957	1.3	1967	-0.1	1977	1.5	1987	2.4	1997	3.6	2007	1.4
1958	0.8	1968	1.2	1978	-0.6	1988	-0.4	1998	0.3	2008	1.6
1959	0.3	1969	0.7	1979	0.0	1989	-0.5	1999	0.9	2009	0.6
Average	0.7 %		0.7 %		0.2 %		0.2 %		0.9 %		0.4 %

26 MONDAY 116 / 249

27 TUESDAY 117 / 248

30 day	Wednesday May 26
60 day	Friday June 25
90 day	Sunday July 25
180 day	Saturday October 23
1 year	Tuesday April 26

30 day	Thursday May 27
60 day	Saturday June 26
90 day	Monday July 26
180 day	Sunday October 24
1 year	Wednesday April 27

28 WEDNESDAY 118 / 247

29 THURSDAY 119 / 246

30 day	Friday May 28
60 day	Sunday June 27
90 day	Tuesday July 27
180 day	Monday October 25
1 year	Thursday April 28

30 day	Saturday May 29
60 day	Monday June 28
90 day	Wednesday July 28
180 day	Tuesday October 26
1 year	Friday April 29

30 FRIDAY 120 / 245

30 day	Sunday May 30
60 day	Tuesday June 29
90 day	Thursday July 29
180 day	Wednesday October 27
1 year	Saturday April 30

Weekly avg closing values- except Fed Funds Rate & CAN overnight tgt rate which are weekly closing values.

WEEK 17

Market Indices & Rates
Weekly Values*

Stock Markets	2008	2009
Dow	12,810	7,946
S&P500	1,386	849
Nasdaq	2,408	1,649
TSX	14,146	9,322
FTSE	6,063	4,037
DAX	6,806	4,559
Nikkei	13,646	8,784
Hang Seng	25,230	15,278

Commodities	2008	2009
Oil	118.63	47.89
Gold	904.40	891.35

Bond Yields	2008	2009
USA 5 Yr Treasury	3.05	1.89
USA 10 Yr T	3.81	2.96
USA 20 Yr T	4.52	3.90
Moody's Aaa	5.58	5.33
Moody's Baa	6.98	8.26
CAN 5 Yr T	3.17	1.91
CAN 10 Yr T	3.69	2.95

Money Market	2008	2009
USA Fed Funds	2.25	0.25
USA 3 Mo T-B	1.29	0.13
CAN tgt overnight rate	3.00	0.25
CAN 3 Mo T-B	2.53	0.26

Foreign Exchange	2008	2009
USD/EUR	1.58	1.30
USD/GBP	1.98	1.46
CAN/USD	1.01	1.23
JPY/USD	103.48	97.99

APRIL

M	T	W	T	F	S	S
		1	2	3	4	
5	6	7	8	9	10	11
12	13	14	15	16	17	18
19	20	21	22	23	24	25
26	27	28	29	30		

MAY

M	T	W	T	F	S	S
					1	2
3	4	5	6	7	8	9
10	11	12	13	14	15	16
17	18	19	20	21	22	23
24	25	26	27	28	29	30
31						

JUNE

M	T	W	T	F	S	S
	1	2	3	4	5	6
7	8	9	10	11	12	13
14	15	16	17	18	19	20
21	22	23	24	25	26	27
28	29	30				

MAY

	MONDAY	TUESDAY	WEDNESDAY
WEEK 18	**3** 28	**4** 27	**5** 26
WEEK 19	**10** 21	**11** 20	**12** 19
WEEK 20	**17** 14	**18** 13	**19** 12
WEEK 21	**24** 7 CAN Market Closed- Victoria Day	**25** 6	**26** 5
WEEK 22	**31** USA Market Closed- Memorial Day	1	2

THURSDAY		FRIDAY	
6	25	**7**	24
13	18	**14**	17
20	11	**21**	10
27	4	**28**	3
3		4	

JUNE

M	T	W	T	F	S	S
	1	2	3	4	5	6
7	8	9	10	11	12	13
14	15	16	17	18	19	20
21	22	23	24	25	26	27
28	29	30				

JULY

M	T	W	T	F	S	S
			1	2	3	4
5	6	7	8	9	10	11
12	13	14	15	16	17	18
19	20	21	22	23	24	25
26	27	28	29	30	31	

AUGUST

M	T	W	T	F	S	S
						1
2	3	4	5	6	7	8
9	10	11	12	13	14	15
16	17	18	19	20	21	22
23	24	25	26	27	28	29
30	31					

SEPTEMBER

M	T	W	T	F	S	S
		1	2	3	4	5
6	7	8	9	10	11	12
13	14	15	16	17	18	19
20	21	22	23	24	25	26
27	28	29	30			

MAY SUMMARY

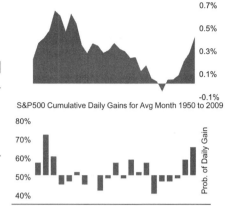

S&P500 Cumulative Daily Gains for Avg Month 1950 to 2009

Prob. of Daily Gain

STRATEGIES	PAGE
STRATEGIES STARTING	
First 3 Days in May – 1/2% Difference	51
Canadian Six 'n' Six – Take a Break for Six Months	59
Six 'n' Six – Take a Break for Six Months	57
Bonds When You Need Them	61
Memorial Day – Be Early and Stay Late	63
STRATEGIES FINISHING	
Platinum Records Solid Results	7
Material Stocks – Material Gains	11
Oil – Equipment and Services	19
Oil – Winter/Spring Strategy I of II	21
First 3 Days in May – 1/2% Difference	51
Risk Sweet Spot Not Just for U.S. Equities	129
Metals & Mining - Don't Melt In Your Portfolio	135

BEST / WORST MAY BROAD MKTS. 2000-2009

BEST MAY MARKETS
- TSX (2009) 11.2%
- Russell 2000 (2003) 10.6%
- Nasdaq (2003) 9.0%

WORST MAY MARKETS
- Nasdaq (2000) -11.9%
- Nasdaq (2006) -6.2%
- Russell 2000 (2000) -5.9%

♦ The first three days in May tend to be positive (see *First 3 Market Days in May* strategy). In 2009 the first few days were positive, mid-month was flat and then the month finished on a strong note. ♦ Oil tends to peak at the beginning to mid-month and in 2009 it peaked once again in May (see oil strategies in February). ♦ The Memorial Day trade produced a strong return in 2009 (see *Memorial Day Be Early Stay Late*).

Index Values End of Month

	2000	2001	2002	2003	2004	2005	2006	2007	2008	2009
Dow	10,522	10,912	9,925	8,850	10,188	10,467	11,168	13,628	12,638	8,500
S&P 500	1,421	1,256	1,067	964	1,121	1,192	1,270	1,531	1,400	919
Nasdaq	3,401	2,110	1,616	1,596	1,987	2,068	2,179	2,605	2,523	1,774
TSX	9,252	8,162	7,656	6,860	8,417	9,607	11,745	14,057	14,715	10,370
Russell 1000	1,444	1,273	1,088	986	1,152	1,239	1,330	1,605	1,477	965
Russell 2000	1,185	1,234	1,211	1,096	1,412	1,533	1,792	2,105	1,860	1,247
Russell 3000 Growth	3,089	2,190	1,729	1,574	1,852	1,895	2,009	2,386	2,344	1,596
Russell 3000 Value	2,074	2,219	2,084	1,873	2,206	2,486	2,742	3,348	2,853	1,790

Percent Gain for May

	2000	2001	2002	2003	2004	2005	2006	2007	2008	2009
Dow	-2.0	1.6	-0.2	4.4	-0.4	2.7	-1.7	4.3	-1.4	4.1
S&P 500	-2.2	0.5	-0.9	5.1	1.2	3.0	-3.1	3.3	1.1	5.3
Nasdaq	-11.9	-0.3	-4.3	9.0	3.5	7.6	-6.2	3.1	4.6	3.3
TSX	-1.0	2.7	-0.1	4.2	2.1	2.5	-3.8	4.8	5.6	11.2
Russell 1000	-2.7	0.5	-1.0	5.5	1.3	3.4	-3.2	3.4	1.6	5.3
Russell 2000	-5.9	2.3	-4.5	10.6	1.5	6.4	-5.7	4.0	4.5	2.9
Russell 3000 Growth	-5.3	-1.2	-2.7	5.3	1.8	4.9	-3.9	3.5	3.7	4.7
Russell 3000 Value	0.6	2.1	0.0	6.4	0.8	2.5	-2.9	3.3	-0.2	5.5

May Market Avg. Performance 2000 to 2009[1]

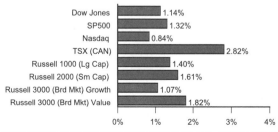

	Dow Jones	1.14%
	SP500	1.32%
	Nasdaq	0.84%
	TSX (CAN)	2.82%
	Russell 1000 (Lg Cap)	1.40%
	Russell 2000 (Sm Cap)	1.61%
	Russell 3000 (Brd Mkt) Growth	1.07%
	Russell 3000 (Brd Mkt) Value	1.82%

Interest Corner May[2]

	Fed Funds % [3]	3 Mo. T-Bill % [4]	10 Yr % [5]	20 Yr % [6]
2009	0.25	0.14	3.47	4.34
2008	2.00	1.89	4.06	4.74
2007	5.25	4.73	4.90	5.10
2006	5.00	4.86	5.12	5.35
2005	3.00	2.99	4.00	4.40

(1) Russell Data provided by Russell (2) Federal Reserve Bank of St. Louis- end of month values (3) Target rate set by FOMC (4)(5)(6) Constant yield maturities.

THACKRAY SECTOR THERMOMETER

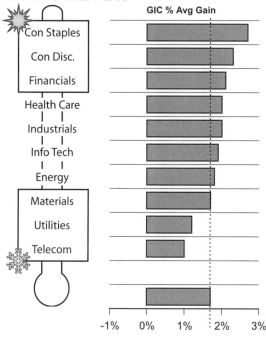

	GIC[2] % Avg Gain	Fq % Gain >S&P 500	
	SP GIC SECTOR 1990-2008[1]		
Con Staples	2.7 %	58 %	Consumer Staples
Con Disc.	2.3	53	Consumer Discretionary
Financials	2.1	47	Financials
Health Care	2.0	42	Health Care
Industrials	2.0	63	Information Technology
Info Tech	1.9	37	Energy
Energy	1.8	42	Industrials
Materials	1.7	37	Materials
Utilities	1.2	42	Utilities
Telecom	1.0	47	Telecom
	1.7 %	N/A %	S&P 500

-1% 0% 1% 2% 3%

Hot Box - 3 Best Sectors
Con Staples ♦ Con Disc. ♦ Financials

May Portfolio

	Avg % Gain	Avg % Gain > S&P 500	Fq % Gain >S&P 500
1990-2008	2.4%	0.7%	58%
2008	-1.5%	-2.6%	

Cold Box - 3 Worst Sectors
Materials ♦ Utilities ♦ Telecom

May Portfolio

	Avg % Gain	Avg % Gain > S&P 500	Fq % Gain >S&P 500
1990-2008	1.3%	-0.4%	37%
2008	3.6%	2.6%	

Commentary

♦ The Consumer Sector of the market tends to do well in May; both the Staples and Discretionary sectors are at the top the Thackray Therometer. ♦ May is often a pivot month in the markets as it slips into a defensive posture. As a result the Consumer Staples sector tends to outperform in this month. ♦ The Financial sector, after typical underperformance for the second half of April, bounces back to do well in May. Although the average return is higher than the S&P 500, its frequency of outperformance is just 47%. ♦ The gains for the Consumer Discretionary sector tend to be made in the first and last few days of the month. ♦ In 2008 the *Cold Box 3 Worst Sectors* produced a surprising combined gain of 3.6% with two of the top performing sectors for the month, Materials and Telecom.

(1) Sector data provided by Standard and Poors (2) GIC is short form for Global Industry Classification (3) Sub Sector data provided by Standard and Poors, except where marked by symbol.

SIX 'N' SIX
Take a Break for Six Months - May 6th to October 27th

☑ **2008 Performance**

This strategy saved investors money big time in 2008 keeping investors out of the market during a 40% drop and helping to establish a position in the market at a very good time to catch the rally in October.

Being out of the market feels good when it is going down. And the market has a habit of going down after the beginning of May. Although sometimes a strong market can continue into July and less frequently into autumn, it has historically made sense to reduce your equity exposure in May.

$852,619 gain on $10,000

The accompanying table uses the S&P 500 to compare the returns made from Oct 28th to May 5th, to the returns made during the remainder of the year. From 1950 to 2008, the October to May time period has produced stunning results.

Starting with $10,000 and investing from October 28th to May 5th every year (1950 to 2008) has produced a gain of $862,619. On the flip side, being invested from May 6th to October 27th, has actually lost money. An initial investment of $10,000 has lost $4,250 over the same time period.

S&P 500 Non-Favorable 6 Month Avg. Gain vs Favorable 6 Month Avg. Gain

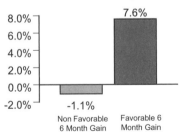

	S&P 500 % May 6 to Oct 27	$10,000 Start	S&P 500 % Oct 28 to May 5	$10,000 Start
1950/51	8.5%	10,851	14.8%	11,477
1951/52	-1.1	10,736	5.4	12,096
1952/53	1.8	10,931	3.9	12,568
1953/54	-3.1	10,595	16.6	14,655
1954/55	13.2	11,992	18.1	17,310
1955/56	12.0	13,425	14.6	19,832
1956/57	-4.6	12,805	0.2	19,862
1957/58	-12.4	11,226	7.9	21,428
1958/59	15.1	12,914	14.5	24,543
1959/60	-0.6	12,840	-4.5	23,449
1960/61	-2.3	12,550	24.1	29,091
1961/62	2.7	12,894	-3.1	28,197
1962/63	-17.7	10,616	28.4	36,205
1963/64	5.7	11,220	9.3	39,566
1964/65	5.1	11,791	5.5	41,758
1965/66	3.1	12,159	-5.0	39,691
1966/67	-8.8	11,094	17.7	46,720
1967/68	0.6	11,155	3.9	48,541
1968/69	5.6	11,782	0.2	48,620
1969/70	-6.1	11,059	-19.8	39,007
1970/71	5.8	11,695	24.9	48,703
1971/72	-9.6	10,570	13.7	55,370
1972/73	3.7	10,965	0.3	55,560
1973/74	0.3	11,003	-18.0	45,539
1974/75	-23.2	8,451	28.5	58,502
1975/76	-0.4	8,418	12.4	65,771
1976/77	0.9	8,492	-1.6	64,705
1977/78	-7.8	7,833	4.5	67,641
1978/79	-2.0	7,675	6.4	72,003
1979/80	-0.1	7,666	5.8	76,162
1980/81	20.2	9,215	1.9	77,616
1981/82	-8.5	8,435	-1.4	76,562
1982/83	15.0	9,699	21.4	92,967
1983/84	0.3	9,732	-3.5	89,736
1984/85	3.9	10,110	8.9	97,765
1985/86	4.1	10,527	26.8	123,942
1986/87	0.4	10,573	23.7	153,307
1987/88	-21.0	8,348	11.0	170,138
1988/89	7.1	8,945	10.9	188,748
1989/90	8.9	9,743	1.0	190,624
1990/91	-10.0	8,773	25.0	238,225
1991/92	0.9	8,852	8.5	258,463
1992/93	0.4	8,887	6.2	274,540
1993/94	4.5	9,288	-2.8	266,922
1994/95	3.2	9,586	11.6	297,794
1995/96	11.5	10,684	10.7	329,608
1996/97	9.2	11,671	18.5	390,445
1997/98	5.6	12,328	27.2	496,632
1998/99	-4.5	11,773	26.5	628,078
1999/00	-3.8	11,331	10.5	693,913
2000/01	-3.7	10,912	-8.2	637,090
2001/02	-12.8	9,516	-2.8	619,107
2002/03	-16.4	7,958	3.2	639,039
2003/04	11.3	8,856	8.8	695,064
2004/05	0.3	8,887	4.2	724,273
2005/06	0.5	8,934	12.5	814,455
2006/07	3.9	9,282	9.3	890,310
2007/08	2.0	9,465	-8.3	816,204
2008/09	-39.7	5,750	6.5	862,619
Total Gain (Loss)	**($-4,250)**			**$852,619**

ⓘ *The above growth rates are geometric averages in order to represent the cumulative growth of a dollar investment over time. These figures differ from the arithmetic mean calculations used in the Six 'N' Six Take a Break Strategy, which are used to represent an average year.*

3 MONDAY	123 / 242

4 TUESDAY	124 / 241

Market Indices & Rates
Weekly Values*

Stock Markets	2008	2009
Dow	12,918	8,122
S&P500	1,399	867
Nasdaq	2,444	1,700
TSX	14,039	9,396
FTSE	6,114	4,188
DAX	6,951	4,694
Nikkei	13,890	8,756
Hang Seng	25,894	14,968

Commodities	2008	2009
Oil	115.34	51.07
Gold	869.60	892.90

Bond Yields	2008	2009
USA 5 Yr Treasury	3.10	1.98
USA 10 Yr T	3.83	3.10
USA 20 Yr T	4.54	4.05
Moody's Aaa	5.56	5.46
Moody's Baa	6.90	8.26
CAN 5 Yr T	3.12	1.99
CAN 10 Yr T	3.64	3.07

Money Market	2008	2009
USA Fed Funds	2.00	0.25
USA 3 Mo T-B	1.45	0.13
CAN tgt overnight rate	3.00	0.25
CAN 3 Mo T-B	2.66	0.21

Foreign Exchange	2008	2009
USD/EUR	1.56	1.32
USD/GBP	1.98	1.47
CAN/USD	1.01	1.20
JPY/USD	104.31	97.44

Monday 3:
30 day	Wednesday June 2
60 day	Friday July 2
90 day	Sunday August 1
180 day	Saturday October 30
1 year	Tuesday May 3

Tuesday 4:
30 day	Thursday June 3
60 day	Saturday July 3
90 day	Monday August 2
180 day	Sunday October 31
1 year	Wednesday May 4

5 WEDNESDAY	125 / 240

6 THURSDAY	126 / 239

MAY

M	T	W	T	F	S	S
					1	2
3	4	5	6	7	8	9
10	11	12	13	14	15	16
17	18	19	20	21	22	23
24	25	26	27	28	29	30
31						

Wednesday 5:
30 day	Friday June 4
60 day	Sunday July 4
90 day	Tuesday August 3
180 day	Monday November 1
1 year	Thursday May 5

Thursday 6:
30 day	Saturday June 5
60 day	Monday July 5
90 day	Wednesday August 4
180 day	Tuesday November 2
1 year	Friday May 6

7 FRIDAY	127 / 238

JUNE

M	T	W	T	F	S	S
	1	2	3	4	5	6
7	8	9	10	11	12	13
14	15	16	17	18	19	20
21	22	23	24	25	26	27
28	29	30				

JULY

M	T	W	T	F	S	S
			1	2	3	4
5	6	7	8	9	10	11
12	13	14	15	16	17	18
19	20	21	22	23	24	25
26	27	28	29	30	31	

Friday 7:
30 day	Sunday June 6
60 day	Tuesday July 6
90 day	Thursday August 5
180 day	Wednesday November 3
1 year	Saturday May 7

* Weekly avg closing values- except Fed Funds Rate & CAN overnight tgt rate which are weekly closing values.

CANADIAN SIX 'N' SIX
Take a Break for Six Months - May 6th to October 27th

In analysing long-term trends for the broad markets such as the S&P 500 or the TSX Composite, a large data set is preferable because it incorporates various economic cycles. The daily data set for the TSX Composite starts in 1977. Over this time period investors have been rewarded for following the six month cycle of investing from October 28th to May 5th, versus the other unfavorable six months, May 6th to October 27th. Starting with an investment of $10,000 in 1977, investing in the unfavorable six months has produced a loss of $4,362, versus investing in the favorable six months which has produced a gain of $164,551.

$164,551 gain on $10,000 since 1977

The TSX Composite Average Year 1977 to 2008 (graph below) indicates that the market tended to peak in mid-July or the end of August. In our book Time In Time Out, Outsmart the Stock Market Using Calendar Investment Strategies, Bruce Lindsay and I analyzed a number of markets over different decades. What we found was that the markets tend to peak at the beginning of May or mid-July. The mid-July peak was usually the result of a strong bull market in place that had a lot of momentum. The main reason that the TSX Composite data shows a peak occurring in July-August is that the data is primarily from the biggest bull market in history, starting in 1982.

Does a later average peak in the stock market mean that the best six month cycle does not work? No. Dividing the year up into six month intervals, the period from October to May is far superior compared with the other half of the year.

The table below illustrates the superiority of the best six months over the worst six months. Going down the table year by year, the period from October 28 to May 5th outperforms the period from May 6th to October 27. In fact, in the few years that the worst six months outperformed, it signalled the start of a serious bull run (1981, 1994, 2004).

	TSX Comp May 6 to Oct 27	$10,000 Start	TSX Comp Oct 28 to May 5	$10,000 Start
1977/78	-3.9 %	9,608	13.1 %	11,313
1978/79	12.1	10,775	21.3	13,728
1979/80	2.9	11,084	23.0	16,883
1980/81	22.5	13,579	-2.4	16,479
1981/82	-17.0	11,272	-18.2	13,488
1982/83	16.6	13,138	34.6	18,150
1983/84	-0.9	13,015	-1.9	17,811
1984/85	1.6	13,226	10.7	19,718
1985/86	0.5	13,299	16.5	22,978
1986/87	-1.9	13,045	24.8	28,666
1987/88	-23.4	9,992	15.3	33,050
1988/89	2.7	10,260	5.7	34,939
1989/90	7.9	11,072	-13.3	30,294
1990/91	-8.4	10,148	13.1	34,266
1991/92	-1.6	9,982	-2.0	33,571
1992/93	-2.3	9,750	15.3	38,704
1993/94	10.8	10,801	1.7	39,365
1994/95	-0.1	10,792	0.3	39,483
1995/96	1.3	10,936	18.2	46,671
1996/97	8.3	11,843	10.8	51,725
1997/98	7.3	12,707	17.0	60,510
1998/99	-22.3	9,870	17.1	70,871
1999/00	-0.2	9,853	36.9	97,009
2000/01	-2.9	9,570	-14.4	83,080
2001/02	-12.2	8,399	9.4	90,875
2002/03	-16.4	7,020	4.0	94,476
2003/04	15.1	8,079	10.3	104,252
2004/05	3.9	8,398	7.8	112,379
2005/06	8.1	9,080	19.8	134,587
2006/07	0.0	9,079	12.2	151,053
2007/08	3.8	9,426	-0.2	150,820
2008/09	-40.2	5,638	15.7	174,551
Total Gain (Loss)	**($-4,362)**			**$164,551**

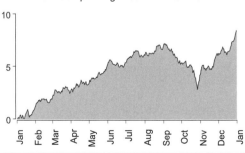

TSX Comp. - Avg. Year 1977 to 2008

In a strong bull market investors always have the choice of using a stop loss or technical indicators to help time the exit point.

10 MONDAY   130 / 235

11 TUESDAY   131 / 234

Market Indices & Rates
Weekly Values*

Stock Markets	2008	2009
Dow	12,883	8,467
S&P500	1,401	913
Nasdaq	2,457	1,746
TSX	14,438	10,020
FTSE	6,238	4,399
DAX	7,044	4,871
Nikkei	13,900	9,409
Hang Seng	25,714	16,851

Commodities	2008	2009
Oil	123.00	56.00
Gold	875.31	909.81

Bond Yields	2008	2009
USA 5 Yr Treasury	3.07	2.09
USA 10 Yr T	3.85	3.23
USA 20 Yr T	4.58	4.17
Moody's Aaa	5.57	5.50
Moody's Baa	6.89	8.14
CAN 5 Yr T	3.15	2.06
CAN 10 Yr T	3.64	3.10

30 day	Wednesday June 9
60 day	Friday July 9
90 day	Sunday August 8
180 day	Saturday November 6
1 year	Tuesday May 10

30 day	Thursday June 10
60 day	Saturday July 10
90 day	Monday August 9
180 day	Sunday November 7
1 year	Wednesday May 11

Money Market	2008	2009
USA Fed Funds	2.00	0.25
USA 3 Mo T-B	1.64	0.19
CAN tgt overnight rate	3.00	0.25
CAN 3 Mo T-B	2.60	0.18

12 WEDNESDAY   132 / 233

13 THURSDAY   133 / 232

Foreign Exchange	2008	2009
USD/EUR	1.54	1.33
USD/GBP	1.96	1.50
CAN/USD	1.01	1.17
JPY/USD	104.55	99.09

MAY

M	T	W	T	F	S	S
					1	2
3	4	5	6	7	8	9
10	11	12	13	14	15	16
17	18	19	20	21	22	23
24	25	26	27	28	29	30
31						

JUNE

M	T	W	T	F	S	S
	1	2	3	4	5	6
7	8	9	10	11	12	13
14	15	16	17	18	19	20
21	22	23	24	25	26	27
28	29	30				

30 day	Friday June 11
60 day	Sunday July 11
90 day	Tuesday August 10
180 day	Monday November 8
1 year	Thursday May 12

30 day	Saturday June 12
60 day	Monday July 12
90 day	Wednesday August 11
180 day	Tuesday November 9
1 year	Friday May 13

14 FRIDAY   134 / 231

JULY

M	T	W	T	F	S	S
			1	2	3	4
5	6	7	8	9	10	11
12	13	14	15	16	17	18
19	20	21	22	23	24	25
26	27	28	29	30	31	

30 day	Sunday June 13
60 day	Tuesday July 13
90 day	Thursday August 12
180 day	Wednesday November 10
1 year	Saturday May 14

* Weekly avg closing values- except Fed Funds Rate & CAN overnight tgt rate which are weekly closing values.

BONDS – WHEN YOU NEED THEM
U.S. Treasuries 7-10 Year - Outperform May 1 to Dec 31

☑ **2008 Performance**

As the global economy slowed and the Fed lowered its target rate, interest rates went down and bonds went up in 2008. Once again the strong seasonal period for bonds (May to December) outperformed the weaker period (January to April).

Since 1982 interest rates have been on a long-term decline and as a result bonds have increased in value. Hidden in this trend is a strong seasonal tendency for bonds to outperform from May 1st to Dec 31st.

6.4% gain &
positive 91% of the time

7-10 Yr. U.S. Treasuries* Total Return 1998 to 2008		
Positive		
	Jan 1- Apr 30	May 1- Dec 31
1998	2.1 %	10.0 %
1999	-2.4	-3.0
2000	2.7	11.7
2001	1.0	5.7
2002	1.5	12.8
2003	1.2	0.6
2004	-0.4	4.8
2005	1.3	1.1
2006	-2.6	5.5
2007	2.2	7.8
2008	3.6	13.9
Avg.	0.9 %	6.4 %

Bonds outperform from the late spring until the end of the year for three reasons. First, companies tend to raise more money through bond issuance at the beginning of the year compared with other times of the year to meet their needs for the rest of the year. With more bonds competing on the market for money, interest rates tend to increase.

Second, optimistic forecasts at the beginning of the year for stronger GDP growth tend to increase inflation expectations and as a result interest rates respond by going up. As GDP expectations tend to decrease in the summer months, interest rates respond by retreating.

ket's entry point can be correspondingly delayed. Nevertheless, May has represented a good time to enter the bond market.

The return in the bond market for the last eight months of the year have far exceeded the returns in the first four months. In fact, the returns are much larger than double.

For the *Barclays U.S. Treasury 7-10 Year Total Return Index*, the period from January 1st to April 30th produces a small average gain of 0.9%, compared with the period from May 1st to December 31st, which produces an average gain of 6.4%.

In addition the favorable period has been positive 91% of the time and has outperformed the less favorable time 73% of the time.

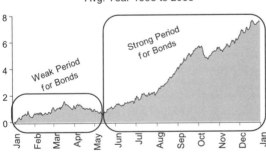

7-10 Yr. U.S. Treasuries Total Return*
Avg. Year 1998 to 2008

Strong Period for Bonds

Weak Period for Bonds

Third, the stock market often peaks in May and investors rotate their money into bonds. As the demand for bonds increases, interest rates decrease and bonds increase in value.

Although the beginning of May has been a good time to increase an allocation to bonds, when the stock market has continued to peak in July, the bond mar-

ⓘ ** Source: Barclays Capital Inc. The U.S. Treasury: 7-10 Year is a total return index, which includes both interest and capital appreciation.*
For more information on fixed income indices, see www.barcap.com.

17 MONDAY   137 / 228

18 TUESDAY   138 / 227

WEEK 20

Market Indices & Rates
Weekly Values*

Stock Markets	2008	2009
Dow	12,917	8,355
S&P500	1,413	895
Nasdaq	2,509	1,696
TSX	14,744	9,899
FTSE	6,241	4,381
DAX	7,083	4,785
Nikkei	14,057	9,290
Hang Seng	25,555	16,927

Commodities	2008	2009
Oil	124.93	58.07
Gold	878.65	921.75

Bond Yields	2008	2009
USA 5 Yr Treasury	3.12	2.01
USA 10 Yr T	3.86	3.14
USA 20 Yr T	4.58	4.09
Moody's Aaa	5.56	5.44
Moody's Baa	6.92	8.00
CAN 5 Yr T	3.16	2.11
CAN 10 Yr T	3.58	3.11

Money Market	2008	2009
USA Fed Funds	2.00	0.25
USA 3 Mo T-B	1.82	0.18
CAN tgt overnight rate	3.00	0.25
CAN 3 Mo T-B	2.65	0.18

Foreign Exchange	2008	2009
USD/EUR	1.55	1.36
USD/GBP	1.95	1.52
CAN/USD	1.00	1.17
JPY/USD	104.52	96.32

17 MONDAY
30 day Wednesday June 16
60 day Friday July 16
90 day Sunday August 15
180 day Saturday November 13
1 year Tuesday May 17

18 TUESDAY
30 day Thursday June 17
60 day Saturday July 17
90 day Monday August 16
180 day Sunday November 14
1 year Wednesday May 18

19 WEDNESDAY   139 / 226

20 THURSDAY   140 / 225

19 WEDNESDAY
30 day Friday June 18
60 day Sunday July 18
90 day Tuesday August 17
180 day Monday November 15
1 year Thursday May 19

20 THURSDAY
30 day Saturday June 19
60 day Monday July 19
90 day Wednesday August 18
180 day Tuesday November 16
1 year Friday May 20

21 FRIDAY   141 / 224

30 day Sunday June 20
60 day Tuesday July 20
90 day Thursday August 19
180 day Wednesday November 17
1 year Saturday May 21

MAY
M	T	W	T	F	S	S
					1	2
3	4	5	6	7	8	9
10	11	12	13	14	15	16
17	18	19	20	21	22	23
24	25	26	27	28	29	30
31						

JUNE
M	T	W	T	F	S	S
	1	2	3	4	5	6
7	8	9	10	11	12	13
14	15	16	17	18	19	20
21	22	23	24	25	26	27
28	29	30				

JULY
M	T	W	T	F	S	S
			1	2	3	4
5	6	7	8	9	10	11
12	13	14	15	16	17	18
19	20	21	22	23	24	25
26	27	28	29	30	31	

Weekly avg closing values- except Fed Funds Rate & CAN overnight tgt rate which are weekly closing values.

MEMORIAL DAY – BE EARLY & STAY LATE
Positive 2 Market Days Before Memorial Day to 5 Market Days into June

---

☑ **2009 Performance**

In 2009 the market rallied strongly off the March low. With strong momentum in the market carrying over into May, the *Memorial Day* trade gained a respectable 4.1%.

A lot of strategies that focus on investing around holidays concentrate on the market performance the day before and the day after a holiday.

Not all holidays were created equal. The typical Memorial Day trade is to invest the day before and sell the day after. If you invested just for these two days you would be missing out on a lot of gains.

1.3% average gain and positive 69% of the time

Memorial Day S&P 500 - 1971 to 2008

1.8%
1.6%
1.4%
1.2%
1.0%
0.8%
0.6%
0.4%
0.2%
0.0%

May 1   May 31   Jun 30

Historically, the best strategy has been to invest two market days before Memorial Day and hold until five market days into June. Extending the investment into June makes sense. The first few days in June tend to be positive...so why sell early?

The graph shows the performance of the S&P 500 on a calendar basis for the months of May and June from 1971 to 2009 (see information box for start year details). The increase from the end of May into June represents the opportunity with the "*Memorial Day - Be Early & Stay Late*" trade. The graph clearly shows a spike in the market that occurs at the end of the month and carries on into June. Investors using the typical Memorial Day trade, miss out on the majority of the gain. The *Memorial Day - Be Early & Stay Late* strategy has produced an average gain of 1.3% and has been positive 69% of the time (S&P 500 1971 to 2009). Not a bad gain for being invested an average of ten market days.

The Memorial Day trade can be extended into June primarily because the first days in June tend to be positive. These days are part of the end of the month effect and are often positive (see *Super Seven* strategy).

2 Market Days Before Memorial Day to 5 Market Days Into June - S&P 500   Positive ▢

		1980	5.1 %	1990	1.1 %	2000	5.2 %
1971	1.5 %	1981	0.2	1991	0.9	2001	-0.9
1972	-2.4	1982	-2.6	1992	-0.5	2002	-5.4
1973	1.7	1983	-2.1	1993	-1.3	2003	7.0
1974	6.3	1984	1.2	1994	0.4	2004	2.3
1975	3.8	1985	4.3	1995	0.9	2005	0.6
1976	-0.7	1986	4.3	1996	0.0	2006	-0.2
1977	1.0	1987	5.5	1997	2.2	2007	-2.1
1978	3.1	1988	4.5	1998	-0.5	2008	-2.2
1979	1.9	1989	2.4	1999	2.3	2009	4.1
Avg.	1.8 %		2.3 %		0.6 %		0.8 %

ⓘ *History of Memorial Day: Originally called Decoration Day in remembrance of those who died in the nation's service. Memorial day was first observed on May 30th 1868 when flowers were placed on the graves of Union and Confederate soldiers at Arlington National Cemetery. The South acknowledged the day after World War I, when the holiday changed from honoring just those who died fighting in the Civil War to honoring Americans who died fighting in any war. In 1971 Congress passed the National Holiday Act recognizing Memorial Day as the last Monday in May.*

24 MONDAY   144 / 221

---

30 day	Wednesday June 23
60 day	Friday July 23
90 day	Sunday August 22
180 day	Saturday November 20
1 year	Tuesday May 24

26 WEDNESDAY   146 / 219

---

30 day	Friday June 25
60 day	Sunday July 25
90 day	Tuesday August 24
180 day	Monday November 22
1 year	Thursday May 26

28 FRIDAY   148 / 217

---

30 day	Sunday June 27
60 day	Tuesday July 27
90 day	Thursday August 26
180 day	Wednesday November 24
1 year	Saturday May 28

25 TUESDAY   145 / 220

---

30 day	Thursday June 24
60 day	Saturday July 24
90 day	Monday August 23
180 day	Sunday November 21
1 year	Wednesday May 25

27 THURSDAY   147 / 218

---

30 day	Saturday June 26
60 day	Monday July 26
90 day	Wednesday August 25
180 day	Tuesday November 23
1 year	Friday May 27

WEEK 21

Market Indices & Rates
Weekly Values*

Stock Markets	2008	2009
Dow	12,713	8,394
S&P500	1,400	899
Nasdaq	2,473	1,716
TSX	14,838	10,069
FTSE	6,207	4,422
DAX	7,080	4,934
Nikkei	14,069	9,233
Hang Seng	25,226	17,261

Commodities	2008	2009
Oil	130.10	60.34
Gold	918.85	936.50

Bond Yields	2008	2009
USA 5 Yr Treasury	3.12	2.13
USA 10 Yr T	3.84	3.29
USA 20 Yr T	4.56	4.22
Moody's Aaa	5.53	5.57
Moody's Baa	6.91	8.04
CAN 5 Yr T	3.21	2.20
CAN 10 Yr T	3.59	3.18

Money Market	2008	2009
USA Fed Funds	2.00	0.25
USA 3 Mo T-B	1.85	0.18
CAN tgt overnight rate	3.00	0.25
CAN 3 Mo T-B	2.64	0.18

Foreign Exchange	2008	2009
USD/EUR	1.57	1.37
USD/GBP	1.97	1.56
CAN/USD	0.99	1.15
JPY/USD	103.63	95.37

MAY

M	T	W	T	F	S	S
					1	2
3	4	5	6	7	8	9
10	11	12	13	14	15	16
17	18	19	20	21	22	23
24	25	26	27	28	29	30
31						

JUNE

M	T	W	T	F	S	S
	1	2	3	4	5	6
7	8	9	10	11	12	13
14	15	16	17	18	19	20
21	22	23	24	25	26	27
28	29	30				

JULY

M	T	W	T	F	S	S
			1	2	3	4
5	6	7	8	9	10	11
12	13	14	15	16	17	18
19	20	21	22	23	24	25
26	27	28	29	30	31	

* Weekly avg closing values- except Fed Funds Rate & CAN overnight tgt rate which are weekly closing values.

1ST DAY OF THE MONTH
Best Day of the Month

The *1st Day of the Month* strategy produced a negative result in 2008. Despite its strong past performance, negative surprises in the economy and markets took their toll.

Not all days are equal. There is one day of the month that has typically been the best – the first day. This day benefits from portfolio managers finishing off their window dressing (making their portfolios look good on the books) and retail investors buying up new positions to start the month on a favorable footing.

0.13% avg. gain & 5 times better than the average market day

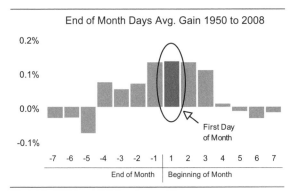

End of Month Days Avg. Gain 1950 to 2008

First Day of Month

End of Month | Beginning of Month

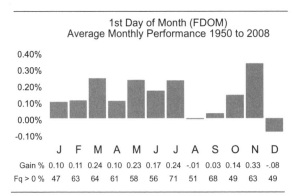

1st Day of Month (FDOM)
Average Monthly Performance 1950 to 2008

	J	F	M	A	M	J	J	A	S	O	N	D
Gain %	0.10	0.11	0.24	0.10	0.23	0.17	0.24	-.01	0.03	0.14	0.33	-.08
Fq > 0 %	47	63	64	61	58	56	71	51	68	49	63	49

sult is that the average daily gain of the first day of the month was almost five times better than the average market day, and yet it had only a slightly higher frequency of being positive. What this means is that when the first day is positive, it has a much higher likelihood of producing extraordinarily large gains. Examining the returns on a monthly basis, only the first day of two months has performed below the average market day from 1950 to 2008. It is not surprising that the months are August and September, two of the worst months in which to invest. On the other hand, the best first day of the month has clearly been November: the traditional start of the six month favorable time period to invest and also one of the best months for a stock market gain.

It is interesting to note that a high frequency positive first day of the month does not necessarily mean that the average gain is high. For example, the first day in September has been positive 68% of the time from 1950 to 2008. Yet, although it is still positive, it is one of the worst first days of the month. As a side note, the month of September has also proved unfriendly to the market and has produced an average negative return from 1950 to 2008.

From 1950 to 2008, the first day of the month (FDOM) has produced an average return of 0.13% and has been positive 59% of the time. This compares to the average market day (all trading days of the year) over the same time period, which has produced a return of 0.03% and has been positive 53% of the time. The interesting re-

⚠ *CAUTION:*
Generally, it is not a wise strategy to invest for just one day: the expected rate of return, combined with the risk from volatility do not justify the expected returns.

31 MONDAY 151 / 214

1 TUESDAY 152 / 213

30 day	Wednesday June 30
60 day	Friday July 30
90 day	Sunday August 29
180 day	Saturday November 27
1 year	Tuesday May 31

30 day	Thursday July 1
60 day	Saturday July 31
90 day	Monday August 30
180 day	Sunday November 28
1 year	Wednesday June 1

2 WEDNESDAY 153 / 212

3 THURSDAY 154 / 211

30 day	Friday July 2
60 day	Sunday August 1
90 day	Tuesday August 31
180 day	Monday November 29
1 year	Thursday June 2

30 day	Saturday July 3
60 day	Monday August 2
90 day	Wednesday September 1
180 day	Tuesday November 30
1 year	Friday June 3

4 FRIDAY 155 / 210

30 day	Sunday July 4
60 day	Tuesday August 3
90 day	Thursday September 2
180 day	Wednesday December 1
1 year	Saturday June 4

* Weekly avg closing values- except Fed Funds Rate & CAN overnight tgt rate which are weekly closing values.

WEEK 22

Market Indices & Rates
Weekly Values*

Stock Markets	2008	2009
Dow	12,607	8,419
S&P500	1,394	907
Nasdaq	2,500	1,752
TSX	14,652	10,252
FTSE	6,062	4,408
DAX	7,020	4,956
Nikkei	13,951	9,414
Hang Seng	24,315	17,542

Commodities	2008	2009
Oil	128.46	64.32
Gold	894.50	957.31

Bond Yields	2008	2009
USA 5 Yr Treasury	3.36	2.38
USA 10 Yr T	4.03	3.59
USA 20 Yr T	4.72	4.47
Moody's Aaa	5.67	5.69
Moody's Baa	7.06	8.03
CAN 5 Yr T	3.34	2.45
CAN 10 Yr T	3.69	3.42

Money Market	2008	2009
USA Fed Funds	2.00	0.25
USA 3 Mo T-B	1.89	0.16
CAN tgt overnight rate	3.00	0.25
CAN 3 Mo T-B	2.66	0.19

Foreign Exchange	2008	2009
USD/EUR	1.57	1.40
USD/GBP	1.98	1.60
CAN/USD	0.99	1.12
JPY/USD	104.48	95.60

JUNE
M	T	W	T	F	S	S
	1	2	3	4	5	6
7	8	9	10	11	12	13
14	15	16	17	18	19	20
21	22	23	24	25	26	27
28	29	30				

JULY
M	T	W	T	F	S	S
			1	2	3	4
5	6	7	8	9	10	11
12	13	14	15	16	17	18
19	20	21	22	23	24	25
26	27	28	29	30	31	

AUGUST
M	T	W	T	F	S	S
						1
2	3	4	5	6	7	8
9	10	11	12	13	14	15
16	17	18	19	20	21	22
23	24	25	26	27	28	29
30	31					

JUNE

	MONDAY	TUESDAY	WEDNESDAY
WEEK 22	31	1 29	2 28
WEEK 23	7 23	8 22	9 21
WEEK 24	14 16	15 15	16 14
WEEK 25	21 9	22 8	23 7
WEEK 26	28 2	29 1	30

THURSDAY		FRIDAY	
3	27	**4**	26
10	20	**11**	19
17	13	**18**	12
24	6	**25**	5
1		2	

JULY

M	T	W	T	F	S	S
		1	2	3	4	
5	6	7	8	9	10	11
12	13	14	15	16	17	18
19	20	21	22	23	24	25
26	27	28	29	30	31	

AUGUST

M	T	W	T	F	S	S
						1
2	3	4	5	6	7	8
9	10	11	12	13	14	15
16	17	18	19	20	21	22
23	24	25	26	27	28	29
30	31					

SEPTEMBER

M	T	W	T	F	S	S
		1	2	3	4	5
6	7	8	9	10	11	12
13	14	15	16	17	18	19
20	21	22	23	24	25	26
27	28	29	30			

OCTOBER

M	T	W	T	F	S	S
				1	2	3
4	5	6	7	8	9	10
11	12	13	14	15	16	17
18	19	20	21	22	23	24
25	26	27	28	29	30	31

JUNE
S U M M A R Y

0.4%

0.2%

0.0%

-0.2%

S&P500 Cumulative Daily Gains for Avg Month 1950 to 2009

STRATEGIES	PAGE
STRATEGIES STARTING	
Biotech Summer Solstice	73
Independence Day – Full Trade Profit	75
STRATEGIES FINISHING	
Memorial Day – Be Early and Stay Late	63

70%

60%

50%

40%

30%

Prob. of Daily Gain

♦ June, on average, is a "see-saw" month. The first half of the month does well and then fades. ♦ The Biotechnology sector usually starts to pick up at the end of the month (see *Biotech Summer Solstice* strategy). ♦ The Nasdaq usually outperforms the S&P 500. ♦ Large Cap Growth (large companies with a growth profile - Russell 1000 Growth) tend to perform well in June. In 2009 all the above occurred and the market ended stronger than usual.

BEST / WORST JUNE BROAD MKTS. 2000-2009

BEST JUNE MARKETS
♦ Nasdaq (2000) 16.6%
♦ TSX (2000) 10.2%
♦ Russell 2000 (2000) 8.6%

WORST JUNE MARKETS
♦ Dow (2008) -10.2%
♦ Russell 3000 Val (2008) -9.8%
♦ Nasdaq (2002) -9.4%

Index Values End of Month

	2000	2001	2002	2003	2004	2005	2006	2007	2008	2009
Dow	10,448	10,502	9,243	8,985	10,435	10,275	11,150	13,409	11,350	8,447
S&P 500	1,455	1,224	990	975	1,141	1,191	1,270	1,503	1,280	919
Nasdaq	3,966	2,161	1,463	1,623	2,048	2,057	2,172	2,603	2,293	1,835
TSX	10,195	7,736	7,146	6,983	8,546	9,903	11,613	13,907	14,467	10,375
Russell 1000	1,479	1,244	1,007	998	1,171	1,242	1,330	1,573	1,352	966
Russell 2000	1,286	1,275	1,150	1,114	1,470	1,590	1,801	2,072	1,714	1,263
Russell 3000 Growth	3,333	2,148	1,569	1,595	1,876	1,892	2,000	2,350	2,175	1,613
Russell 3000 Value	1,987	2,177	1,967	1,894	2,258	2,515	2,757	3,265	2,574	1,773

Percent Gain for June

	2000	2001	2002	2003	2004	2005	2006	2007	2008	2009
Dow	-0.7	-3.8	-6.9	1.5	2.4	-1.8	-0.2	-1.6	-10.2	-0.6
S&P 500	2.4	-2.5	-7.2	1.1	1.8	0.0	0.0	-1.8	-8.6	0.0
Nasdaq	16.6	2.4	-9.4	1.7	3.1	-0.5	-0.3	0.0	-9.1	3.4
TSX	10.2	-5.2	-6.7	1.8	1.5	3.1	-1.1	-1.1	-1.7	0.0
Russell 1000	2.5	-2.3	-7.5	1.2	1.7	0.3	0.0	-2.0	-8.5	0.1
Russell 2000	8.6	3.3	-5.1	1.7	4.1	3.7	0.5	-1.6	-7.8	1.3
Russell 3000 Growth	7.9	-1.9	-9.3	1.3	1.3	-0.1	-0.5	-1.5	-7.2	1.1
Russell 3000 Value	-4.2	-1.9	-5.6	1.1	2.4	1.2	0.5	-2.5	-9.8	-0.9

June Market Avg. Performance 1999 to 2009 [1]

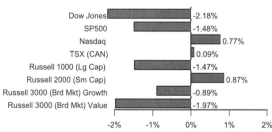

Dow Jones	-2.18%
SP500	-1.48%
Nasdaq	0.77%
TSX (CAN)	0.09%
Russell 1000 (Lg Cap)	-1.47%
Russell 2000 (Sm Cap)	0.87%
Russell 3000 (Brd Mkt) Growth	-0.89%
Russell 3000 (Brd Mkt) Value	-1.97%

-2%   -1%   0%   1%   2%

Interest Corner Jun[2]

	Fed Funds % [3]	3 Mo. T-Bill % [4]	10 Yr % [5]	20 Yr % [6]
2009	0.25	0.19	3.53	4.30
2008	2.00	1.90	3.99	4.59
2007	5.25	4.82	5.03	5.21
2006	5.25	5.01	5.15	5.31
2005	3.25	3.13	3.94	4.28

(1) Russell Data provided by Russell (2) Federal Reserve Bank of St. Louis- end of month values (3) Target rate set by FOMC (4)(5)(6) Constant yield maturities

JUNE SECTOR PERFORMANCE

THACKRAY SECTOR THERMOMETER

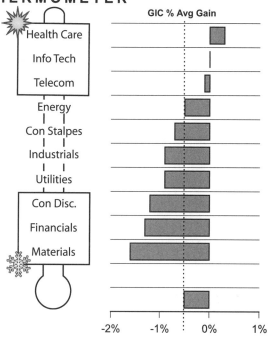

	GIC(2) % Avg Gain	Fq % Gain >S&P 500	SP GIC SECTOR 1990-2008(1)
Health Care	0.3 %	53 %	Health Care
Info Tech	0.0	42	Information Technology
Telecom	-0.1	58	Telecom
Energy	-0.5	42	Energy
Con Stalpes	-0.7	32	Consumer Staples
Industrials	-0.9	42	Industrials
Utilities	-0.9	42	Utilities
Con Disc.	-1.2	42	Consumer Discretionary
Financials	-1.3	42	Financials
Materials	-1.6	32	Materials
	-0.5 %	N/A %	S&P 500

-2% -1% 0% 1%

Hot Box - 3 Best Sectors
Health Care ♦ Info Tech ♦ Telecom
June Portfolio

	Avg % Gain	Avg % Gain > S&P 500	Fq % Gain >S&P 500
1990-2008	0.1 %	0.5 %	58 %
2008	-8.5 %	0.1 %	

Cold Box - 3 Worst Sectors
Con Disc. ♦ Financials ♦ Materials
June Portfolio

	Avg % Gain	Avg % Gain > S&P 500	Fq % Gain >S&P 500
1990-2008	-1.4 %	-0.9 %	26 %
2008	-12.2 %	-3.6 %	

Commentary

♦ At the sector level, the market has not had a lot of leadership. There is only one positive sector for the month: Health Care. ♦ The Information Technology sector, next on the list, has only outperformed the S&P 500, 42% of the time, not making it an attractive investment. ♦ Keep an eye on the bottom sector, Materials, as it moves up the list next month. ♦ In 2008 the energy sector was the top sector and the only positive sector. This is the time that oil was hitting its all time high. All of the other sectors heading "south" should have raised concern for oil, especially since oil had finished up its seasonally strong cycle. ♦ The *Hot Box 3 Best Sectors* produced a loss of 8.5% in 2008, but managed to marginally beat the S&P 500.

(1) Sector data provided by Standard and Poors (2) GIC is short form for Global Industry Classification (3) Sub Sector data provided by Standard and Poors, except where marked by symbol.

7 MONDAY   158 / 207

30 day   Wednesday July 7
60 day   Friday August 6
90 day   Sunday September 5
180 day   Saturday December 4
1 year   Tuesday June 7

9 WEDNESDAY   160 / 205

30 day   Friday July 9
60 day   Sunday August 8
90 day   Tuesday September 7
180 day   Monday December 6
1 year   Thursday June 9

11 FRIDAY   162 / 203

30 day   Sunday July 11
60 day   Tuesday August 10
90 day   Thursday September 9
180 day   Wednesday December 8
1 year   Saturday June 11

8 TUESDAY   159 / 206

30 day   Thursday July 8
60 day   Saturday August 7
90 day   Monday September 6
180 day   Sunday December 5
1 year   Wednesday June 8

10 THURSDAY   161 / 204

30 day   Saturday July 10
60 day   Monday August 9
90 day   Wednesday September 8
180 day   Tuesday December 7
1 year   Friday June 10

WEEK 23

Market Indices & Rates
Weekly Values*

Stock Markets	2008	2009
Dow	12,422	8,730
S&P500	1,381	940
Nasdaq	2,500	1,838
TSX	14,837	10,506
FTSE	5,988	4,438
DAX	6,948	5,097
Nikkei	14,383	9,712
Hang Seng	24,398	18,607

Commodities	2008	2009
Oil	128.14	68.10
Gold	884.05	974.25

Bond Yields	2008	2009
USA 5 Yr Treasury	3.26	2.58
USA 10 Yr T	3.98	3.70
USA 20 Yr T	4.70	4.55
Moody's Aaa	5.63	5.68
Moody's Baa	7.01	7.80
CAN 5 Yr T	3.22	2.49
CAN 10 Yr T	3.65	3.41

Money Market	2008	2009
USA Fed Funds	2.00	0.25
USA 3 Mo T-B	1.85	0.15
CAN tgt overnight rate	3.00	0.25
CAN 3 Mo T-B	2.53	0.21

Foreign Exchange	2008	2009
USD/EUR	1.55	1.42
USD/GBP	1.96	1.64
CAN/USD	1.01	1.09
JPY/USD	105.22	95.93

JUNE

M	T	W	T	F	S	S
	1	2	3	4	5	6
7	8	9	10	11	12	13
14	15	16	17	18	19	20
21	22	23	24	25	26	27
28	29	30				

JULY

M	T	W	T	F	S	S
			1	2	3	4
5	6	7	8	9	10	11
12	13	14	15	16	17	18
19	20	21	22	23	24	25
26	27	28	29	30	31	

AUGUST

M	T	W	T	F	S	S
						1
2	3	4	5	6	7	8
9	10	11	12	13	14	15
16	17	18	19	20	21	22
23	24	25	26	27	28	29
30	31					

* Weekly avg closing values- except Fed Funds Rate & CAN overnight tgt rate which are weekly closing values.

BIOTECH SUMMER SOLSTICE
June 23rd to Sep 13th

☑ 2008 Performance

Biotech once again pulled off a strong performance during its seasonal cycle. On a timely basis the market started to fall apart at the end of the biotech cycle. Although the sector produced an 11.4% gain, the technicals on the market and the sector were falling apart in September and I recommended in my monthly newsletter to take profits early.

The *Biotech Summer Solstice* trade starts on June 23rd and lasts until September 13th. The trade is aptly named as its outperformance starts approximately on the day of the summer solstice – the longest day of the year. There are two main drivers of the trade: biotech is a good substitute for technology stocks in the summer, and investors taking a position in the biotech sector before the autumn conferences.

14% extra & 15 out of 17 times better than the S&P 500

Biotech vs. S&P 500 1992 to 2008			
Performance > S&P 500			
Jun 23 to Sep 13	Biotech	S&P 500	Diff
1992	17.9 %	4.0 %	13.8 %
1993	3.6	3.6	0.0
1994	24.2	3.2	21.0
1995	31.5	5.0	26.5
1996	7.0	2.1	4.9
1997	-18.9	2.8	-21.7
1998	20.6	-8.5	29.1
1999	64.3	0.6	63.7
2000	7.6	2.3	5.4
2001	-3.6	-10.8	7.2
2002	8.1	-10.0	18.2
2003	6.4	2.3	4.1
2004	8.9	-0.8	9.6
2005	26.0	1.4	24.5
2006	7.4	5.8	1.6
2007	6.0	-1.2	7.2
2008	11.4	-5.0	16.5
Avg	13.4 %	-0.2 %	13.6 %

nology sector is viewed as being largely dependent on the economy. The biotech sector is viewed as being much less dependent on the economy. The end product of biotechnology companies is mainly medicine, which is not economically sensitive. As a result, in the softer summer months, investors are more willing to commit speculative money into the biotech sector, compared with the technology sector.

Second, the biotech sector is one of the few sectors that starts its outperformance in June. This is in part because of the biotech conferences that occur in autumn. With positive announcements, biotech companies can increase dramatically. As a result, investors try to lock in positions early.

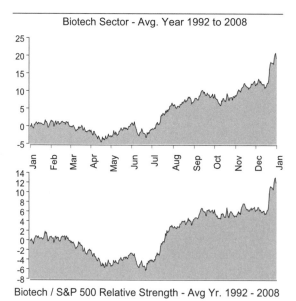

Biotech Sector - Avg. Year 1992 to 2008

Biotech / S&P 500 Relative Strength - Avg Yr. 1992 - 2008

First, the biotechnology sector is often considered the cousin of the technology sector, a good place for speculative investments. The sectors are similar as both include concept companies (companies without a product but with good potential). Despite their similarity, investors view the sectors differently. The tech-

ⓘ *Biotech SP GIC Sector # 352010: Companies primarily engaged in the research, development, manufacturing and/or marketing of products based on genetic analysis and genetic engineering. This includes companies specializing in protein-based therapeutics to treat human diseases.*

14 MONDAY   165 / 200

15 TUESDAY   166 / 199

30 day	Wednesday July 14
60 day	Friday August 13
90 day	Sunday September 12
180 day	Saturday December 11
1 year	Tuesday June 14

30 day	Thursday July 15
60 day	Saturday August 14
90 day	Monday September 13
180 day	Sunday December 12
1 year	Wednesday June 15

16 WEDNESDAY   167 / 198

17 THURSDAY   168 / 197

30 day	Friday July 16
60 day	Sunday August 15
90 day	Tuesday September 14
180 day	Monday December 13
1 year	Thursday June 16

30 day	Saturday July 17
60 day	Monday August 16
90 day	Wednesday September 15
180 day	Tuesday December 14
1 year	Friday June 17

18 FRIDAY   169 / 196

30 day	Sunday July 18
60 day	Tuesday August 17
90 day	Thursday September 16
180 day	Wednesday December 15
1 year	Saturday June 18

WEEK 24

Market Indices & Rates
Weekly Values*

Stock Markets	2008	2009
Dow	12,221	8,767
S&P500	1,351	942
Nasdaq	2,432	1,855
TSX	14,759	10,611
FTSE	5,804	4,430
DAX	6,743	5,046
Nikkei	14,050	9,952
Hang Seng	23,080	18,556

Commodities	2008	2009
Oil	134.73	70.83
Gold	875.75	947.65

Bond Yields	2008	2009
USA 5 Yr Treasury	3.57	2.88
USA 10 Yr T	4.15	3.89
USA 20 Yr T	4.78	4.67
Moody's Aaa	5.68	5.80
Moody's Baa	7.08	7.69
CAN 5 Yr T	3.52	2.73
CAN 10 Yr T	3.83	3.55

Money Market	2008	2009
USA Fed Funds	2.00	0.25
USA 3 Mo T-B	1.97	0.19
CAN tgt overnight rate	3.00	0.25
CAN 3 Mo T-B	2.71	0.23

Foreign Exchange	2008	2009
USD/EUR	1.55	1.40
USD/GBP	1.96	1.62
CAN/USD	1.02	1.11
JPY/USD	107.20	98.23

JUNE

M	T	W	T	F	S	S
	1	2	3	4	5	6
7	8	9	10	11	12	13
14	15	16	17	18	19	20
21	22	23	24	25	26	27
28	29	30				

JULY

M	T	W	T	F	S	S
			1	2	3	4
5	6	7	8	9	10	11
12	13	14	15	16	17	18
19	20	21	22	23	24	25
26	27	28	29	30	31	

AUGUST

M	T	W	T	F	S	S
						1
2	3	4	5	6	7	8
9	10	11	12	13	14	15
16	17	18	19	20	21	22
23	24	25	26	27	28	29
30	31					

* Weekly avg closing values- except Fed Funds Rate & CAN overnight tgt rate which are weekly closing values.

Two Market Days Before June Month End To 5 Market Days After Independence Day

---

☒ **2009 Performance**

The Independence Day trade lost over 4%. This is the second year in a row that this trade has not worked. Over the long-term it is still a good trade. If you combined this trade with the Memorial Day trade for 2009, the result would be a wash. The lesson here is that it is better to implement more trades for less money.

The beginning of July is a time for celebration and the markets tend to agree.

Based on previous market data, the best way to take advantage of this trend is to be invested for the two market days prior to the June month end and hold until five market days after Independence Day. This time period has produced above average returns on a fairly consistent basis.

0.8% avg. gain & 70% of the time positive

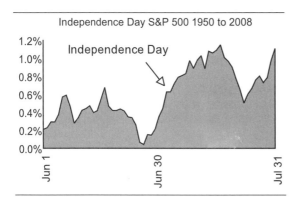

Independence Day S&P 500 1950 to 2008

The typical Independence Day trade put forward by quite a few pundits has been to invest one or two days before the holiday and take profits one or two days after the holiday. Although this strategy has produced profits, it has left a lot of money on the table. This strategy misses out on the positive days at the end of June and on the full slate of positive days after Independence Day. The beginning part of the Independence Day positive trend is driven by two combining factors. First, portfolio managers "window dress" (buying stocks that have a favorable perception in the market); thereby pushing stock prices up at the end of the month. Second, investors becoming "wise" to the Independence Day Trade and try to jump in before everyone else.

ⓘ *History of Independence Day: Independence Day is celebrated on July 4th because that is the day when the Continental Congress adopted the final draft of the Declaration of Independence in 1776. Independence Day was made an official holiday at the end of the War of Independence in 1783. In 1941 Congress declared the 4th of July a federal holiday.*

S&P 500, 2 Market Days Before June Month End To 5 Market Days after Independence Day % Gain 1950 to 2008 — Positive

1950	-4.4 %	1960	-0.1 %	1970	1.5 %	1980	1.4 %	1990	1.7 %	2000	1.8 %
1951	1.5	1961	1.7	1971	3.2	1981	-2.4	1991	1.4	2001	-2.6
1952	0.9	1962	9.8	1972	0.3	1982	-0.6	1992	2.8	2002	-4.7
1953	0.8	1963	0.5	1973	2.1	1983	1.5	1993	-0.6	2003	1.2
1954	2.9	1964	2.3	1974	-8.8	1984	-0.7	1994	0.4	2004	-1.7
1955	4.9	1965	5.0	1975	-0.2	1985	1.5	1995	1.8	2005	1.5
1956	3.4	1966	2.1	1976	2.4	1986	-2.6	1996	-2.8	2006	2.1
1957	3.8	1967	1.3	1977	-0.6	1987	0.4	1997	3.7	2007	0.8
1958	2.0	1968	2.3	1978	0.6	1988	-0.6	1998	2.7	2008	-3.4
1959	3.3	1969	-1.5	1979	1.3	1989	0.9	1999	5.1	2009	-4.3
Average	1.9 %		2.3 %		0.2 %		-0.1 %		1.8 %		-0.9 %

21 MONDAY 172 / 193

22 TUESDAY 173 / 192

30 day	Wednesday July 21
60 day	Friday August 20
90 day	Sunday September 19
180 day	Saturday December 18
1 year	Tuesday June 21

30 day	Thursday July 22
60 day	Saturday August 21
90 day	Monday September 20
180 day	Sunday December 19
1 year	Wednesday June 22

23 WEDNESDAY 174 / 191

24 THURSDAY 175 / 190

30 day	Friday July 23
60 day	Sunday August 22
90 day	Tuesday September 21
180 day	Monday December 20
1 year	Thursday June 23

30 day	Saturday July 24
60 day	Monday August 23
90 day	Wednesday September 22
180 day	Tuesday December 21
1 year	Friday June 24

25 FRIDAY 176 / 189

30 day	Sunday July 25
60 day	Tuesday August 24
90 day	Thursday September 23
180 day	Wednesday December 22
1 year	Saturday June 25

* Weekly avg closing values- except Fed Funds Rate & CAN overnight tgt rate which are weekly closing values.

WEEK 25

Market Indices & Rates
Weekly Values*

Stock Markets	2008	2009
Dow	12,073	8,542
S&P500	1,342	917
Nasdaq	2,446	1,811
TSX	14,891	10,236
FTSE	5,749	4,312
DAX	6,711	4,852
Nikkei	14,246	9,825
Hang Seng	22,991	18,089

Commodities	2008	2009
Oil	134.37	70.61
Gold	893.55	934.50

Bond Yields	2008	2009
USA 5 Yr Treasury	3.64	2.76
USA 10 Yr T	4.20	3.75
USA 20 Yr T	4.81	4.54
Moody's Aaa	5.74	5.61
Moody's Baa	7.14	7.42
CAN 5 Yr T	3.55	2.66
CAN 10 Yr T	3.85	3.49

Money Market	2008	2009
USA Fed Funds	2.00	0.25
USA 3 Mo T-B	1.95	0.18
CAN tgt overnight rate	3.00	0.25
CAN 3 Mo T-B	2.64	0.23

Foreign Exchange	2008	2009
USD/EUR	1.55	1.39
USD/GBP	1.96	1.63
CAN/USD	1.02	1.13
JPY/USD	108.00	96.81

JUNE

M	T	W	T	F	S	S
	1	2	3	4	5	6
7	8	9	10	11	12	13
14	15	16	17	18	19	20
21	22	23	24	25	26	27
28	29	30				

JULY

M	T	W	T	F	S	S
			1	2	3	4
5	6	7	8	9	10	11
12	13	14	15	16	17	18
19	20	21	22	23	24	25
26	27	28	29	30	31	

AUGUST

M	T	W	T	F	S	S
						1
2	3	4	5	6	7	8
9	10	11	12	13	14	15
16	17	18	19	20	21	22
23	24	25	26	27	28	29
30	31					

Seasonal Investment Time Line*

Investment	Seasonal	Jul	Aug	Sep	Oct	Nov	Dec	Jan	Feb	Mar	Apr	May	Jun
Major Market Indices													
S&P 500	Oct 28 - May 5												
TSX Comp	Oct 28 - May 5												
Russell 2000	Dec 19 - Mar 7												
Primary Sectors													
Energy	Jul 24 - Oct 3												
Energy (2)	Feb 25 - May 9												
Materials	Nov 19 - May 5												
Industrials	Mkt Perform												
Consumer Disc.	Oct 28 - Apr 22												
Consumer Staples	Apr 23 - Oct 27												
Health Care	Aug 15 - Oct18												
Financial	Jan 19- Apr 13												
Information Tech	Oct 9 - Jan 17												
Utilities	Jul 17 - Oct 3												
Secondary Sectors													
Gold (Metal)	Jul 12 - Oct 9												
Platinum	Jan 1 - May 31												
Retail	Oct 28 - Nov 29												
Retail (2)	Jan 21 - Apr 12												
Biotech	Jun 23 - Sep 13												
Agriculture	Aug 1 - Dec 31												
Natural Gas	Aug 1 - Dec 21												
Transportation	Sep 24 - Nov 13												
Metals and Mining	Nov 19 - May 5												
Bonds	May 1 - Dec 31												
U.S Dollar	Jan 1 - Jan 31												
Canadian Dollar	Apr 1 - Apr 30												
Large Cap Value	Jan 1 - Apr 30												
Large Cap Growth	Oct 1 - Dec 31												
Small Cap Value	Jan 1 - Aug 31												
Small Cap Growth	Sep 1 - Dec 31												
Oil E&P	Jan 30 - Apr 13												
Oil E&S	Apr 14 - May 17												

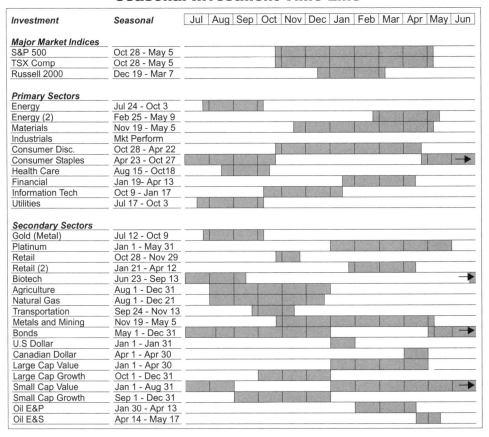

* Holiday, End of Month, Witches' Hangover, Yearly Cycles (Presidential Cycle) and Predictor Trades (January Predictor) not included

JUNE/JULY

28 MONDAY 179 / 186

29 TUESDAY 180 / 185

30 day	Wednesday July 28
60 day	Friday August 27
90 day	Sunday September 26
180 day	Saturday December 25
1 year	Tuesday June 28

30 day	Thursday July 29
60 day	Saturday August 28
90 day	Monday September 27
180 day	Sunday December 26
1 year	Wednesday June 29

30 WEDNESDAY 181 / 184

1 THURSDAY 182 / 183

30 day	Friday July 30
60 day	Sunday August 29
90 day	Tuesday September 28
180 day	Monday December 27
1 year	Thursday June 30

30 day	Saturday July 31
60 day	Monday August 30
90 day	Wednesday September 29
180 day	Tuesday December 28
1 year	Friday July 1

2 FRIDAY 183 / 182

30 day	Sunday August 1
60 day	Tuesday August 31
90 day	Thursday September 30
180 day	Wednesday December 29
1 year	Saturday July 2

* Weekly avg closing values- except Fed Funds Rate & CAN overnight tgt rate which are weekly closing values.

WEEK 26

Market Indices & Rates
Weekly Values*

Stock Markets	2008	2009
Dow	11,652	8,375
S&P 500	1,303	906
Nasdaq	2,358	1,798
TSX	14,438	10,115
FTSE	5,603	4,248
DAX	6,525	4,763
Nikkei	13,781	9,728
Hang Seng	22,461	18,073

Commodities	2008	2009
Oil (WTI)	137.26	68.52
Gold (London PM)	896.45	930.55

Bond Yields	2008	2009
USA 5 Yr Treasury	3.50	2.66
USA 10 Yr Treasury	4.09	3.63
USA 20 Yr Treasury	4.69	4.37
Moody's Aaa Corporate	5.67	5.43
Moody's Baa Corporate	7.08	7.20
CAN 5 Yr Treasury	3.43	2.54
CAN 10 Yr Treasury	3.73	3.43

Money Market	2008	2009
USA Fed Funds	2.00	0.25
USA 3 Mo T-Bill	1.79	0.19
CAN tgt overnight rate	3.00	0.25
CAN 3 Mo T-Bill	2.57	0.24

Foreign Exchange	2008	2009
USD / EUR	1.56	1.40
USD / GBP	1.97	1.64
CAN / USD	1.01	1.15
JPY / USD	107.57	95.71

JULY

M	T	W	T	F	S	S
			1	2	3	4
5	6	7	8	9	10	11
12	13	14	15	16	17	18
19	20	21	22	23	24	25
26	27	28	29	30	31	

AUGUST

M	T	W	T	F	S	S
						1
2	3	4	5	6	7	8
9	10	11	12	13	14	15
16	17	18	19	20	21	22
23	24	25	26	27	28	29
30	31					

SEPTEMBER

M	T	W	T	F	S	S
		1	2	3	4	5
6	7	8	9	10	11	12
13	14	15	16	17	18	19
20	21	22	23	24	25	26
27	28	29	30			

JULY

	MONDAY	TUESDAY	WEDNESDAY
WEEK 26	28	29	30
WEEK 27	**5** 26 USA Market Closed - Independence Day	**6** 25	**7** 24
WEEK 28	**12** 19	**13** 18	**14** 17
WEEK 29	**19** 12	**20** 11	**21** 10
WEEK 30	**26** 5	**27** 4	**28** 3

THURSDAY		FRIDAY	
1 30		**2** 29	
CAN Market Closed- Canada Day			
8 23		**9** 22	
15 16		**16** 15	
22 9		**23** 8	
29 2		**30** 1	

AUGUST

M	T	W	T	F	S	S
						1
2	3	4	5	6	7	8
9	10	11	12	13	14	15
16	17	18	19	20	21	22
23	24	25	26	27	28	29
30	31					

SEPTEMBER

M	T	W	T	F	S	S
		1	2	3	4	5
6	7	8	9	10	11	12
13	14	15	16	17	18	19
20	21	22	23	24	25	26
27	28	29	30			

OCTOBER

M	T	W	T	F	S	S
				1	2	3
4	5	6	7	8	9	10
11	12	13	14	15	16	17
18	19	20	21	22	23	24
25	26	27	28	29	30	31

NOVEMBER

M	T	W	T	F	S	S
1	2	3	4	5	6	7
8	9	10	11	12	13	14
15	16	17	18	19	20	21
22	23	24	25	26	27	28
29	30					

JULY
S U M M A R Y

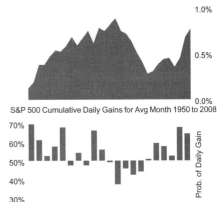

1.0%

0.5%

0.0%

S&P 500 Cumulative Daily Gains for Avg Month 1950 to 2008

STRATEGIES	PAGE
STRATEGIES STARTING	
18 Day Earnings Month Effect	39
Utilities – Summer Bounce	83
Gold (Metal) Shines	85
Golden Times	87
Oil – Summer/Autumn Strategy II of II	89
Mid-Summer Triple Combo	91
STRATEGIES FINISHING	
18 Day Earnings Month Effect	39
Independence Day – Full Trade Profit	75

70%
60%
50%
40%
30%

Prob. of Daily Gain

♦ When a summer rally does occur, the bulk of the gains are made in July. ♦ In the last half of the month the energy, gold and utility stocks tend to start their seasonal rallies (see strategies in this month). ♦ In 2009 the market shot up like a rocket after Independence Day as the earnings of companies were better than expected. Gold started its rally on que and utilities and energy turned in a lack lustre performance at best.

BEST / WORST JULY BROAD MKTS. 1999-2008

BEST JULY MARKETS
♦ Nasdaq (2003) 6.9%
♦ Russell 2000 (2005) 6.3%
♦ Nasdaq (2005) 6.2%

WORST JULY MARKETS
♦ Russell 2000 (2002) -15.2%
♦ Russell 3000 Val (2002) -9.9%
♦ Nasdaq (2002) -9.2%

Index Values End of Month

	1999	2000	2001	2002	2003	2004	2005	2006	2007	2008
Dow	10,655	10,522	10,523	8,737	9,234	10,140	10,641	11,186	13,212	11,378
S&P 500	1,329	1,431	1,211	912	990	1,102	1,234	1,277	1,455	1,267
Nasdaq	2,638	3,767	2,027	1,328	1,735	1,887	2,185	2,091	2,546	2,326
TSX	7,081	10,406	7,690	6,605	7,258	8,458	10,423	11,831	13,869	13,593
Russell 1000	1,328	1,454	1,225	931	1,016	1,129	1,288	1,331	1,523	1,334
Russell 2000	1,108	1,244	1,205	975	1,183	1,370	1,689	1,741	1,929	1,776
Russell 3000 Growth	2,577	3,183	2,084	1,471	1,639	1,764	1,988	1,955	2,305	2,139
Russell 3000 Value	2,149	2,012	2,166	1,773	1,922	2,216	2,589	2,809	3,099	2,570

Percent Gain for July

	1999	2000	2001	2002	2003	2004	2005	2006	2007	2008
Dow	-2.9	0.7	0.2	-5.5	2.8	-2.8	3.6	0.3	-1.5	0.2
S&P 500	-3.2	-1.6	-1.1	-7.9	1.6	-3.4	3.6	0.5	-3.2	-1.0
Nasdaq	-1.8	-5.0	-6.2	-9.2	6.9	-7.8	6.2	-3.7	-2.2	1.4
TSX	1.0	2.1	-0.6	-7.6	3.9	-1.0	5.3	1.9	-0.3	-6.0
Russell 1000	-3.1	-1.7	-1.5	-7.5	1.8	-3.6	3.8	0.1	-3.2	-1.3
Russell 2000	-2.8	-3.3	-5.5	-15.2	6.2	-6.8	6.3	-3.3	-6.9	3.6
Russell 3000 Growth	-3.2	-4.5	-3.0	-6.2	2.8	-6.0	5.0	-2.2	-1.9	-1.6
Russell 3000 Value	-3.0	1.3	-0.5	-9.9	1.5	-1.9	2.9	1.9	-5.1	-0.2

July Market Avg. Performance 1999 to 2008 [1]

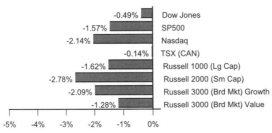

-0.49% Dow Jones
-1.57% SP500
-2.14% Nasdaq
-0.14% TSX (CAN)
-1.62% Russell 1000 (Lg Cap)
-2.78% Russell 2000 (Sm Cap)
-2.09% Russell 3000 (Brd Mkt) Growth
-1.28% Russell 3000 (Brd Mkt) Value

-5%   -4%   -3%   -2%   -1%   0%

Interest Corner Jul[2]

	Fed Funds % [3]	3 Mo. T-Bill % [4]	10 Yr % [5]	20 Yr % [6]
2008	2.00	1.68	3.99	4.63
2007	5.25	4.96	4.78	5.00
2006	5.25	5.10	4.99	5.17
2005	3.25	3.42	4.28	4.56
2004	1.25	1.45	4.50	5.24

(1) Russell Data provided by Russell (2) Federal Reserve Bank of St. Louis - end of month values (3) Target rate set by FOMC (4)(5)(6) Constant yield maturities.

THACKRAY SECTOR THERMOMETER

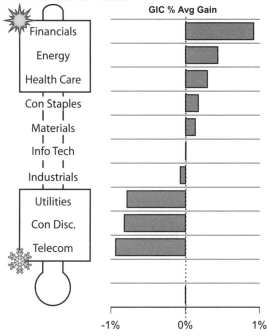

	GIC % Avg Gain	Fq % Gain >S&P 500	SP GIC SECTOR 1990-2008(1)
Financials	0.9	53	Financials
Energy	0.4	63	Energy
Health Care	0.3	47	Health Care
Con Staples	0.2	63	Consumer Staples
Materials	0.1	63	Materials
Info Tech	0.0	42	Information Technology
Industrials	-0.1	47	Industrials
Utilities	-0.8	42	Utilities
Con Disc.	-0.8	42	Consumer Discretionary
Telecom	-0.9	47	Telecom
	0.0 %	N/A %	S&P 500

GIC(2) % Avg Gain   Fq % Gain >S&P 500

-1%   0%   1%

Hot Box - 3 Best Sectors
Financials ♦ Energy ♦ Health Care

July Portfolio

	Avg % Gain	Avg % Gain > S&P 500	Fq % Gain >S&P 500
1990-2008	0.6%	0.5%	58%
2008	-0.8%	0.2%	

Cold Box - 3 Worst Sectors
Utilities ♦ Con Disc. ♦ Telecom

July Portfolio

	Avg % Gain	Avg % Gain > S&P 500	Fq % Gain >S&P 500
1990-2008	-0.8%	-0.9%	37%
2008	-4.2%	-3.2%	

Commentary

♦ From 1990 to 2008, July has been "flat," although it has had more negative months than positive. ♦ July's performance is really the tale of two half months. In the first half of the month, the broad market tends to do very well (see *18 Day Earnings Month Effect*). In the second half the performance tends to wither away. ♦ This is the time that the Energy sector tends to do well relative to the broad market. Investors should be cautious with this sector as it typically does not start to outperform until the end of the month. ♦ In 2008 the energy sector produced a loss of almost 14%. Despite Energy's bad performance the *Hot Box 3 Best Sectors* marginally outperformed the S&P 500 as the other two sectors in the trio were the top two sectors for the month.

(1) Sector data provided by Standard and Poors (2) GIC is short form for Global Industry Classification (3) Sub Sector data provided by Standard and Poors, except where marked by symbol.

UTILITIES – SUMMER BOUNCE
July 17th to Oct 3rd

☒ 2008 Performance

Not only did the lights go off for the S&P 500 in 2008, but also for utility companies. The utilities sector suffered indiscriminate selling like many other sectors in the market.

Utility stocks are a long forgotten part of the market. Very seldom do you hear pundits singing their virtues. They lost out to the hype of tech stocks in the 90's and are still shunned by a large number of investors because of the fear of rising interest rates. Despite the environment of neglect, utility stocks have managed to outperform the S&P 500 on a fairly consistent basis from July 17th to October 3rd.

3.3% better and positive at a time
when the S&P 500 has been negative

Utilities' outperformance from the end of July to the beginning of October fits in very well with the theme of investors taking a defensive position during this time of year. At this time the broad market tends to produce a negative return and investors are looking for a safe place to invest. Utilities fit the bill.

S&P Utilities Sector vs. S&P 500 1990 to 2008			
Jul 17 to Oct 3	Utilities	Positive SP500	Diff
1990	-3.4 %	-15.6 %	12.2 %
1991	9.2	0.8	8.5
1992	-0.9	-1.7	0.8
1993	3.6	3.5	0.1
1994	-1.6	1.7	-3.3
1995	6.6	4.0	2.5
1996	-0.9	10.3	-11.2
1997	2.6	3.0	-0.4
1998	6.8	-15.3	22.1
1999	-5.5	-9.6	4.1
2000	23.0	-5.5	28.5
2001	-13.6	-10.8	-2.8
2002	-12.0	-9.1	-2.9
2003	7.2	3.6	3.6
2004	5.1	2.7	2.4
2005	6.0	-0.1	6.1
2006	5.3	7.9	-2.6
2007	0.6	-0.6	1.2
2008	-17.6	-11.7	-5.9
Avg.	1.1 %	-2.2 %	3.3 %

been negative. Also, during this time period the utilities sector beat the S&P 500, 12 out of 19 times. Not bad for a defensive sector. The utilities sector is considered defensive because it is a slow growth mature industry that has stable income from long term contracts. When the market gets "spooked," investors typically switch their money into companies with stable earnings. There is an added bonus of investing in utilities – dividends. Because the sector is mature with stable earnings they tend to pay out a higher dividend yield.

In the last two decades there have been two periods of two back-to-back years of negative performance. In 1996 and 1997 the utilities sector underperformed as dividends and defensive positions did not matter much. In 2001 and 2002 the utilities sector underperformed as a few scandal ridden utilities companies hit the newspaper headlines. The most notorious being Enron.

Utilities Sector - Avg. Year 1990 to 2008

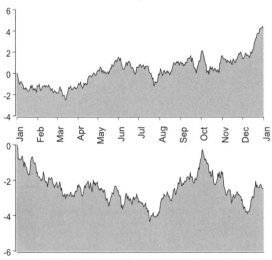

Utilities / S&P 500 Relative Strength - Avg Yr. 1990 - 2008

From July 17th to October 3rd, during the years 1990 to 2007, the utilities sector has produced an average return of 2.1%, while the S&P 500 reached into the negative territory with a -1.7% return. Utilities have produced 3.8% more when the S&P 500 has typically

 Utilities SP GIC Sector 55:
An index designed to represent a cross section of utility companies.
For more information on the utilities sector, see www.standardandpoors.com.

5 MONDAY	186 / 179

6 TUESDAY	187 / 178

Market Indices & Rates
Weekly Values*

Stock Markets	2007	2008
Dow	13,573	11,309
S&P 500	1,525	1,272
Nasdaq	2,650	2,274
TSX	14,081	14,164
FTSE	6,646	5,484
DAX	8,024	6,333
Nikkei	18,165	13,347
Hang Seng	22,289	21,618

Commodities	2007	2008
Oil (WTI)	71.78	142.46
Gold (London PM)	652.58	933.65

Bond Yields	2007	2008
USA 5 Yr Treasury	5.00	3.32
USA 10 Yr Treasury	5.10	4.00
USA 20 Yr Treasury	5.27	4.59
Moody's Aaa Corporate	5.80	5.60
Moody's Baa Corporate	6.69	7.06
CAN 5 Yr Treasury	4.62	3.45
CAN 10 Yr Treasury	4.60	3.74

Money Market	2007	2008
USA Fed Funds	5.25	2.00
USA 3 Mo T-Bill	4.95	1.86
CAN tgt overnight rate	4.25	3.00
CAN 3 Mo T-Bill	4.43	2.44

Foreign Exchange	2007	2008
USD / EUR	1.36	1.58
USD / GBP	2.01	1.99
CAN / USD	1.06	1.02
JPY / USD	122.68	106.11

30 day	Wednesday August 4
60 day	Friday September 3
90 day	Sunday October 3
180 day	Saturday January 1
1 year	Tuesday July 5

30 day	Thursday August 5
60 day	Saturday September 4
90 day	Monday October 4
180 day	Sunday January 2
1 year	Wednesday July 6

7 WEDNESDAY	188 / 177

8 THURSDAY	189 / 176

JULY

M	T	W	T	F	S	S
			1	2	3	4
5	6	7	8	9	10	11
12	13	14	15	16	17	18
19	20	21	22	23	24	25
26	27	28	29	30	31	

AUGUST

M	T	W	T	F	S	S
						1
2	3	4	5	6	7	8
9	10	11	12	13	14	15
16	17	18	19	20	21	22
23	24	25	26	27	28	29
30	31					

30 day	Friday August 6
60 day	Sunday September 5
90 day	Tuesday October 5
180 day	Monday January 3
1 year	Thursday July 7

30 day	Saturday August 7
60 day	Monday September 6
90 day	Wednesday October 6
180 day	Tuesday January 4
1 year	Friday July 8

9 FRIDAY	190 / 175

SEPTEMBER

M	T	W	T	F	S	S
		1	2	3	4	5
6	7	8	9	10	11	12
13	14	15	16	17	18	19
20	21	22	23	24	25	26
27	28	29	30			

30 day	Sunday August 8
60 day	Tuesday September 7
90 day	Thursday October 7
180 day	Wednesday January 5
1 year	Saturday July 9

* Weekly avg closing values- except Fed Funds Rate & CAN overnight tgt rate which are weekly closing values.

GOLD SHINES
(Metal) Gold (Metal) Outperforms – July 12th to October 9th

"Foul cankering rust the hidden treasure frets, but gold that's put to use more gold begets."

(William Shakespeare, *Venus and Adonis*)

☑ **2008 Performance**

One of the reasons that investors buy gold is for disaster protection. What is often forgotten is that in the initial stages of a major fall in the market, everything gets sold. Gold is no exception. Although it turned in a negative performance during its seasonal time in 2008, it substantially outperformed the S&P 500.

For many years gold was thought to be a dead investment. It was only the "gold bugs" that espoused the virtues of investing in the precious metal. Investors were mesmerized with technology stocks and central bankers, confident of their currencies, were selling gold, "left, right and center."

3.2% when the S&P 500 has been negative & 64% of the time positive

Gold (Metal) London PM vs S&P 500 1984 to 2008

Jul 12 to Oct 9th	Gold	S&P 500	Positive Diff
1984	0.5 %	7.4 %	-6.9 %
1985	4.1	-5.4	9.5
1986	25.2	-2.6	27.8
1987	3.9	0.9	3.0
1988	-7.5	2.8	-10.3
1989	-4.2	9.4	-13.6
1990	12.1	-15.5	27.6
1991	-2.9	0.0	-2.8
1992	0.4	-2.9	3.3
1993	-8.8	2.7	-11.5
1994	1.6	1.6	0.0
1995	-0.1	4.3	-4.3
1996	-0.4	7.9	-8.3
1997	4.4	5.9	-1.5
1998	2.8	-15.5	18.2
1999	25.6	-4.8	30.4
2000	-4.5	-5.3	0.8
2001	8.4	-10.5	18.8
2002	1.7	-16.2	17.9
2003	7.8	4.1	3.8
2004	3.8	0.8	2.9
2005	11.4	-1.9	13.4
2006	-8.8	6.1	-14.9
2007	11.0	3.1	8.0
2008	-8.2	-26.6	18.4
Avg.	3.2 %	-2.0 %	5.2 %

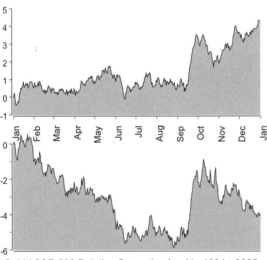

Gold (metal) Sector - Avg. Year 1984 to 2008

Gold / S&P 500 Relative Strength - Avg Yr. 1984 - 2008

Golden Times strategy page. The movement of gold stock prices, represented by the index (XAU) on the Philadelphia Exchange, coincides closely with the price of gold (metal). Although there is a strong correlation between gold and gold stocks, there are other factors, such as company operations and hedging policies which determine each company's price in the market.

Gold (metal) has typically started its seasonal strong period a few weeks earlier than gold stocks and finished just after gold stocks have turned down.

Times have changed and investors have taken a shine to gold (metal). In the last few years gold has substantially outperformed the stock market. On a seasonal basis, on average from 1984 to 2007, gold has done well relative to the stock market from July 12th to October 9th. The reasons for gold's seasonal changes in price movements, jewellery production and central bank selling cycles, have been put forward in the

 Cliff Warning -- Similar to the XAU pattern, the price of gold tends to correct severely in October.

ⓘ *Source: Bank of England London PM is recognized as the world benchmark for gold prices. London PM represents the close value of gold in afternoon trading in London.*

12 MONDAY	193 / 172	**13** TUESDAY	194 / 171

WEEK 28

Market Indices & Rates
Weekly Values*

Stock Markets	2007	2008
Dow	13,700	11,219
S&P 500	1,532	1,253
Nasdaq	2,674	2,254
TSX	14,266	13,717
FTSE	6,675	5,430
DAX	8,017	6,309
Nikkei	18,157	13,110
Hang Seng	22,844	21,789

Commodities	2007	2008
Oil (WTI)	72.80	140.04
Gold (London PM)	663.94	933.45

Bond Yields	2007	2008
USA 5 Yr Treasury	5.00	3.18
USA 10 Yr Treasury	5.10	3.90
USA 20 Yr Treasury	5.27	4.51
Moody's Aaa Corporate	5.81	5.53
Moody's Baa Corporate	6.69	7.03
CAN 5 Yr Treasury	4.64	3.39
CAN 10 Yr Treasury	4.63	3.72

Monday 12:
30 day	Wednesday August 11
60 day	Friday September 10
90 day	Sunday October 10
180 day	Saturday January 8
1 year	Tuesday July 12

Tuesday 13:
30 day	Thursday August 12
60 day	Saturday September 11
90 day	Monday October 11
180 day	Sunday January 9
1 year	Wednesday July 13

Money Market	2007	2008
USA Fed Funds	5.25	2.00
USA 3 Mo T-Bill	4.96	1.77
CAN tgt overnight rate	4.50	3.00
CAN 3 Mo T-Bill	4.50	2.35

14 WEDNESDAY	195 / 170	**15** THURSDAY	196 / 169

Foreign Exchange	2007	2008
USD / EUR	1.37	1.57
USD / GBP	2.03	1.97
CAN / USD	1.05	1.02
JPY / USD	122.58	107.18

JULY

M	T	W	T	F	S	S
			1	2	3	4
5	6	7	8	9	10	11
12	13	14	15	16	17	18
19	20	21	22	23	24	25
26	27	28	29	30	31	

Wednesday 14:
30 day	Friday August 13
60 day	Sunday September 12
90 day	Tuesday October 12
180 day	Monday January 10
1 year	Thursday July 14

Thursday 15:
30 day	Saturday August 14
60 day	Monday September 13
90 day	Wednesday October 13
180 day	Tuesday January 11
1 year	Friday July 15

16 FRIDAY	197 / 168

AUGUST

M	T	W	T	F	S	S
						1
2	3	4	5	6	7	8
9	10	11	12	13	14	15
16	17	18	19	20	21	22
23	24	25	26	27	28	29
30	31					

Friday 16:
30 day	Sunday August 15
60 day	Tuesday September 14
90 day	Thursday October 14
180 day	Wednesday January 12
1 year	Saturday July 16

SEPTEMBER

M	T	W	T	F	S	S
		1	2	3	4	5
6	7	8	9	10	11	12
13	14	15	16	17	18	19
20	21	22	23	24	25	26
27	28	29	30			

Weekly avg closing values- except Fed Funds Rate & CAN overnight tgt rate which are weekly closing values.

GOLDEN TIMES

(Stocks) Gold Stocks Outperform – July 27th to September 25th

Investors often view gold stocks as an asset class for disaster protection. This does not work when a large number of hedge funds hold gold stocks in their leveraged portfolios and need money quickly. As the world was falling apart in late 2008 hedge funds and investors sold almost everything to raise money, including gold stocks. Normally gold stocks do well from July 27th to September 25th.

Gold stocks were shunned for many years. It is only recently that interest has sparked again. What few investors know is that even during the twenty year bear market in gold that started in 1981, it was possible to make money in gold stocks.

6.8% when the S&P 500 has been negative

XAU (Gold Stocks) vs S&P 500 1984 to 2008			
Jul 27 to Sep 25	XAU	Positive S&P 500	Diff
1984	20.8 %	10.4 %	10.4 %
1985	-5.5	-6.1	0.6
1986	36.9	-3.5	40.4
1987	23.0	3.5	19.5
1988	-11.9	1.7	-13.7
1989	10.5	1.8	8.7
1990	3.8	-13.4	17.2
1991	-11.9	1.6	-13.5
1992	-3.8	0.7	-4.5
1993	-7.3	1.9	-9.2
1994	18.2	1.4	16.8
1995	-1.0	3.6	-4.6
1996	-1.0	7.9	-8.9
1997	8.7	-0.1	8.8
1998	12.0	-8.4	20.5
1999	16.9	-5.2	22.1
2000	-2.8	-0.9	-1.9
2001	3.2	-15.8	19.0
2002	29.8	-1.5	31.4
2003	11.0	0.5	10.5
2004	16.5	2.4	14.1
2005	20.5	-1.3	21.8
2006	-11.9	4.6	-16.8
2007	14.0	2.3	11.7
2008	-18.5	-3.9	-14.6
Avg.	6.8 %	-0.6 %	7.5 %

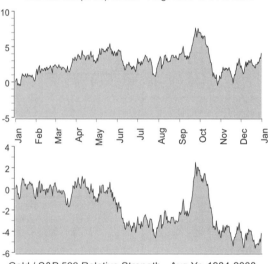

Gold stocks (XAU) Sector - Avg. Year 1984 to 2008

Gold / S&P 500 Relative Strength - Avg Yr. 1984-2008

On average from 1984 (start of the XAU index) to 2008, gold stocks as represented by the XAU index, have outperformed the S&P 500 from July 27th to September 25th. One factor that has led to a rise in the price of gold stocks in August and September is the Indian festival and wedding season that starts in October and finishes in November during Diwali. The Asian culture places a great emphasis on gold as a store of value and a lot of it is "consumed" as jewellery during the festival and wedding season. The price of gold tends to increase in the months preceding this season as the jewellery fabricators purchase gold to make their final product.

The August-September increase in gold stocks coincides with the time that a lot of investors are pulling their money out of the broad market and are looking for a place to invest. If you believe in the merits of gold stocks, this is definitely a great time to consider.

Be careful. Just as the gold stocks tend to go up in August-September, they also tend to go down in October. The fall can be rather abrupt so getting out a little early might be prudent.

XAU is an index traded on the Philadelphia exchange. It consists of 12 precious metal mining companies.

JULY

19 MONDAY	200 / 165		**20** TUESDAY	201 / 164

Market Indices & Rates
Weekly Values*

Stock Markets	2007	2008
Dow	13,938	11,240
S&P 500	1,546	1,242
Nasdaq	2,703	2,262
TSX	14,503	13,516
FTSE	6,630	5,257
DAX	7,981	6,218
Nikkei	18,127	12,843
Hang Seng	23,032	21,604

Commodities	2007	2008
Oil (WTI)	74.94	135.34
Gold (London PM)	671.07	971.35

Bond Yields	2007	2008
USA 5 Yr Treasury	4.93	3.26
USA 10 Yr Treasury	5.03	3.98
USA 20 Yr Treasury	5.19	4.62
Moody's Aaa Corporate	5.74	5.67
Moody's Baa Corporate	6.62	7.18
CAN 5 Yr Treasury	4.63	3.34
CAN 10 Yr Treasury	4.60	3.74

Money Market	2007	2008
USA Fed Funds	5.25	2.00
USA 3 Mo T-Bill	4.97	1.44
CAN tgt overnight rate	4.50	3.00
CAN 3 Mo T-Bill	4.49	2.25

Foreign Exchange	2007	2008
USD / EUR	1.38	1.59
USD / GBP	2.05	2.00
CAN / USD	1.04	1.00
JPY / USD	122.01	105.47

Monday 19:
30 day	Wednesday August 18
60 day	Friday September 17
90 day	Sunday October 17
180 day	Saturday January 15
1 year	Tuesday July 19

Tuesday 20:
30 day	Thursday August 19
60 day	Saturday September 18
90 day	Monday October 18
180 day	Sunday January 16
1 year	Wednesday July 20

21 WEDNESDAY	202 / 163		**22** THURSDAY	203 / 162

Wednesday 21:
30 day	Friday August 20
60 day	Sunday September 19
90 day	Tuesday October 19
180 day	Monday January 17
1 year	Thursday July 21

Thursday 22:
30 day	Saturday August 21
60 day	Monday September 20
90 day	Wednesday October 20
180 day	Tuesday January 18
1 year	Friday July 22

23 FRIDAY	204 / 161

Friday 23:
30 day	Sunday August 22
60 day	Tuesday September 21
90 day	Thursday October 21
180 day	Wednesday January 19
1 year	Saturday July 23

JULY
M	T	W	T	F	S	S
			1	2	3	4
5	6	7	8	9	10	11
12	13	14	15	16	17	18
19	20	21	22	23	24	25
26	27	28	29	30	31	

AUGUST
M	T	W	T	F	S	S
						1
2	3	4	5	6	7	8
9	10	11	12	13	14	15
16	17	18	19	20	21	22
23	24	25	26	27	28	29
30	31					

SEPTEMBER
M	T	W	T	F	S	S
		1	2	3	4	5
6	7	8	9	10	11	12
13	14	15	16	17	18	19
20	21	22	23	24	25	26
27	28	29	30			

* Weekly avg closing values- except Fed Funds Rate & CAN overnight tgt rate which are weekly closing values.

OIL – SUMMER/AUTUMN STRATEGY
IInd of II Oil Stock Strategies for the Year
July 24th to October 3rd

(Stocks)

☒ **2008 Performance**

In the summer months of 2008 there were grave concerns that the global economy was going to implode. As a result, the demand for oil decreased and the energy sector underperformed the S&P 500 by 3.8%.

Oil stocks tend to outperform the market once again (see *Oil - Winter/Spring Strategy* for first wave of outperformance from late February to early May, and for details on the XOI oil index). Although the first wave has had an incredible record of outperformance, the second wave is still noteworthy. While the first wave has more to do with inventories during the switch from producing heating oil to gasoline, the second wave is more related to the conversion of production from gasoline to heating oil and the effects of the hurricane season.

Extra 2.7 % &
60% of the time better than S&P 500

XOI vs. S&P 500 1984 to 2008			
Jul 24 to Oct 3	XOI	Positive S&P 500	Diff
1984	9.0	9.1	-0.1
1985	6.7	-4.3	11.0
1986	15.7	-2.1	17.7
1987	-1.2	6.6	-7.8
1988	-3.6	3.0	-6.6
1989	5.7	5.6	0.1
1990	-0.5	-12.4	11.8
1991	0.7	1.3	-0.7
1992	2.9	-0.4	3.3
1993	7.8	3.2	4.6
1994	-3.6	1.9	-5.5
1995	-2.2	5.2	-7.4
1996	7.7	10.5	-2.8
1997	8.9	3.0	5.9
1998	1.4	-12.0	13.5
1999	-2.1	-5.5	3.3
2000	12.2	-3.6	15.8
2001	-5.1	-10.0	4.8
2002	7.3	2.7	4.6
2003	5.5	4.2	1.4
2004	10.9	4.2	6.7
2005	14.3	-0.6	14.9
2006	-8.5	7.6	-16.9
2007	-4.2	-0.1	-4.1
2008	-18.1	-14.3	-3.8
Avg	2.7 %	0.1 %	2.6 %

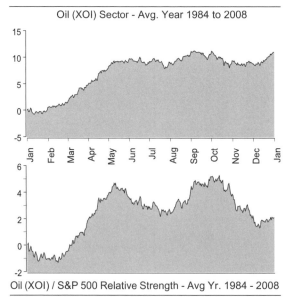

Oil (XOI) Sector - Avg. Year 1984 to 2008

Oil (XOI) / S&P 500 Relative Strength - Avg Yr. 1984 - 2008

First, there is a large difference between how heating oil and gasoline is stored and consumed. For the average individual and business, gasoline is consumed in a fairly immediate fashion. It is stored by the local distributor and the supplies are drawn upon as needed. Heating oil, on the other hand is largely inventoried by individuals, farms and business operations in rural areas in large amounts. The inventory process starts well before the cold weather arrives. Further down the line the production facilities have to start switching from gasoline to heating oil, dropping their inventory levels and boosting prices.

Second, hurricane season can play havoc with the production of oil and drive up prices substantially. The official duration of the hurricane season in the Gulf of Mexico is from June 1st to November 30th, but most major hurricanes occur in September and early October. The threat of a strong hurricane can shut down the oil platforms temporarily, interrupting production. If a strong hurricane strikes the oil platforms it can do significant damage and put the platform out of commission for an extended period of time.

26 MONDAY	207 / 158

27 TUESDAY	208 / 157

Market Indices & Rates
Weekly Values*

Stock Markets	2007	2008
Dow	13,637	11,484
S&P 500	1,502	1,266
Nasdaq	2,628	2,300
TSX	14,047	13,486
FTSE	6,409	5,387
DAX	7,681	6,456
Nikkei	17,762	13,359
Hang Seng	23,197	22,805

Commodities	2007	2008
Oil (WTI)	75.22	125.97
Gold (London PM)	674.31	939.40

Bond Yields	2007	2008
USA 5 Yr Treasury	4.74	3.44
USA 10 Yr Treasury	4.88	4.11
USA 20 Yr Treasury	5.09	4.72
Moody's Aaa Corporate	5.64	5.78
Moody's Baa Corporate	6.61	7.27
CAN 5 Yr Treasury	4.59	3.43
CAN 10 Yr Treasury	4.55	3.83

Money Market	2007	2008
USA Fed Funds	5.25	2.00
USA 3 Mo T-Bill	4.96	1.60
CAN tgt overnight rate	4.50	3.00
CAN 3 Mo T-Bill	4.55	2.39

Foreign Exchange	2007	2008
USD / EUR	1.37	1.58
USD / GBP	2.05	2.00
CAN / USD	1.05	1.01
JPY / USD	120.35	107.17

30 day	Wednesday August 25
60 day	Friday September 24
90 day	Sunday October 24
180 day	Saturday January 22
1 year	Tuesday July 26

30 day	Thursday August 26
60 day	Saturday September 25
90 day	Monday October 25
180 day	Sunday January 23
1 year	Wednesday July 27

28 WEDNESDAY	209 / 156

29 THURSDAY	210 / 155

JULY

M	T	W	T	F	S	S
			1	2	3	4
5	6	7	8	9	10	11
12	13	14	15	16	17	18
19	20	21	22	23	24	25
26	27	28	29	30	31	

AUGUST

M	T	W	T	F	S	S
						1
2	3	4	5	6	7	8
9	10	11	12	13	14	15
16	17	18	19	20	21	22
23	24	25	26	27	28	29
30	31					

30 day	Friday August 27
60 day	Sunday September 26
90 day	Tuesday October 26
180 day	Monday January 24
1 year	Thursday July 28

30 day	Saturday August 28
60 day	Monday September 27
90 day	Wednesday October 27
180 day	Tuesday January 25
1 year	Friday July 29

30 FRIDAY	211 / 154

SEPTEMBER

M	T	W	T	F	S	S
		1	2	3	4	5
6	7	8	9	10	11	12
13	14	15	16	17	18	19
20	21	22	23	24	25	26
27	28	29	30			

30 day	Sunday August 29
60 day	Tuesday September 28
90 day	Thursday October 28
180 day	Wednesday January 26
1 year	Saturday July 30

* Weekly avg closing values- except Fed Funds Rate & CAN overnight tgt rate which are weekly closing values.

(Stocks) + (Stocks) +

MID-SUMMER TRIPLE COMBO
Oil Stocks, Gold Stocks and Utility Stocks
Prosper from July 27th to September 25th

☒ 2008 Performance

In 2008 all three elements of the combo under-performed the S&P 500.

Would you like some utilities with your oil and gold stocks? Why not! Unlike fast food this combination has been good for you. The full meal deal (gold, oil and utility stocks) is a good order for the summer time as all three sectors have typically increased at the same time of year (July 27th to September 25th).

2.3% average return & 63% of the time better than the S&P 500

Part of the value of this combination is that the sectors have not always increased together in the same year. For example, in 2000 during the seasonal combo time period, gold stocks lost 2.8% as the gold market failed to gain traction in its new bull market. During the same time period, oil stocks were up 8.9% and utility stocks were up 17.3%, producing an overall blended combination return of 7.8%. This was 8.7% better than the S&P 500. In 2001 and 2002 the tables turned with gold stocks making up for the performance of the oil and utility stocks. The end result in both cases was the *Mid-Summer Triple Combo* outperforming the S&P 500.

From 1990 to 2007 the gold, oil and utility stock combo has produced a positive return of 3.0%, which is 4.1% better than the S&P 500 over the same time period. What makes this combo so attractive is that it occurs during the summer months when the market typically has a negative return.

Although the gold stocks are clearly the outper-forming winner, they have typically been more volatile. Adding oil stocks and utilities to the order, despite lowering the return, has added to the frequency of outperforming the S&P 500. Gold stocks have outperformed the S&P 500 61% of the time, oil stocks 61% and utility stocks 61%. The combination of all three has produced an outperformance 63% of the time.

Combo Gold Stocks & Oil Stocks & Utility Stocks vs S&P 500 Jul 27 to Sep 25, 1990 to 2008

Performance > S&P 500

Year	XAU	XOI	Utilities	Avg Combo	SP500
1990	3.8 %	2.1 %	-4.3 %	0.5 %	-13.4 %
1991	-11.9	0.5	4.8	-2.2	1.6
1992	-3.8	3.5	0.0	-0.1	0.7
1993	-7.3	1.5	2.3	-1.2	1.9
1994	18.2	-3.8	-2.8	3.9	1.4
1995	-1.0	-2.0	2.2	-0.3	3.6
1996	-1.0	6.7	1.5	2.4	7.9
1997	8.7	6.8	3.3	6.3	-0.1
1998	12.0	2.4	4.6	6.4	-8.4
1999	16.9	-2.1	-7.5	2.4	-5.2
2000	-2.8	8.9	17.3	7.8	-0.9
2001	3.2	-14.3	-13.0	-8.0	-15.8
2002	29.8	-1.8	-3.5	8.2	-1.5
2003	11.0	2.9	2.7	5.5	0.5
2004	16.5	9.0	6.0	10.5	2.4
2005	20.5	13.1	2.6	12.1	-1.3
2006	-11.9	-12.8	-0.1	-8.3	4.6
2007	14.0	4.1	5.6	7.9	2.3
2008	-18.5	-2.3	-8.0	-9.6	3.9
Avg.	5.1 %	1.2 %	0.7 %	2.3 %	-1.3 %

For convenience we have made the triple combo 1/3 gold, 1/3 oil and 1/3 utilities. An investor's mix depends on risk toler-ance and expectations. At the time of this writing, using the S&P GIC sector weights, the energy (oil) sector represent-ed 11% of the market, utilities 4%, and gold under 2% of the S&P 500. If you are managing your portfolio relative to these benchmarks, oil stocks should generally be favored as it is the largest sector.

When you are finished your seasonal tri-ple combo, make sure that you do not come back for seconds at the end of Sep-tember - it is not good for you. All three sectors have typically started their under-performance relative to the S&P 500 at this time.

For a detailed analysis of each sector in the combo, please see the proceeding strategy pages in the month of July.

AUGUST

2 MONDAY — 214 / 151

3 TUESDAY — 215 / 150

30/60/90/180 day – 1 year (Monday)
30 day	Wednesday September 1
60 day	Friday October 1
90 day	Sunday October 31
180 day	Saturday January 29
1 year	Tuesday August 2

30/60/90/180 day – 1 year (Tuesday)
30 day	Thursday September 2
60 day	Saturday October 2
90 day	Monday November 1
180 day	Sunday January 30
1 year	Wednesday August 3

4 WEDNESDAY — 216 / 149

5 THURSDAY — 217 / 148

30/60/90/180 day – 1 year (Wednesday)
30 day	Friday September 3
60 day	Sunday October 3
90 day	Tuesday November 2
180 day	Monday January 31
1 year	Thursday August 4

30/60/90/180 day – 1 year (Thursday)
30 day	Saturday September 4
60 day	Monday October 4
90 day	Wednesday November 3
180 day	Tuesday February 1
1 year	Friday August 5

6 FRIDAY — 218 / 147

30/60/90/180 day – 1 year (Friday)
30 day	Sunday September 5
60 day	Tuesday October 5
90 day	Thursday November 4
180 day	Wednesday February 2
1 year	Saturday August 6

WEEK 31

Market Indices & Rates — Weekly Values*

Stock Markets	2007	2008
Dow	13,316	11,363
S&P 500	1,460	1,262
Nasdaq	2,554	2,310
TSX	13,753	13,484
FTSE	6,268	5,364
DAX	7,497	6,417
Nikkei	17,075	13,270
Hang Seng	22,672	22,646

Commodities	2007	2008
Oil (WTI)	76.78	124.57
Gold (London PM)	665.90	913.65

Bond Yields	2007	2008
USA 5 Yr Treasury	4.60	3.31
USA 10 Yr Treasury	4.77	4.04
USA 20 Yr Treasury	5.00	4.66
Moody's Aaa Corporate	5.63	5.73
Moody's Baa Corporate	6.62	7.21
CAN 5 Yr Treasury	4.56	3.31
CAN 10 Yr Treasury	4.52	3.75

Money Market	2007	2008
USA Fed Funds	5.25	2.00
USA 3 Mo T-Bill	4.91	1.70
CAN tgt overnight rate	4.50	3.00
CAN 3 Mo T-Bill	4.55	2.40

Foreign Exchange	2007	2008
USD / EUR	1.37	1.57
USD / GBP	2.03	1.98
CAN / USD	1.06	1.02
JPY / USD	118.72	107.80

AUGUST
M	T	W	T	F	S	S
						1
2	3	4	5	6	7	8
9	10	11	12	13	14	15
16	17	18	19	20	21	22
23	24	25	26	27	28	29
30	31					

SEPTEMBER
M	T	W	T	F	S	S
		1	2	3	4	5
6	7	8	9	10	11	12
13	14	15	16	17	18	19
20	21	22	23	24	25	26
27	28	29	30			

OCTOBER
M	T	W	T	F	S	S
				1	2	3
4	5	6	7	8	9	10
11	12	13	14	15	16	17
18	19	20	21	22	23	24
25	26	27	28	29	30	31

* Weekly avg closing values- except Fed Funds Rate & CAN overnight tgt rate which are weekly closing values.

AUGUST

	MONDAY	TUESDAY	WEDNESDAY
WEEK 31	**2** 29 CAN Market Closed- Civic Day	**3** 28	**4** 27
WEEK 32	**9** 22	**10** 21	**11** 20
WEEK 33	**16** 15	**17** 14	**18** 13
WEEK 34	**23** 8	**24** 7	**25** 6
WEEK 35	**30** 1	**31**	1

THURSDAY		FRIDAY	
5	26	**6**	25
12	19	**13**	18
19	12	**20**	11
26	5	**27**	4
2		3	

SEPTEMBER

M	T	W	T	F	S	S
		1	2	3	4	5
6	7	8	9	10	11	12
13	14	15	16	17	18	19
20	21	22	23	24	25	26
27	28	29	30			

OCTOBER

M	T	W	T	F	S	S
				1	2	3
4	5	6	7	8	9	10
11	12	13	14	15	16	17
18	19	20	21	22	23	24
25	26	27	28	29	30	31

NOVEMBER

M	T	W	T	F	S	S
1	2	3	4	5	6	7
8	9	10	11	12	13	14
15	16	17	18	19	20	21
22	23	24	25	26	27	28
29	30					

DECEMBER

M	T	W	T	F	S	S
		1	2	3	4	5
6	7	8	9	10	11	12
13	14	15	16	17	18	19
20	21	22	23	24	25	26
27	28	29	30	31		

AUGUST
S U M M A R Y

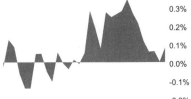

S&P 500 Cumulative Daily Gains for Avg Month 1950 to 2008

♦ If there is a summer rally, it is often in jeopardy in August. ♦ The best August over the last ten years occurred in 2000 (Nasdaq 11.7%; Russell 3000, 9.1%, and the TSX (Canada) 8.1%. ♦ Since 1950 the S&P 500 has produced an average gain of 0.1% and has been positive 56% of the time. Over the same time period it is ranked as the 9th best month. ♦ August is hardly a month to get excited about, especially considering the typical performance of the following month, September.

BEST / WORST AUGUST BROAD MKTS. 1999-2008

BEST AUGUST MARKETS
- ♦ Nasdaq (2000) 11.7%
- ♦ Russell 3000 Gr (2000) 9.1%
- ♦ TSX (2000) 8.1%

WORST AUGUST MARKETS
- ♦ Nasdaq (2001) -10.9%
- ♦ Russell 3000 Gr (2001) -8.1%
- ♦ S&P500 (2001) -6.4%

Index Values End of Month

	1999	2000	2001	2002	2003	2004	2005	2006	2007	2008
Dow	10,829	11,215	9,950	8,664	9,416	10,174	10,482	11,381	13,358	11,544
S&P 500	1,320	1,518	1,134	916	1,008	1,104	1,220	1,304	1,474	1,283
Nasdaq	2,739	4,206	1,805	1,315	1,810	1,838	2,152	2,184	2,596	2,368
TSX	6,971	11,248	7,399	6,612	7,510	8,377	10,669	12,074	13,660	13,771
Russell 1000	1,314	1,559	1,149	934	1,035	1,132	1,275	1,360	1,540	1,350
Russell 2000	1,066	1,337	1,165	972	1,236	1,362	1,656	1,791	1,970	1,838
Russell 3000 Growth	2,608	3,473	1,915	1,474	1,682	1,751	1,959	2,013	2,341	2,613
Russell 3000 Value	2,065	2,118	2,080	1,780	1,951	2,242	2,567	2,851	3,127	2,613

Percent Gain for August

	1999	2000	2001	2002	2003	2004	2005	2006	2007	2008
Dow	1.6	6.6	-5.4	-0.8	2.0	0.3	-1.5	1.7	1.1	1.5
S&P 500	-0.6	6.1	-6.4	0.5	1.8	0.2	-1.1	2.1	1.3	1.2
Nasdaq	3.8	11.7	-10.9	-1.0	4.3	-2.6	-1.5	4.4	2.0	1.8
TSX	-1.6	8.1	-3.8	0.1	3.5	-1.0	2.4	2.1	-1.5	1.3
Russell 1000	-1.1	7.3	-6.2	0.4	1.9	0.3	-1.1	2.2	1.1	1.2
Russell 2000	-3.8	7.5	-3.3	-0.4	4.5	-0.6	-1.9	2.8	2.2	3.5
Russell 3000 Growth	1.2	9.1	-8.1	0.2	2.6	-0.8	-1.4	3.0	1.5	1.0
Russell 3000 Value	-3.9	5.3	-4.0	0.4	1.5	1.2	-0.9	1.5	0.9	1.7

August Market Avg. Performance 1999 to 2008[(1)]

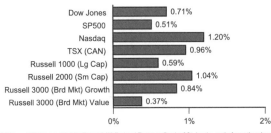

Dow Jones	0.71%
SP500	0.51%
Nasdaq	1.20%
TSX (CAN)	0.96%
Russell 1000 (Lg Cap)	0.59%
Russell 2000 (Sm Cap)	1.04%
Russell 3000 (Brd Mkt) Growth	0.84%
Russell 3000 (Brd Mkt) Value	0.37%

Interest Corner Aug[(2)]

	Fed Funds % [(3)]	3 Mo. T-Bill % [(4)]	10 Yr % [(5)]	20 Yr % [(6)]
2008	2.00	1.72	3.83	4.47
2007	5.25	4.01	4.54	4.87
2006	5.25	5.05	4.74	4.95
2005	3.50	3.52	4.02	4.30
2004	1.50	1.59	4.13	4.93

(1) Russell Data provided by Russell (2) Federal Reserve Bank of St. Louis- end of month values (3) Target rate set by FOMC (4)(5)(6) Constant yield maturities.

THACKRAY SECTOR THERMOMETER

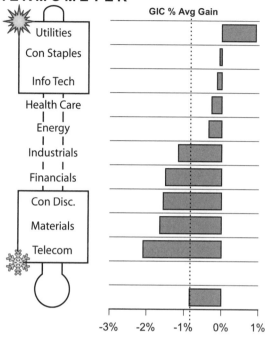

GIC% Avg Gain	SP GIC SECTOR 1990-2008[1]	
GIC[2] % Avg Gain	Fq % Gain >S&P 500	
0.9 %	68 %	Utilities
-0.1	68	Consumer Staples
-0.1	58	Information Technology
-0.3	74	Health Care
-0.3	47	Energy
-1.2	32	Industrials
-1.5	37	Financials
-1.6	32	Consumer Discretionary
-1.6	42	Materials
-2.1	42	Telecom
-0.8 %	N/A %	S&P 500

Thermometer labels (top to bottom): Utilities, Con Staples, Info Tech, Health Care, Energy, Industrials, Financials, Con Disc., Materials, Telecom

Axis: -3% -2% -1% 0% 1%

Commentary

♦ On average, there has only been one positive sector in the month of August – Utilities. Investors use this sector as a safe-haven. Not knowing where to put their money in the summer months, investors are attracted to the stability and safety of the high dividend yielding utilities sector. ♦ In 2008 July was a positive month and as a result, investors shunned safe-havens and took on more of an appetite for risk. Utilities ended up with a loss for the month. ♦ The *Cold Box 3 Worst Sectors* ended up with a strong performance for the month based upon the performance of the Consumer Discretionary and Telecom sectors. Materials was the worst sector for the month, producing a loss of almost 3%.

Hot Box - 3 Best Sectors
Utilities ♦ Con Staples ♦ Info Tech
August Portfolio

	Avg % Gain	Fq % Gain
Avg % Gain	> S&P 500	>S&P 500
1990-2008	0.2%	1.1%	74%
2008	0.9%	-0.3%	

Cold Box - 3 Worst Sectors
Con Disc. ♦ Materials ♦ Telecom
August Portfolio

	Avg % Gain	Fq % Gain
Avg % Gain	> S&P 500	>S&P 500
1990-2008	-1.8%	-0.9%	32%
2008	2.6%	1.4%	

(1) Sector data provided by Standard and Poors (2) GIC is short form for Global Industry Classification (3) Sub Sector data provided by Standard and Poors, except where marked by symbol.

AGRICULTURE MOOOVES
LAST 5 MONTHS OF THE YEAR – Aug to Dec

☑ 2008 Performance

In early 2008 the agriculture sector was the "hot" sector. Like the rest of the market, agriculture corrected. A major portion of its correction occurred before the seasonal strong period. In the end, the sector had a nominal gain during its strong seasonal cycle. Investors should take note that there are large differences between the ETFs in this sector.

Agriculture, one of the hot sectors in recent years, has typically been hot during the last five months of the year (August to December). This is the result of the major summer growing season in the northern hemisphere producing cash for the growers and subsequently increasing sales for the farming suppliers (fertilizer, farming machinery - see note at bottom of page for description of sector).

Agriculture vs. S&P 500 1994 to 2008

Aug 1 to Dec 31	Agri	Positive S&P 500	Diff
1994 %	8.0 %	0.2 %	7.8 %
1995	31.7	9.6	22.1
1996	30.2	15.7	14.5
1997	14.6	1.7	13.0
1998	-3.4	9.7	-13.1
1999	-2.6	10.6	-13.2
2000	68.0	-7.7	75.7
2001	12.5	-5.2	17.7
2002	6.0	-3.5	9.5
2003	15.8	12.3	3.5
2004	44.6	10.0	34.6
2005	7.5	1.1	6.4
2006	-27.4	11.1	-38.5
2007	38.2	0.9	37.3
2008	0.7	-28.7	29.4
Avg.	16.3 %	2.5 %	13.8 %

80% of the time
better than the S&P 500

Although this sector can represent a good opportunity, investors should be wary of the wide performance swings. Out of the fifteen cycles from August to December (1994 to 2008), there have been six years with absolute returns +/- 25%, and nine years +/- 10%

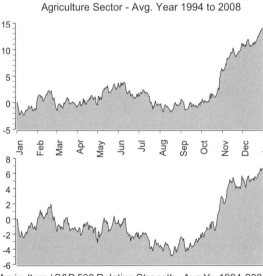

Agriculture Sector - Avg. Year 1994 to 2008

Agriculture / S&P 500 Relative Strength - Avg Yr. 1994-2008

On a year by year basis, the year 2000 produced the biggest return at 68%; the same year the technology bubble burst. The agriculture sector benefited from

the market correction because investors were looking for a safe haven to invest in – people need to eat, regardless of the performance of worldwide stock markets. The negative performance of 2006 was a correction from the rapid rise of the sector in the first half of the year. This time period was the start of investors having an epiphany that the world might be running out of food and as the market marched upwards, it produced some big swings.

In 2007 and the first half of 2008, the agriculture sector rocketed upwards due to the increase in prices of agricultural products, which in turn were a result of worldwide food shortages.

Although food prices have had some reprieve with the global slowdown, the world population is still increasing and imbalances in food supply and demand will continue to exist in the future. Investors should consider "moooving" into the agriculture sector for the last five months of the year.

> (i) *The SP GICS Agriculture Sector*
> *# 30202010*
> *For more information on the agriculture sector, see www.standardandpoors.com*

- 97 -

9 MONDAY · 221 / 144

10 TUESDAY · 222 / 143

Market Indices & Rates
Weekly Values*

Stock Markets	2007	2008
Dow	13,428	11,544
S&P 500	1,470	1,277
Nasdaq	2,565	2,357
TSX	13,566	13,356
FTSE	6,240	5,446
DAX	7,472	6,507
Nikkei	16,960	13,079
Hang Seng	22,123	22,114

Commodities	2007	2008
Oil (WTI)	71.94	118.88
Gold (London PM)	669.22	878.25

Bond Yields	2007	2008
USA 5 Yr Treasury	4.60	3.24
USA 10 Yr Treasury	4.79	3.99
USA 20 Yr Treasury	5.06	4.63
Moody's Aaa Corporate	5.78	5.74
Moody's Baa Corporate	6.66	7.22
CAN 5 Yr Treasury	4.55	3.17
CAN 10 Yr Treasury	4.51	3.66

For Monday 9:

30 day	Wednesday September 8
60 day	Friday October 8
90 day	Sunday November 7
180 day	Saturday February 5
1 year	Tuesday August 9

For Tuesday 10:

30 day	Thursday September 9
60 day	Saturday October 9
90 day	Monday November 8
180 day	Sunday February 6
1 year	Wednesday August 10

Money Market	2007	2008
USA Fed Funds	5.25	2.00
USA 3 Mo T-Bill	4.83	1.70
CAN tgt overnight rate	4.50	3.00
CAN 3 Mo T-Bill	4.56	2.48

11 WEDNESDAY · 223 / 142

12 THURSDAY · 224 / 141

Foreign Exchange	2007	2008
USD / EUR	1.38	1.54
USD / GBP	2.03	1.95
CAN / USD	1.06	1.05
JPY / USD	118.48	108.76

AUGUST

M	T	W	T	F	S	S
						1
2	3	4	5	6	7	8
9	10	11	12	13	14	15
16	17	18	19	20	21	22
23	24	25	26	27	28	29
30	31					

For Wednesday 11:

30 day	Friday September 10
60 day	Sunday October 10
90 day	Tuesday November 9
180 day	Monday February 7
1 year	Thursday August 11

For Thursday 12:

30 day	Saturday September 11
60 day	Monday October 11
90 day	Wednesday November 10
180 day	Tuesday February 8
1 year	Friday August 12

SEPTEMBER

M	T	W	T	F	S	S
		1	2	3	4	5
6	7	8	9	10	11	12
13	14	15	16	17	18	19
20	21	22	23	24	25	26
27	28	29	30			

13 FRIDAY · 225 / 140

For Friday 13:

30 day	Sunday September 12
60 day	Tuesday October 12
90 day	Thursday November 11
180 day	Wednesday February 9
1 year	Saturday August 13

OCTOBER

M	T	W	T	F	S	S
				1	2	3
4	5	6	7	8	9	10
11	12	13	14	15	16	17
18	19	20	21	22	23	24
25	26	27	28	29	30	31

Weekly avg closing values- except Fed Funds Rate & CAN overnight tgt rate which are weekly closing values.

GAS FOR 5 MONTHS

Natural Gas (Commodity) – Outperforms last 5 months
Cash price increases from Aug 1st to Dec 21st

☒ 2008 Performance

When large macro events take place, they can overcome fundamentals, technicals and seasonals influences – 2008 was such a year for natural gas. Halfway through it was struck with a double whammy; decreasing demand caused by the global slowdown and increasing supply caused by the large output of natural gas from the shale reserves. The poor 2008 performance does not necessarily mean that this seasonal is no longer working. Natural gas is extremely volatile and any large returns in the future are more likely to occur from August 1st to December 21st.

We may not use natural gas ourselves, but most of us depend on it in one way or another. It is used for furnaces and hot water tanks and is usually responsible for producing some portion of the electrical power that we consume. As a result, there are two high consumption times for natural gas: winter and summer. The colder it gets in winter, the more natural gas is consumed to keep the furnaces going. The warmer it gets in the summer, the more natural gas is used to produce power for air conditioners.

On the supply side, weather also plays a large factor in determining price. During the hurricane season in the Gulf of Mexico, the price of natural gas is effected by the forecast for the number, severity and impact of hurricanes. The tail end of the hurricane season occurs in late autumn and early winter, at the same time distributors are accumulating natural gas inventories for the winter heating season. As a result the price of natural gas tends to rise in the last five months of the year. As the price is very dependent on the weather, it is also extremely volatile. Large percentage moves are not uncommon. Caution and a shorting possibility should be noted. As a result of hurricane season ending and the slowdown in accumulating natural gas inventories for winter heating, the price of natural gas frequently decreases during the last part of December.

Natural Gas (Cash) Henry Hub LA
Seasonal Gains 1995 to 2008

	Negative	Positive	Negative
	Jan 1 to Jul 31	Aug 1 to Dec 21	Dec 22 to Dec 31
1995		144.6 %	-11.9 %
1996	-16.0 %	90.0	-7.7
1997	-45.2	6.8	-4.6
1998	-18.1	10.8	-4.0
1999	32.1	1.2	-12.9
2000	62.6	180.7	5.4
2001	-68.2	-19.3	5.8
2002	11.0	67.2	-9.1
2003	0.9	49.5	-16.8
2004	4.7	13.3	-15.7
2005	28.9	74.7	-31.0
2006	-15.5	-24.3	-14.5
2007	18.7	7.7	-1.1
2008	29.3	-38.7	-0.9
Avg.	1.9 %	40.3 %	-8.5 %

Natural Gas (Cash) Henry Hub LA
Avg. Year 1996 to 2008

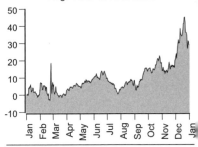

⚠ *Caution:*
The cash price for natural gas is extremely volatile and extreme caution should be used. Care must be taken to ensure that investments are within risk tolerances.

ⓘ *Source: New York Mercantile Exchange. NYMX is an exchange provider of futures and options.*

Natural Gas (Cash Price) Henry Hub Louisiana % Month Gain

	Jan	Feb	Mar	Apr	May	Jun	Jul	Aug	Sep	Oct	Nov	Dec	Year
1997	-28	-39	6	13	6	-6	3	22	16	3	-25	-6	-44
1998	-6	3	5	-5	-4	12	-22	-14	38	-19	-9	18	-15
1999	-6	-8	19	13	0	4	10	13	-20	21	-22	6	19
2000	17	0	7	8	45	-4	-14	27	8	-15	46	64	353
2001	-44	-11	3	-12	-21	-21	12	-34	-17	68	-40	47	-74
2002	-21	16	28	15	-14	2	-6	3	31	7	-5	10	69
2003	22	94	-54	5	14	-11	-13	5	-4	-15	22	19	25
2004	1	-9	7	3	11	-7	0	-16	26	1	6	-11	5
2005	2	8	13	-11	-5	11	11	64	17	-18	-4	-19	58
2006	-8	-23	4	-5	-10	-2	38	-28	-37	81	25	-34	-42
2007	41	-7	4	3	1	-18	2	-16	12	18	0	-2	29
2008	13	12	8	10	6	15	-30	-11	-13	-13	4	-13	-21
Avg	1 %	2 %	4 %	1 %	3 %	-1 %	-2 %	-1 %	5 %	13 %	3 %	6 %	31 %

16 MONDAY 228 / 137

17 TUESDAY 229 / 136

Market Indices & Rates
Weekly Values*

Stock Markets	2007	2008
Dow	13,010	11,647
S&P 500	1,429	1,294
Nasdaq	2,491	2,441
TSX	13,123	13,241
FTSE	6,079	5,495
DAX	7,399	6,501
Nikkei	16,308	13,147
Hang Seng	21,267	21,469

Commodities	2007	2008
Oil (WTI)	72.06	114.45
Gold (London PM)	664.82	818.65

Bond Yields	2007	2008
USA 5 Yr Treasury	4.42	3.18
USA 10 Yr Treasury	4.70	3.91
USA 20 Yr Treasury	5.05	4.58
Moody's Aaa Corporate	5.85	5.68
Moody's Baa Corporate	6.70	7.17
CAN 5 Yr Treasury	4.36	3.11
CAN 10 Yr Treasury	4.44	3.60

Money Market	2007	2008
USA Fed Funds	5.25	2.00
USA 3 Mo T-Bill	4.23	1.86
CAN tgt overnight rate	4.50	3.00
CAN 3 Mo T-Bill	4.33	2.49

Foreign Exchange	2007	2008
USD / EUR	1.35	1.49
USD / GBP	1.99	1.89
CAN / USD	1.07	1.07
JPY / USD	116.13	109.83

16 MONDAY
30 day	Wednesday September 15
60 day	Friday October 15
90 day	Sunday November 14
180 day	Saturday February 12
1 year	Tuesday August 16

17 TUESDAY
30 day	Thursday September 16
60 day	Saturday October 16
90 day	Monday November 15
180 day	Sunday February 13
1 year	Wednesday August 17

18 WEDNESDAY 230 / 135

19 THURSDAY 231 / 134

AUGUST
M	T	W	T	F	S	S
						1
2	3	4	5	6	7	8
9	10	11	12	13	14	15
16	17	18	19	20	21	22
23	24	25	26	27	28	29
30	31					

18 WEDNESDAY
30 day	Friday September 17
60 day	Sunday October 17
90 day	Tuesday November 16
180 day	Monday February 14
1 year	Thursday August 18

19 THURSDAY
30 day	Saturday September 18
60 day	Monday October 18
90 day	Wednesday November 17
180 day	Tuesday February 15
1 year	Friday August 19

20 FRIDAY 232 / 133

SEPTEMBER
M	T	W	T	F	S	S
		1	2	3	4	5
6	7	8	9	10	11	12
13	14	15	16	17	18	19
20	21	22	23	24	25	26
27	28	29	30			

OCTOBER
M	T	W	T	F	S	S
				1	2	3
4	5	6	7	8	9	10
11	12	13	14	15	16	17
18	19	20	21	22	23	24
25	26	27	28	29	30	31

20 FRIDAY
30 day	Sunday September 19
60 day	Tuesday October 19
90 day	Thursday November 18
180 day	Wednesday February 16
1 year	Saturday August 20

* Weekly avg closing values- except Fed Funds Rate & CAN overnight tgt rate which are weekly closing values.

☑2008 Performance

The small cap strategy outperformed the S&P 500 in 2008 when the market was taking a beating. Usually during major downdrafts small caps underperform. Knowing whether to be in growth companies or value companies during their respective seasons can help provide some downside protection.

Over the long-term, small companies have produced better returns than large companies. Most pundits agree that this outcome is a result of investors being rewarded for taking on greater risks. From 1979 to 2008, if an investor had invested in small value companies for the first eight months of the year and then switched to small growth companies for the last four months, they would have increased their returns even more.

For definitions of value and growth, information on the Russell small cap indices, and the trend of value outperforming growth at the beginning of the year and growth outperforming at the end, see *Value For First Four Months of Year - Growth For Last 3 Months* strategy.

It is important to note that the performance for this strategy has been very volatile. Sometimes value or growth small caps can outperform significantly in their seasonal time and other times not. Even within the year there can be a large difference in performance.

Small Cap Value & Small Cap Growth Switch Strategy*

Val>Gr   Gr>Val   8n4> S&P 500

	Jan to Aug		Sep to Dec		Yr. % Gain	
Year	Sm Cap Gr	Sm Cap Val	Sm Cap Val	Sm Cap Gr	S&P 500	Sm Cap 8n4
1979	36.2%	35.7%	-5.0%	8.1%	12.3%	46.7%
1980	27.4	15.6	2.9	17.3	25.8	35.6
1981	-8.9	9.4	1.0	-1.8	-9.7	7.5
1982	-12.4	-1.6	24.4	35.2	14.8	33.1
1983	28.2	31.8	1.7	-7.3	17.3	22.2
1984	-9.3	-1.2	-0.1	-8.5	1.4	-9.6
1985	19.4	17.2	8.0	8.2	26.3	26.8
1986	10.9	10.4	-5.0	-7.4	14.6	2.2
1987	31.2	28.2	-29.1	-32.5	2.0	-13.5
1988	17.0	24.7	1.0	1.5	12.4	26.6
1989	22.4	18.8	-7.7	-2.8	27.3	15.5
1990	-16.1	-18.0	-7.7	-2.8	-6.6	-20.3
1991	36.6	34.6	2.5	9.6	26.3	47.4
1992	-10.9	10.3	14.5	19.8	4.5	32.2
1993	6.4	16.4	4.4	5.8	7.1	23.1
1994	-2.6	1.2	-4.8	-0.6	-1.5	0.6
1995	25.9	18.5	3.6	3.3	34.1	22.4
1996	5.1	5.7	12.1	5.3	20.3	11.2
1997	13.6	19.7	7.6	-1.0	31.0	18.5
1998	-25.9	-19.9	14.2	36.0	26.7	8.9
1999	5.0	-2.6	-1.4	35.8	19.5	32.3
2000	2.1	12.3	6.5	-24.2	-10.1	-14.9
2001	-14.4	8.2	3.0	5.7	-13.0	14.3
2002	-30.3	-10.2	-3.4	-0.6	-23.4	-10.7
2003	34.6	25.3	14.3	9.6	26.4	37.4
2004	-6.1	2.8	16.8	21.3	9.0	24.6
2005	1.4	3.0	-0.2	2.2	3.0	5.3
2006	3.2	10.9	9.3	9.3	13.6	21.2
2007	5.9	-4.3	-7.6	0.5	3.5	-3.7
2008	-4.9	-2.1	-29.1	-35.8	-38.5	-37.5
Avg.	6.4%	10.0%	1.6%	3.6%	9.2%	13.2%
Fq >		60%		60%		63%

* Small Cap Growth (Russell 2000 Growth)
Small Cap Value (Russell 2000 Value)

⚠ CAUTION: The small cap sector can be very volatile. There can also be large performance differences between the two different styles of management, value and growth. Like all strategies in this book, proper care should be taken so that risk tolerances are not exceeded.

Total Gains From 1979 to 2008

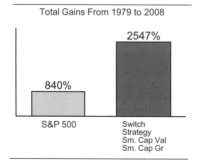

2547%

840%

S&P 500   Switch Strategy Sm. Cap Val Sm. Cap Gr

Russell 2000 Growth less Russell 2000 Value 1979-2008

J F M A M J J A S O N D

23 MONDAY   235 / 130   **24** TUESDAY   236 / 129

30 day	Wednesday September 22
60 day	Friday October 22
90 day	Sunday November 21
180 day	Saturday February 19
1 year	Tuesday August 23

30 day	Thursday September 23
60 day	Saturday October 23
90 day	Monday November 22
180 day	Sunday February 20
1 year	Wednesday August 24

25 WEDNESDAY   237 / 128   **26** THURSDAY   238 / 127

30 day	Friday September 24
60 day	Sunday October 24
90 day	Tuesday November 23
180 day	Monday February 21
1 year	Thursday August 25

30 day	Saturday September 25
60 day	Monday October 25
90 day	Wednesday November 24
180 day	Tuesday February 22
1 year	Friday August 26

27 FRIDAY   239 / 126

30 day	Sunday September 26
60 day	Tuesday October 26
90 day	Thursday November 25
180 day	Wednesday February 23
1 year	Saturday August 27

Weekly avg closing values- except Fed Funds Rate & CAN overnight tgt rate which are weekly closing values.

WEEK 34

Market Indices & Rates
Weekly Values*

Stock Markets	2007	2008
Dow	13,213	11,461
S&P 500	1,460	1,278
Nasdaq	2,540	2,397
TSX	13,357	13,304
FTSE	6,156	5,404
DAX	7,470	6,322
Nikkei	16,020	12,860
Hang Seng	22,312	20,685

Commodities	2007	2008
Oil (WTI)	70.24	115.51
Gold (London PM)	659.62	811.65

Bond Yields	2007	2008
USA 5 Yr Treasury	4.34	3.07
USA 10 Yr Treasury	4.62	3.83
USA 20 Yr Treasury	5.00	4.48
Moody's Aaa Corporate	5.85	5.58
Moody's Baa Corporate	6.68	7.11
CAN 5 Yr Treasury	4.28	3.10
CAN 10 Yr Treasury	4.39	3.58

Money Market	2007	2008
USA Fed Funds	5.25	2.00
USA 3 Mo T-Bill	3.70	1.75
CAN tgt overnight rate	4.50	3.00
CAN 3 Mo T-Bill	3.95	2.49

Foreign Exchange	2007	2008
USD / EUR	1.35	1.47
USD / GBP	1.99	1.86
CAN / USD	1.06	1.06
JPY / USD	115.44	109.59

AUGUST

M	T	W	T	F	S	S
						1
2	3	4	5	6	7	8
9	10	11	12	13	14	15
16	17	18	19	20	21	22
23	24	25	26	27	28	29
30	31					

SEPTEMBER

M	T	W	T	F	S	S
		1	2	3	4	5
6	7	8	9	10	11	12
13	14	15	16	17	18	19
20	21	22	23	24	25	26
27	28	29	30			

OCTOBER

M	T	W	T	F	S	S
				1	2	3
4	5	6	7	8	9	10
11	12	13	14	15	16	17
18	19	20	21	22	23	24
25	26	27	28	29	30	31

HEALTH CARE
AUGUST PRESCRIPTION RENEWAL
August 15th to October 18th

☑ 2008 Performance

The big question for the health care sector in 2008 was, "were investors going to shy away from the sector given the imminent arrival of the democrats." The democrats usually "talk" health care reform which can hurt the health care stocks, especially pharmaceuticals. In 2008 investors were much more concerned with the first aid of their investment portfolios, than focusing on health care reform. As a result, health care outperformed the S&P 500 during its seasonal time.

Health care stocks have traditionally been classified as defensive stocks because of the stability of their earnings. Pharmaceutical and other health care companies typically still do well in an economic downturn. Even in tough times, people still need to take their medication. As a result, investors have typically found comfort in this sector starting in the late summer doldrums and riding the momentum into early December.

3.4% more & 14 out of 19 times better than the S&P 500

Health Care vs. S&P 500 Performance 1990 to 2008			
Aug 15 to Oct 18	Health Care	Positive S&P 500	Diff
1990	-1.3 %	-9.9 %	8.6 %
1991	1.3	0.7	0.6
1992	-9.0	-1.9	-7.1
1993	13.5	4.1	9.5
1994	7.2	1.2	6.0
1995	11.7	4.9	6.7
1996	9.4	7.4	2.1
1997	5.8	2.1	3.7
1998	3.0	-0.6	3.6
1999	-0.5	-5.5	5.0
2000	6.9	-10.0	16.9
2001	-0.4	-10.0	9.6
2002	2.4	-3.8	6.2
2003	-0.5	4.9	-5.4
2004	-0.8	4.6	-5.4
2005	-3.1	-4.2	1.2
2006	6.4	7.7	-1.3
2007	6.0	8.0	-2.0
2008	-20.4	-27.3	6.8
Avg	2.0 %	-1.5 %	3.4 %

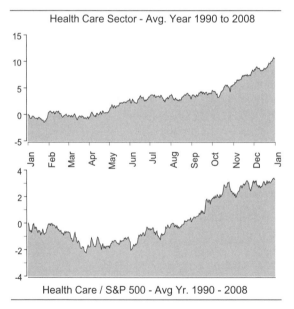

Health Care Sector - Avg. Year 1990 to 2008

Health Care / S&P 500 - Avg Yr. 1990 - 2008

From August 15th to October 18th (1990 to 2008), health care stocks have had a tendency to outperform the S&P 500 on a yearly basis. During this time period, the broad market (S&P 500) has produced an av-

erage return of 0.0%, compared with the health care stocks that produced 3.2%. Despite competing with a runaway market in 2003 and legal problems which required drugs to be withdrawn from the market in 2004, the sector has beaten the S&P 500 fourteen out of nineteen times from 1990 to 2008. The real benefit of investing in this sector has been the positive returns that have been generated when the market has typically been negative. Since 1950 August and September have been the worst two-month combination for gains in the broad stock market.

Ⓨ *Alternate Strategy—As the health care sector has had a tendency to perform at par with the broad market from late October to early December, an alternative strategy is to continue holding the health care sector during this time period if the fundamentals or technicals are favorable.*

ⓘ *Health Care SP GIC Sector# 35: An index designed to represent a cross section of utility companies. For more information on the materials sector, see www.standardandpoors.com.*

AUGUST/SEPTEMBER

30 MONDAY	242 / 123	**31** TUESDAY	243 / 122

WEEK 35

Market Indices & Rates
Weekly Values*

Stock Markets	2007	2008
Dow	13,250	11,512
S&P 500	1,459	1,281
Nasdaq	2,557	2,378
TSX	13,470	13,528
FTSE	6,187	5,559
DAX	7,503	6,360
Nikkei	16,265	12,850
Hang Seng	23,486	21,172

Commodities	2007	2008
Oil (WTI)	72.92	116.04
Gold (London PM)	667.06	831.31

Bond Yields	2007	2008
USA 5 Yr Treasury	4.28	3.06
USA 10 Yr Treasury	4.55	3.79
USA 20 Yr Treasury	4.90	4.43
Moody's Aaa Corporate	5.77	5.54
Moody's Baa Corporate	6.60	7.09
CAN 5 Yr Treasury	4.29	3.06
CAN 10 Yr Treasury	4.36	3.54

Money Market	2007	2008
USA Fed Funds	5.25	2.00
USA 3 Mo T-Bill	4.17	1.72
CAN tgt overnight rate	4.50	3.00
CAN 3 Mo T-Bill	3.89	2.43

Foreign Exchange	2007	2008
USD / EUR	1.36	1.47
USD / GBP	2.01	1.84
CAN / USD	1.06	1.05
JPY / USD	115.72	109.28

Monday 30
- 30 day Wednesday September 29
- 60 day Friday October 29
- 90 day Sunday November 28
- 180 day Saturday February 26
- 1 year Tuesday August 30

Tuesday 31
- 30 day Thursday September 30
- 60 day Saturday October 30
- 90 day Monday November 29
- 180 day Sunday February 27
- 1 year Wednesday August 31

1 WEDNESDAY	244 / 121	**2** THURSDAY	245 / 120

Wednesday 1
- 30 day Friday October 1
- 60 day Sunday October 31
- 90 day Tuesday November 30
- 180 day Monday February 28
- 1 year Thursday September 1

Thursday 2
- 30 day Saturday October 2
- 60 day Monday November 1
- 90 day Wednesday December 1
- 180 day Tuesday March 1
- 1 year Friday September 2

3 FRIDAY	246 / 119

Friday 3
- 30 day Sunday October 3
- 60 day Tuesday November 2
- 90 day Thursday December 2
- 180 day Wednesday March 2
- 1 year Saturday September 3

SEPTEMBER

M	T	W	T	F	S	S
		1	2	3	4	5
6	7	8	9	10	11	12
13	14	15	16	17	18	19
20	21	22	23	24	25	26
27	28	29	30			

OCTOBER

M	T	W	T	F	S	S
				1	2	3
4	5	6	7	8	9	10
11	12	13	14	15	16	17
18	19	20	21	22	23	24
25	26	27	28	29	30	31

NOVEMBER

M	T	W	T	F	S	S
1	2	3	4	5	6	7
8	9	10	11	12	13	14
15	16	17	18	19	20	21
22	23	24	25	26	27	28
29	30					

Weekly avg closing values- except Fed Funds Rate & CAN overnight tgt rate which are weekly closing values.

SEPTEMBER

	MONDAY	TUESDAY	WEDNESDAY
WEEK 35	30	31	1 29
WEEK 36	6 24 USA Market Closed- Labour Day CAN Market Closed- Labour Day	7 23	8 22
WEEK 37	13 17	14 16	15 15
WEEK 38	20 10	21 9	22 8
WEEK 39	27 3	28 2	29 1

THURSDAY		FRIDAY	
2	28	**3**	27
9	21	**10**	20
16	14	**17**	13
23	7	**24**	6
30		1	

OCTOBER

M	T	W	T	F	S	S
				1	2	3
4	5	6	7	8	9	10
11	12	13	14	15	16	17
18	19	20	21	22	23	24
25	26	27	28	29	30	31

NOVEMBER

M	T	W	T	F	S	S
1	2	3	4	5	6	7
8	9	10	11	12	13	14
15	16	17	18	19	20	21
22	23	24	25	26	27	28
29	30					

DECEMBER

M	T	W	T	F	S	S
		1	2	3	4	5
6	7	8	9	10	11	12
13	14	15	16	17	18	19
20	21	22	23	24	25	26
27	28	29	30	31		

JANUARY

M	T	W	T	F	S	S
					1	2
3	4	5	6	7	8	9
10	11	12	13	14	15	16
17	18	19	20	21	22	23
24	25	26	27	28	29	30
31						

SEPTEMBER
S U M M A R Y

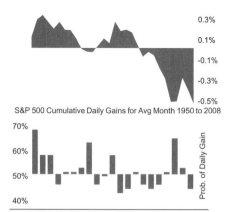

S&P 500 Cumulative Daily Gains for Avg Month 1950 to 2008

BEST / WORST SEPTEMBER BROAD MKTS. 1999-2008

BEST SEPTEMBER MARKETS
- Russell 2000 (2004) 4.6%
- Nasdaq (2007) 4.0%
- Dow (2007) 4.0%

WORST SEPTEMBER MARKETS
- Nasdaq (2001) -17.0%
- TSX (2008) -14.7%
- Russell 2000 (2001) -13.6%

♦ September earns the sad face award (see *September Not A Favorable Month*). ♦ Although it is not always negative, overall it has not fared well. ♦ Gold is golden until month end when it tends to lose its shine (see *Golden Times* strategy). In 2008 investors, particularly hedge funds, started to sell their gold earlier in the month. ♦ The year 2008 for the broad stock market indexes was a disaster but not as bad as 2002 when the S&P 500 lost 11%.

Index Values End of Month

	1999	2000	2001	2002	2003	2004	2005	2006	2007	2008
Dow	10,337	10,651	8,848	7,592	9,275	10,080	10,569	11,679	13,896	10,85
S&P 500	1,283	1,437	1,041	815	996	1,115	1,229	1,336	1,527	1,16
Nasdaq	2,746	3,673	1,499	1,172	1,787	1,897	2,152	2,258	2,702	2,09
TSX	6,958	10,378	6,839	6,180	7,421	8,668	11,012	11,761	14,099	11,75
Russell 1000	1,276	1,486	1,050	833	1,023	1,145	1,285	1,391	1,597	1,21
Russell 2000	1,064	1,296	1,006	900	1,212	1,424	1,660	1,803	2,002	1,68
Russell 3000 Growth	2,558	3,154	1,714	1,322	1,660	1,772	1,967	2,063	2,434	1,91
Russell 3000 Value	1,992	2,132	1,925	1,584	1,928	2,277	2,595	2,901	3,220	2,42

Percent Gain for September

	1999	2000	2001	2002	2003	2004	2005	2006	2007	2008
Dow	-4.5	-5.0	-11.1	-12.4	-1.5	-0.9	0.8	2.6	4.0	-6.0
S&P 500	-2.9	-5.3	-8.2	-11.0	-1.2	0.9	0.7	2.5	3.6	-9.1
Nasdaq	0.2	-12.7	-17.0	-10.9	-1.3	3.2	0.0	3.4	4.0	-11.6
TSX	-0.2	-7.7	-7.6	-6.5	-1.2	3.5	3.2	-2.6	3.2	-14.7
Russell 1000	-2.9	-4.7	-8.6	-10.9	-1.2	1.1	0.8	2.3	3.7	-9.7
Russell 2000	-0.1	-3.1	-13.6	-7.3	-2.0	4.6	0.2	0.7	1.6	-8.1
Russell 3000 Growth	-1.9	-9.2	-10.5	-10.3	-1.3	1.2	0.4	2.5	4.0	-11.7
Russell 3000 Value	-3.6	0.7	-7.5	-11.0	-1.2	1.5	1.1	1.7	3.0	-7.4

September Market Avg. Performance 1999 to 2008

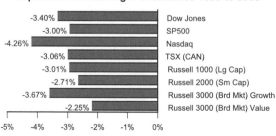

	-3.40%	Dow Jones
	-3.00%	SP500
-4.26%		Nasdaq
	-3.06%	TSX (CAN)
	-3.01%	Russell 1000 (Lg Cap)
	-2.71%	Russell 2000 (Sm Cap)
	-3.67%	Russell 3000 (Brd Mkt) Growth
	-2.25%	Russell 3000 (Brd Mkt) Value

Interest Corner Sep[2]

	Fed Funds % [3]	3 Mo. T-Bill % [4]	10 Yr % [5]	20 Yr % [6]
2008	2.00	0.92	3.85	4.43
2007	4.75	3.82	4.59	4.89
2006	5.25	4.89	4.64	4.84
2005	3.75	3.55	4.34	4.62
2004	1.75	1.71	4.14	4.89

(1) Russell Data provided by Russell (2) Federal Reserve Bank of St. Louis - end of month values (3) Target rate set by FOMC (4)(5)(6) Constant yield maturities

SEPTEMBER SECTOR PERFORMANCE

THACKRAY SECTOR THERMOMETER

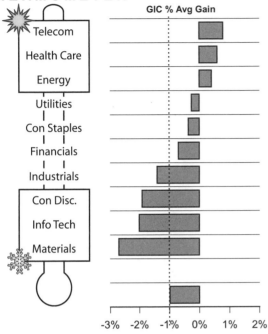

	GIC[2] % Avg Gain	Fq % Gain >S&P 500	SP GIC SECTOR 1990-2008[1]
Telecom	0.8 %	68 %	Telecom
Health Care	0.6	63	Health Care
Energy	0.4	58	Energy
Utilities	-0.3	37	Utilities
Con Staples	-0.4	63	Consumer Staples
Financials	-0.7	63	Financials
Industrials	-1.4	42	Industrials
Con Disc.	-1.9	42	Consumer Discretionary
Info Tech	-2.0	63	Information Technology
Materials	-2.7	16	Materials
	-1.0 %	N/A %	S&P 500

GIC % Avg Gain: -3% -2% -1% 0% 1% 2%

Commentary

♦ Defensive sectors rule this month. As investors look for a safe place to park their money, they turn to defensive sectors. The performance of the Consumer Staples sector has been in the grey area. Although it has outperformed the S&P 500, 63% of the time, it has produced a return of -0.4%. ♦ The worst performer by far has been the Materials sector, with a -2.7% return; it has only beaten the market a dismal 16% of the time. ♦ If the Gold sub-sector were factored out of the Materials sector, the performance would be a travesty. ♦ In 2008 every sector produced a loss as investors were anticipating the "end of the world." The best performing sector was Consumer Staples with a marginal loss. The worst performing sector was the Materials sector with a loss of 17%.

Hot Box - 3 Best Sectors
Telecom ♦ Health Care ♦ Energy
September Portfolio

	Avg % Gain	Avg % Gain > S&P 500	Fq % Gain >S&P 500
1990-2008	0.6 %	1.6 %	74 %
2008	-10.3 %	-1.3 %	

Cold Box - 3 Worst Sectors
Con Disc. ♦ Info Tech ♦ Materials
September Portfolio

	Avg % Gain	Avg % Gain > S&P 500	Fq % Gain >S&P 500
1990-2008	-2.2 %	-1.2 %	32 %
2008	-12.6 %	-3.6 %	

(1) Sector data provided by Standard and Poors (2) GIC is short form for Global Industry Classification (3) Sub Sector data provided by Standard and Poors, except where marked by symbol.

SEPTEMBER NOT A FAVORABLE MONTH

Wake Me Up When September Ends...
Green Day (2005)

☑ 2008 Performance

After a few years of positive performances, September crashed and burned and lost 9.1%. September is "reality check" month and investors definitely checked their reality in 2008. After slowly declining throughout the year, the market plummeted in September.

A lot of investors feel the same way as the rock group Green Day. September has not been the best month for the markets: in fact it has been the worst.

-0.7% return & only positive 42% of the time

You have to ask yourself why you would want to be invested up to your risk tolerance during the month of September. It has been positive less than half the time from 1950 to 2008 and has produced an average negative return (42% of the time positive and a return of -0.7%).

Over the years, numerous explanations have been suggested as to why September is a poor performer. The most commonly accepted reason is that in the month of September investors return from their summer vacations and get serious about their portfolios. They sell off securities that they had previously intended to sell, and generally "clean house." The result has been an under-performing September.

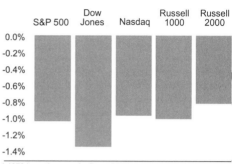

September Avg. Returns
1979 to 2008*

S&P 500 · Dow Jones · Nasdaq · Russell 1000 · Russell 2000

* 1979 inception year for Russell indices

Another reason that the markets tend to under-perform in September is that mutual fund companies clean their bad stocks from their books in September in order to purchase "good" stocks in October. This makes their year end holdings on their annual statements look good at the end of October.

The good news is that there are parts of the market in which you can hide. The basic defensive sectors: telecom, energy, health care and utilities have all produced an average positive return from 1990 to 2008 (see *September Sector/Sub-Sector Performance* page).

September's negative performance has been fairly well spread out over the decades. There have only been two decades with an average positive performance: the 1950s and the 1990s. September's performance in the 1950s was barely positive and in the 1990s it was influenced by an extremely strong bull market.

S&P 500 September Monthly % Gain 1950 to 2008   ☐ Negative

1950	5.6 %	1960	-6.0 %	1970	3.4 %	1980	2.5 %	1990	-5.1 %	2000	-5.3 %
1951	-0.1	1961	-2.0	1971	-0.7	1981	-5.4	1991	-1.9	2001	-8.2
1952	-2.0	1962	-4.8	1972	-0.5	1982	0.8	1992	0.9	2002	-11.0
1953	0.1	1963	-1.1	1973	4.0	1983	1.0	1993	-1.0	2003	-1.2
1954	8.3	1964	2.9	1974	-11.9	1984	-0.3	1994	-2.7	2004	0.9
1955	1.1	1965	3.2	1975	-3.5	1985	-3.5	1995	4.0	2005	0.7
1956	-4.5	1966	-0.7	1976	2.3	1986	-8.5	1996	5.4	2006	2.5
1957	-6.2	1967	3.3	1977	-0.2	1987	-2.4	1997	5.3	2007	3.6
1958	4.8	1968	3.9	1978	-0.7	1988	4.0	1998	6.2	2008	-9.1
1959	-4.6	1969	-2.5	1979	0.0	1989	-0.7	1999	-2.9		
Average	0.3 %		-0.4 %		-0.8 %		-1.3 %		0.8 %		-3.0 %

6 MONDAY	249 / 116

7 TUESDAY	250 / 115

Market Indices & Rates
Weekly Values*

Stock Markets	2007	2008
Dow	13,308	11,365
S&P 500	1,473	1,258
Nasdaq	2,604	2,299
TSX	13,721	13,017
FTSE	6,293	5,465
DAX	7,603	6,363
Nikkei	16,297	12,581
Hang Seng	23,978	20,571

Commodities	2007	2008
Oil (WTI)	75.95	108.30
Gold (London PM)	684.03	807.70

Bond Yields	2007	2008
USA 5 Yr Treasury	4.16	2.93
USA 10 Yr Treasury	4.48	3.69
USA 20 Yr Treasury	4.82	4.34
Moody's Aaa Corporate	5.73	5.49
Moody's Baa Corporate	6.55	7.04
CAN 5 Yr Treasury	4.30	2.99
CAN 10 Yr Treasury	4.36	3.49

30 day	Wednesday October 6
60 day	Friday November 5
90 day	Sunday December 5
180 day	Saturday March 5
1 year	Tuesday September 6

30 day	Thursday October 7
60 day	Saturday November 6
90 day	Monday December 6
180 day	Sunday March 6
1 year	Wednesday September 7

Money Market	2007	2008
USA Fed Funds	5.25	2.00
USA 3 Mo T-Bill	4.30	1.70
CAN tgt overnight rate	4.50	3.00
CAN 3 Mo T-Bill	4.05	2.39

8 WEDNESDAY	251 / 114

9 THURSDAY	252 / 113

Foreign Exchange	2007	2008
USD / EUR	1.36	1.44
USD / GBP	2.02	1.78
CAN / USD	1.05	1.07
JPY / USD	115.49	108.01

SEPTEMBER

M	T	W	T	F	S	S
	1	2	3	4	5
6	7	8	9	10	11	12
13	14	15	16	17	18	19
20	21	22	23	24	25	26
27	28	29	30			

OCTOBER

M	T	W	T	F	S	S
				1	2	3
4	5	6	7	8	9	10
11	12	13	14	15	16	17
18	19	20	21	22	23	24
25	26	27	28	29	30	31

30 day	Friday October 8
60 day	Sunday November 7
90 day	Tuesday December 7
180 day	Monday March 7
1 year	Thursday September 8

30 day	Saturday October 9
60 day	Monday November 8
90 day	Wednesday December 8
180 day	Tuesday March 8
1 year	Friday September 9

10 FRIDAY	253 / 112

NOVEMBER

M	T	W	T	F	S	S
1	2	3	4	5	6	7
8	9	10	11	12	13	14
15	16	17	18	19	20	21
22	23	24	25	26	27	28
29	30					

30 day	Sunday October 10
60 day	Tuesday November 9
90 day	Thursday December 9
180 day	Wednesday March 9
1 year	Saturday September 10

Weekly avg closing values- except Fed Funds Rate & CAN overnight tgt rate which are weekly closing values.

SEPTEMBER PAIR TRADE
Long Gold – Short Metals and Mining in September

☑ 2008 Performance

The metals and mining sector melted down in September on concerns of a dramatically falling global GDP. Gold started to fall off at the end of September but managed to maintain a positive performance for the month.

6.1% extra gain & positive 79% of the time

How a pair trade works

The trade requires buying one security in the expectation that it will go up (long position) and buying a second security in the expectation that it will go down (short position). The short position can be achieved by selling a position short (selling a position before buying it), or buying a bear fund that buys the short positions.

Most retail investors shy away from taking a short position because of the perceived risk. But selling a position short can help reduce risk, especially when it is used in a pair trade.

Taking a long position in gold (expecting the price of gold to increase), and taking a short position in the metals and mining sector (expecting a decrease in price), has paid handsome rewards in the month of September from 1990 to 2008. This trade has netted an average return of 6.1% and has been positive 79% of the time. The pair trade results have been better than if you just entered a long position for gold or a short position for the metals and mining sector.

There is a good reason that this pair trade makes sense. The metals and mining and the gold sector have a lot of the same factors driving their performance, at least on the supply side of the equation. If it costs more to get "stuff" out of the ground, then both sectors are effected.

Where the metals and mining sector and gold differ is in their demand cycle. Demand in the metals and mining sector slows down in the summer months as industrial production decreases during the holiday months. Gold on the other hand has a large spike in demand in the late summer from the gold fabricators having to buy enough gold for the Indian wedding and festival season.

Over the long-term, gold and the metals and mining sector have monthly averages that generally move together. September presents an exception to this trend and a profitable opportunity for a pair trade.

Sept	Gold	Positive M&M	Diff
1990	5.3 %	-4.0 %	9.3 %
1991	2.2	-2.9	5.0
1992	2.6	-1.2	3.9
1993	-4.3	-8.0	3.6
1994	2.4	3.7	-1.4
1995	0.4	-1.7	2.1
1996	-1.9	-2.1	0.2
1997	2.1	1.3	0.8
1998	7.5	26.8	-19.3
1999	17.3	3.0	14.3
2000	-1.2	-15.3	14.1
2001	7.4	-13.0	20.4
2002	3.5	-16.7	20.1
2003	3.3	-4.2	7.5
2004	2.1	5.5	-3.4
2005	9.2	7.3	1.9
2006	-3.9	-5.4	1.5
2007	10.6	11.9	-1.3
2008	6.2	-31.1	37.3
Avg	3.7 %	-2.4 %	6.1 %

Gold vs. Metals and Mining Performance 1990 to 2008

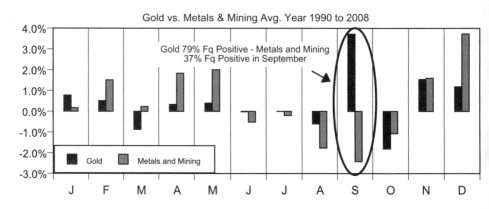

Gold vs. Metals & Mining Avg. Year 1990 to 2008

Gold 79% Fq Positive - Metals and Mining 37% Fq Positive in September

Gold — Metals and Mining

13 MONDAY	256 / 109		**14** TUESDAY	257 / 108

Market Indices & Rates
Weekly Values*

Stock Markets	2007	2008
Dow	13,319	11,373
S&P 500	1,473	1,245
Nasdaq	2,590	2,246
TSX	13,755	12,532
FTSE	6,275	5,393
DAX	7,468	6,224
Nikkei	15,878	12,338
Hang Seng	24,339	20,005

Commodities	2007	2008
Oil (WTI)	78.96	102.79
Gold (London PM)	706.90	771.30

Bond Yields	2007	2008
USA 5 Yr Treasury	4.12	2.92
USA 10 Yr Treasury	4.42	3.66
USA 20 Yr Treasury	4.73	4.28
Moody's Aaa Corporate	5.66	5.46
Moody's Baa Corporate	6.54	7.05
CAN 5 Yr Treasury	4.26	3.01
CAN 10 Yr Treasury	4.32	3.50

Money Market	2007	2008
USA Fed Funds	5.25	2.00
USA 3 Mo T-Bill	4.04	1.62
CAN tgt overnight rate	4.50	3.00
CAN 3 Mo T-Bill	3.93	2.37

Foreign Exchange	2007	2008
USD / EUR	1.39	1.41
USD / GBP	2.03	1.76
CAN / USD	1.04	1.07
JPY / USD	114.19	107.69

Monday 13:
30 day	Wednesday October 13
60 day	Friday November 12
90 day	Sunday December 12
180 day	Saturday March 12
1 year	Tuesday September 13

Tuesday 14:
30 day	Thursday October 14
60 day	Saturday November 13
90 day	Monday December 13
180 day	Sunday March 13
1 year	Wednesday September 14

15 WEDNESDAY	258 / 107		**16** THURSDAY	259 / 106

SEPTEMBER

M	T	W	T	F	S	S
		1	2	3	4	5
6	7	8	9	10	11	12
13	14	15	16	17	18	19
20	21	22	23	24	25	26
27	28	29	30			

OCTOBER

M	T	W	T	F	S	S
				1	2	3
4	5	6	7	8	9	10
11	12	13	14	15	16	17
18	19	20	21	22	23	24
25	26	27	28	29	30	31

Wednesday 15:
30 day	Friday October 15
60 day	Sunday November 14
90 day	Tuesday December 14
180 day	Monday March 14
1 year	Thursday September 15

Thursday 16:
30 day	Saturday October 16
60 day	Monday November 15
90 day	Wednesday December 15
180 day	Tuesday March 15
1 year	Friday September 16

17 FRIDAY	260 / 105

NOVEMBER

M	T	W	T	F	S	S
1	2	3	4	5	6	7
8	9	10	11	12	13	14
15	16	17	18	19	20	21
22	23	24	25	26	27	28
29	30					

Friday 17:
30 day	Sunday October 17
60 day	Tuesday November 16
90 day	Thursday December 16
180 day	Wednesday March 16
1 year	Saturday September 17

* Weekly avg closing values- except Fed Funds Rate & CAN overnight tgt rate which are weekly closing values.

TRANSPORTATION – ON A ROLL
September 24th to November 13th

☑ **2008 Performance**

In 2008, during its seasonal time, the transportation sector was hurt by the decrease in demand and helped by the cost of lower oil. In the end the sector was down, but it still outperformed the market by almost 6%.

Many investors believe that transportation stocks measure the health of the economy. When the economy is expanding there is a greater need for companies to move goods and people, and transportation stocks respond accordingly. In fact, the Dow Theory, one of the oldest market timing models is built on the relationship between rail stocks (transportation) and industrial stocks. The basic premise of the theory is that the direction of the transportation and industrial indexes lead the overall direction of the market.

3.5% extra compared with the S&P 500

Transportation vs. S&P 500
Sep. 27th to Nov. 6th 1990-2008

| Sep 27 to Nov 6 | Positive | | |
	Trans	S&P 500	Diff
1990	0.3 %	2.0 %	-1.8 %
1991	10.6	3.0	7.7
1992	9.3	1.2	8.2
1993	6.4	1.7	4.7
1994	-1.9	0.6	-2.5
1995	2.1	1.8	0.3
1996	4.5	6.5	-2.0
1997	-5.4	-3.7	-1.7
1998	-0.8	5.6	-6.4
1999	8.5	9.0	-0.5
2000	15.4	-6.7	22.1
2001	21.3	17.9	3.3
2002	1.9	5.9	-4.0
2003	9.9	2.9	7.1
2004	15.8	6.8	9.0
2005	10.9	1.6	9.3
2006	10.2	5.3	5.0
2007	0.1	-2.9	3.1
2008	-17.4	-23.3	5.9
Avg	5.4 %	1.8 %	3.5 %

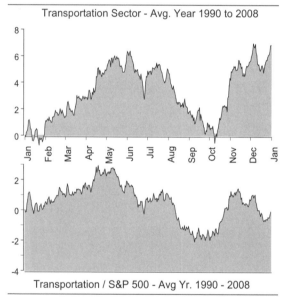

Transportation Sector - Avg. Year 1990 to 2008

Transportation / S&P 500 - Avg Yr. 1990 - 2008

From a seasonal perspective the transportation sector tends to do well starting in late September, ahead of the broad market. This trend appears in both the absolute graph (top graph) and the relative performance graph (bottom graph). Investors should be attentive to the trade, as on average, the transportation sector puts in a definitive bottom at the end of September, and then puts in a solid performance for a short period of time. The transportation sector is "driven" by two factors: increased movement of goods in autumn and de-

clining fuel prices. In autumn, the rail and truck sectors are busy moving harvest crops, and retail goods for the Christmas holiday season. This increased activity leads to greater projections of future earnings. In addition, one of the biggest cost components of the transportation sector is fuel. In the "shoulder season" between summer driving season and the heating season, there is often a reprieve in fuel prices. As a result, transportation stocks benefit.

The airline industry just coming off its busiest time of year, does very well in the transportation seasonal period as a large portion of its costs are fuel costs. Although airlines are long-term poor performers, often going bankrupt, if there were one time of the year to consider investing in the sector, this would be it.

ⓘ *Transportation Sector*
GIC # 2030
An index designed to represent a cross section of widely held corporations involved in various phases of the transportation industry.

SEPTEMBER

20 MONDAY	263 / 102		**21** TUESDAY	264 / 101

WEEK 38

Market Indices & Rates
Weekly Values*

Stock Markets	2007	2008
Dow	13,709	10,999
S&P 500	1,514	1,205
Nasdaq	2,645	2,192
TSX	13,907	12,267
FTSE	6,362	5,067
DAX	7,667	5,989
Nikkei	16,227	11,692
Hang Seng	25,255	18,224

Commodities	2007	2008
Oil (WTI)	82.15	97.29
Gold (London PM)	726.08	819.90

Bond Yields	2007	2008
USA 5 Yr Treasury	4.25	2.69
USA 10 Yr Treasury	4.57	3.54
USA 20 Yr Treasury	4.87	4.20
Moody's Aaa Corporate	5.77	5.63
Moody's Baa Corporate	6.65	7.28
CAN 5 Yr Treasury	4.29	2.95
CAN 10 Yr Treasury	4.38	3.50

Money Market	2007	2008
USA Fed Funds	4.75	2.00
USA 3 Mo T-Bill	3.92	0.62
CAN tgt overnight rate	4.50	3.00
CAN 3 Mo T-Bill	4.04	1.85

Foreign Exchange	2007	2008
USD / EUR	1.40	1.43
USD / GBP	2.00	1.80
CAN / USD	1.02	1.07
JPY / USD	115.34	105.51

Monday 20:
30 day Wednesday October 20
60 day Friday November 19
90 day Sunday December 19
180 day Saturday March 19
1 year Tuesday September 20

Tuesday 21:
30 day Thursday October 21
60 day Saturday November 20
90 day Monday December 20
180 day Sunday March 20
1 year Wednesday September 21

22 WEDNESDAY	265 / 100		**23** THURSDAY	266 / 099

Wednesday 22:
30 day Friday October 22
60 day Sunday November 21
90 day Tuesday December 21
180 day Monday March 21
1 year Thursday September 22

Thursday 23:
30 day Saturday October 23
60 day Monday November 22
90 day Wednesday December 22
180 day Tuesday March 22
1 year Friday September 23

24 FRIDAY	267 / 098

Friday 24:
30 day Sunday October 24
60 day Tuesday November 23
90 day Thursday December 23
180 day Wednesday March 23
1 year Saturday September 24

SEPTEMBER
M	T	W	T	F	S	S
		1	2	3	4	5
6	7	8	9	10	11	12
13	14	15	16	17	18	19
20	21	22	23	24	25	26
27	28	29	30			

OCTOBER
M	T	W	T	F	S	S
				1	2	3
4	5	6	7	8	9	10
11	12	13	14	15	16	17
18	19	20	21	22	23	24
25	26	27	28	29	30	31

NOVEMBER
M	T	W	T	F	S	S
1	2	3	4	5	6	7
8	9	10	11	12	13	14
15	16	17	18	19	20	21
22	23	24	25	26	27	28
29	30					

* Weekly avg closing values- except Fed Funds Rate & CAN overnight tgt rate which are weekly closing values.

ODD COUPLE
CONSUMER STAPLES & INFO TECH
Live Together for the Month of October

☑ 2008 Performance

October was a disaster in 2008, but the combination of consumer staples and technology performed less poorly. The technology sector went down a bit more than the market and the staples sector went down less. The net outperformance for the combo relative to the S&P 500 was 2.5%.

The consumer staples and information technology sectors make an odd couple for the month of October.

Usually stocks of a similar type move together. For example, the growth sectors of the market tend to rise and fall together. The defensive sectors tend to rise and fall together. Although this relationship is not always true, it is true more often than not.

1.5% extra and 68% of the time better than the S&P 500

October is considered a transition month, where the market bottoms and new sectors tend to rotate into positions of outperformance. It also tends to be the most volatile month of the year. In this month two unlikely sectors tend to outperform the market: consumer staples and information technology.

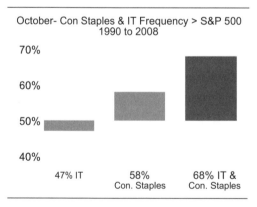

October- Con Staples & IT Frequency > S&P 500
1990 to 2008

47% IT   58% Con. Staples   68% IT & Con. Staples

Why does this odd couple outperform? It is a combination of two factors. First, investors seek the stability of earnings from the consumer staples sector during volatile times. Second, investors desire to establish a position in information technology before the best three months of

Consumer Staples & Information Technology
October Performance vs S&P 500- 1990-2008

% Gain > S&P 500			
		Consumer	
	Consumer	Info	Staples &
	Staples	Tech	Info Tech	S&P 500
1990	5.1 %	-4.2 %	0.5 %	-0.7 %
1991	-0.1	-0.1	-0.1	1.2
1992	-0.1	-0.4	-0.3	0.2
1993	6.8	2.6	4.7	1.9
1994	3.1	8.9	6.0	2.1
1995	2.5	3.8	3.2	-0.5
1996	1.5	1.1	1.3	2.6
1997	-2.1	-9.2	-5.6	-3.4
1998	14.9	6.7	10.8	8.0
1999	7.1	1.8	4.5	6.3
2000	11.6	-5.8	2.9	-0.5
2001	-0.6	17.4	8.4	1.8
2002	3.4	22.3	12.9	8.6
2003	4.8	8.1	6.5	5.5
2004	0.6	5.2	2.9	1.4
2005	-0.4	-2.2	-1.3	-1.8
2006	1.8	4.1	3.0	3.2
2007	1.7	7.1	4.4	1.5
2008	-11.1	-17.8	-14.4	-16.9
Avg	2.7 %	2.6 %	2.6 %	1.1 %

the market in a row- November, December and January (see *Three Stars* strategy). Another month of transition is May. The market tends to peak at the beginning of the month and take on a defensive posture. It is no surprise that the consumer staples sector tends to do well during this month. The "Odd Couple" (consumer staples and information technology) does not work in May because the market is starting to get defensive and looks for an opportunity to sell off some of the growth sectors. As a result, the information technology sector underperforms in May.

In the transition month of October the *Odd Couple* sectors of consumer staples and information technology have the same approximate gain, 2.7% and 2.6% respectively. The real value of the odd couple comes in its combined performance of how often it outperforms the S&P 500.

> (i) *Odd Couple Strategy is similar to a Barbell Strategy- The term barbell strategy is usually reserved for fixed income managers who overweight both short-term and long-term bonds. The odd couple strategy is similar in that it combines sectors that are totally different*

27 MONDAY 270 / 095

---

28 TUESDAY 271 / 094

30 day	Wednesday October 27
60 day	Friday November 26
90 day	Sunday December 26
180 day	Saturday March 26
1 year	Tuesday September 27

30 day	Thursday October 28
60 day	Saturday November 27
90 day	Monday December 27
180 day	Sunday March 27
1 year	Wednesday September 28

29 WEDNESDAY 272 / 093

---

30 THURSDAY 273 / 092

30 day	Friday October 29
60 day	Sunday November 28
90 day	Tuesday December 28
180 day	Monday March 28
1 year	Thursday September 29

30 day	Saturday October 30
60 day	Monday November 29
90 day	Wednesday December 29
180 day	Tuesday March 29
1 year	Friday September 30

1 FRIDAY 274 / 091

30 day	Sunday October 31
60 day	Tuesday November 30
90 day	Thursday December 30
180 day	Wednesday March 30
1 year	Saturday October 1

WEEK 39

Market Indices & Rates
Weekly Values*

Stock Markets	2007	2008
Dow	13,845	10,972
S&P 500	1,524	1,201
Nasdaq	2,692	2,172
TSX	14,044	12,471
FTSE	6,450	5,151
DAX	7,815	6,093
Nikkei	16,614	12,026
Hang Seng	26,797	19,017

Commodities	2007	2008
Oil (WTI)	81.77	110.41
Gold (London PM)	733.60	894.90

Bond Yields	2007	2008
USA 5 Yr Treasury	4.26	3.02
USA 10 Yr Treasury	4.61	3.84
USA 20 Yr Treasury	4.92	4.48
Moody's Aaa Corporate	5.79	5.91
Moody's Baa Corporate	6.63	7.66
CAN 5 Yr Treasury	4.26	3.15
CAN 10 Yr Treasury	4.39	3.67

Money Market	2007	2008
USA Fed Funds	4.75	2.00
USA 3 Mo T-Bill	3.78	0.84
CAN tgt overnight rate	4.50	3.00
CAN 3 Mo T-Bill	3.97	1.98

Foreign Exchange	2007	2008
USD / EUR	1.41	1.47
USD / GBP	2.02	1.85
CAN / USD	1.00	1.04
JPY / USD	115.08	105.83

OCTOBER

M	T	W	T	F	S	S
				1	2	3
4	5	6	7	8	9	10
11	12	13	14	15	16	17
18	19	20	21	22	23	24
25	26	27	28	29	30	31

NOVEMBER

M	T	W	T	F	S	S
1	2	3	4	5	6	7
8	9	10	11	12	13	14
15	16	17	18	19	20	21
22	23	24	25	26	27	28
29	30					

DECEMBER

M	T	W	T	F	S	S
		1	2	3	4	5
6	7	8	9	10	11	12
13	14	15	16	17	18	19
20	21	22	23	24	25	26
27	28	29	30	31		

* Weekly avg closing values- except Fed Funds Rate & CAN overnight tgt rate which are weekly closing values.

OCTOBER

	MONDAY	TUESDAY	WEDNESDAY
WEEK 39	27	28	29
WEEK 40	**4** 27	**5** 26	**6** 25

WEEK 41	**11** 20
	
	USA Bond Market Closed-
	        Columbus Day
	
	CAN Market Closed-
	        Thanksgiving Day
		12 19	**13** 18

WEEK 42	**18** 13	**19** 12	**20** 11
WEEK 43	**25** 6	**26** 5	**27** 4

THURSDAY	FRIDAY

30	1	30

7	24	8	23

14	17	15	16

21	10	22	9

28	3	29	2

NOVEMBER

M	T	W	T	F	S	S
1	2	3	4	5	6	7
8	9	10	11	12	13	14
15	16	17	18	19	20	21
22	23	24	25	26	27	28
29	30					

DECEMBER

M	T	W	T	F	S	S
		1	2	3	4	5
6	7	8	9	10	11	12
13	14	15	16	17	18	19
20	21	22	23	24	25	26
27	28	29	30	31		

JANUARY

M	T	W	T	F	S	S
					1	2
3	4	5	6	7	8	9
10	11	12	13	14	15	16
17	18	19	20	21	22	23
24	25	26	27	28	29	30
31						

FEBRUARY

M	T	W	T	F	S	S
	1	2	3	4	5	6
7	8	9	10	11	12	13
14	15	16	17	18	19	20
21	22	23	24	25	26	27
28						

OCTOBER
SUMMARY

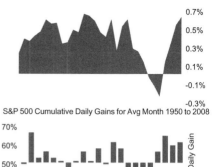

S&P 500 Cumulative Daily Gains for Avg Month 1950 to 2008

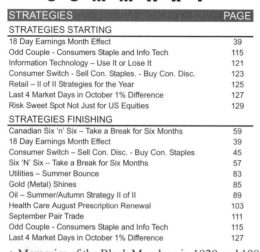

BEST / WORST OCTOBER BROAD MKTS. 1999-2008

BEST OCTOBER MARKETS
- Nasdaq (2002) 13.5%
- Nasdaq (2001) 12.8%
- Dow (2002) 10.6%

WORST OCTOBER MARKETS
- Russell 2000 (2008) -20.9%
- Russell 3000 Gr (2008) -18.0%
- Russell 3000 Val (2008) -17.8%

♦ Memories of the Black Mondays in 1929 and 1987 still haunt investors. Despite its bad reputation, October has a positive average return. ♦ The market tends to bottom on approximately October 9th and October 27th (see *Information Technology - Use It or Lose It*).

Index Values End of Month

	1999	2000	2001	2002	2003	2004	2005	2006	2007	2008
Dow	10,730	10,971	9,075	8,397	9,801	10,027	10,440	12,081	13,930	9,325
S&P 500	1,363	1,429	1,060	886	1,051	1,130	1,207	1,378	1,549	969
Nasdaq	2,966	3,370	1,690	1,330	1,932	1,975	2,120	2,367	2,859	1,721
TSX	7,256	9,640	6,886	6,249	7,773	8,871	10,383	12,345	14,625	9,763
Russell 1000	1,361	1,467	1,071	900	1,081	1,162	1,261	1,437	1,623	1,004
Russell 2000	1,068	1,237	1,064	928	1,313	1,451	1,607	1,906	2,058	1,336
Russell 3000 Growth	2,742	2,997	1,808	1,439	1,756	1,800	1,942	2,140	2,518	1,566
Russell 3000 Value	2,092	2,178	1,910	1,691	2,045	2,310	2,526	2,996	3,219	1,991

Percent Gain for October

	1999	2000	2001	2002	2003	2004	2005	2006	2007	2008
Dow	3.8	3.0	2.6	10.6	5.7	-0.5	-1.2	3.4	0.2	-14.1
S&P 500	6.3	-0.5	1.8	8.6	5.5	1.4	-1.8	3.2	1.5	-16.9
Nasdaq	8.0	-8.3	12.8	13.5	8.1	4.1	-1.5	4.8	5.8	-17.7
TSX	4.3	-7.1	0.7	1.1	4.7	2.3	-5.7	5.0	3.7	-16.9
Russell 1000	6.6	-1.3	2.0	8.1	5.7	1.5	-1.9	3.3	1.6	-17.6
Russell 2000	0.3	-4.6	5.8	3.1	8.3	1.9	-3.2	5.7	2.8	-20.9
Russell 3000 Growth	7.2	-5.0	5.5	8.8	5.8	1.6	-1.3	3.7	3.4	-18.0
Russell 3000 Value	5.0	2.1	-0.8	6.7	6.1	1.5	-2.7	3.3	-0.1	-17.8

October Market Avg. Performance 1999 to 2008 (1)

Dow Jones	1.35%
SP500	0.90%
Nasdaq	2.9
TSX (CAN)	-0.79%
Russell 1000 (Lg Cap)	0.81%
Russell 2000 (Sm Cap)	-0.08%
ussell 3000 (Brd Mkt) Growth	1.17%
Russell 3000 (Brd Mkt) Value	0.34%

Interest Corner Oct(2)

	Fed Funds % (3)	3 Mo. T-Bill % (4)	10 Yr % (5)	20 Yr % (6)
2008	1.00	0.46	4.01	4.74
2007	4.50	3.94	4.48	4.79
2006	5.25	5.08	4.61	4.81
2005	3.75	3.98	4.57	4.84
2004	1.75	1.91	4.05	4.79

(1) Russell Data provided by Russell (2) Federal Reserve Bank of St. Louis- end of month values (3) Target rate set by FOMC (4)(5)(6) Constant yield maturities

THACKRAY SECTOR THERMOMETER

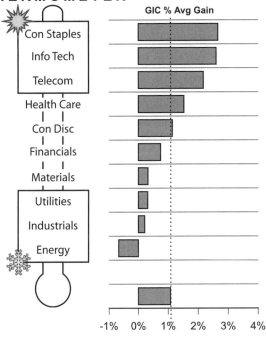

	GIC(2) % Avg Gain	Fq % Gain >S&P 500	
	SP GIC SECTOR 1990-2008(1)		
Con Staples	2.7 %	58 %	Consumer Staples
Info Tech	2.6	47	Information Technology
Telecom	2.2	47	Telecom
Health Care	1.5	53	Health Care
Con Disc	1.1	47	Consumer Discretionary
Financials	0.7	42	Financials
Materials	0.3	47	Materials
Utilities	0.3	42	Utilities
Industrials	0.2	32	Industrials
Energy	-0.7	37	Energy
	1.1 %	N/A %	S&P 500

-1% 0% 1% 2% 3% 4%

Hot Box - 3 Best Sectors
Con Staples ♦ Info Tech ♦ Telecom

October Portfolio

	Avg % Gain	Avg % Gain > S&P 500	Fq % Gain >S&P 500
1990-2008	2.5%	1.4%	68%
2008	-12.8%	4.1%	

Cold Box - 3 Worst Sectors
Utilities ♦ Industrials ♦ Energy

October Portfolio

	Avg % Gain	Avg % Gain > S&P 500	Fq % Gain >S&P 500
1990-2008	0.0%	-1.1%	53%
2008	-16.3%	0.7%	

Commentary

♦ Consumer Staples and Information Technology live together at the top of the ranks for this month (see *Odd Couple* strategy). ♦ Information Technology, although it has a better average return than the S&P 500, outperforms the market less than half of the time during the month. Information Technology's outperformance has typically started after September's spell has worn off (see *Information Technology Use It Or Lose It* strategy). ♦ In 2008 every sector produced large losses as the S&P 500 was down almost 17%. Consumer Staples did relatively well compared with the S&P 500 and helped balance the underperformance of the Information Technology sector.

(1) Sector data provided by Standard and Poors (2) GIC is short form for Global Industry Classification (3) Sub Sector data provided by Standard and Poors, except where marked by symbol.

- 120 -

INFORMATION TECHNOLOGY
USE IT OR LOSE IT
October 9th to January 17th

☑ **2008 Performance**

During this seasonal period in 2008, technology stocks beat the S&P 500 by 1.6%. The outperformance of the technology sector over the S&P 500 was somewhat of an anomaly. In previous years, an absolute negative performance meant underperformance relative to the S&P 500. It is possible that the outperformance in 2008 was forecasting the March low.

Information technology....the sector that investors love to love and love to hate. In recent times most investors have made and lost money in this sector. When the sector is good, it can be really good. When it is bad, it can be really bad.

5.9% extra compared with the S&P 500

Technology stocks get bid up at the end of the year for three reasons:

First, a lot of companies operate with year end budgets and if they do not spend the money in their budget, they lose it. In the last few months of the year, whatever money they have they spend. Hence, the saying "use it or lose it." The number one purchase item for this budget flush is technology equipment. An upgrade in technology equipment is something in which a large number of employees in the company can benefit and is easy to justify.

Second, consumers indirectly help push up technology stocks by purchasing electronic items during the holiday season. Retail sales ramp up significantly on Black Friday, the Friday after Thanksgiving. Investors anticipate the upswing in sales and increase money flows into technology stocks.

Third, the "Conference Effect" helps maintain the momentum in January. This phenomenon is the result of investors increasing positions ahead of major conferences in order to benefit from positive announcements. In the case of Information Technology, investors increase their holdings ahead of the Las Vegas Consumer Electronics Conference in the second week of January.

Info Tech & Nasdaq vs S&P 500
Oct 9 to Jan 17, 1990-2008

	Info Tech	Nas daq	S&P 500	Positive ▢ Diff IT to S&P	Diff Nas to S&P
1990	-6.9 %	-9.3 %	-6.0 %	-1.0 %	-3.3 %
1991	13.4	8.0	4.6	8.8	3.3
1992	16.4	21.2	10.0	6.4	11.2
1993	11.2	21.5	7.2	4.0	14.3
1994	12.5	3.7	2.8	9.7	0.8
1995	16.0	3.0	3.3	12.7	-0.3
1996	-8.9	-1.4	4.1	-13.0	-5.5
1997	21.2	8.8	10.8	10.4	-2.0
1998	-14.2	-10.3	-1.3	-12.9	-9.0
1999	71.8	65.5	29.6	42.2	35.9
2000	29.2	40.8	9.7	19.5	31.1
2001	-21.7	-20.2	-5.6	-16.1	-14.5
2002	26.8	23.7	7.2	19.6	16.5
2003	30.0	21.9	12.9	17.0	8.9
2004	14.2	13.0	10.3	4.0	2.8
2005	6.8	8.7	5.6	1.2	3.2
2006	9.7	10.2	7.3	2.4	2.9
2007	7.1	7.8	6.0	1.1	1.8
2008	-14.9	-15.8	-14.1	-0.7	-1.7
2009	-12.0	-12.1	-13.7	1.6	1.6
Avg	10.4 %	9.4 %	4.5 %	5.9 %	4.9 %

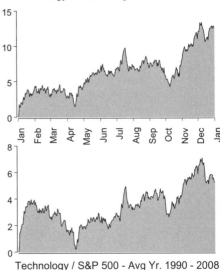

Technology Sector - Avg. Year 1990 to 2008

Technology / S&P 500 - Avg Yr. 1990 - 2008

ⓘ *Information Technology SP GIC Sector 45: An index designed to represent a cross section of information technology companies.*
For more information on the information technology sector, see www.standardandpoors.com.

OCTOBER

4 MONDAY	277 / 088

5 TUESDAY	278 / 087

WEEK 40

Market Indices & Rates
Weekly Values*

Stock Markets	2007	2008
Dow	14,029	10,571
S&P 500	1,547	1,129
Nasdaq	2,746	2,014
TSX	14,147	11,291
FTSE	6,537	4,906
DAX	7,954	5,780
Nikkei	17,050	11,293
Hang Seng	27,621	17,948

Commodities	2007	2008
Oil (WTI)	80.58	96.68
Gold (London PM)	733.25	869.90

Bond Yields	2007	2008
USA 5 Yr Treasury	4.25	2.77
USA 10 Yr Treasury	4.57	3.70
USA 20 Yr Treasury	4.86	4.30
Moody's Aaa Corporate	5.72	5.96
Moody's Baa Corporate	6.55	7.86
CAN 5 Yr Treasury	4.24	3.03
CAN 10 Yr Treasury	4.35	3.64

Money Market	2007	2008
USA Fed Funds	4.75	2.00
USA 3 Mo T-Bill	3.96	0.77
CAN tgt overnight rate	4.50	3.00
CAN 3 Mo T-Bill	3.97	1.55

Foreign Exchange	2007	2008
USD / EUR	1.42	1.41
USD / GBP	2.04	1.78
CAN / USD	1.00	1.06
JPY / USD	116.19	105.58

Monday 4:
30 day	Wednesday November 3
60 day	Friday December 3
90 day	Sunday January 2
180 day	Saturday April 2
1 year	Tuesday October 4

Tuesday 5:
30 day	Thursday November 4
60 day	Saturday December 4
90 day	Monday January 3
180 day	Sunday April 3
1 year	Wednesday October 5

6 WEDNESDAY	279 / 086

7 THURSDAY	280 / 085

Wednesday 6:
30 day	Friday November 5
60 day	Sunday December 5
90 day	Tuesday January 4
180 day	Monday April 4
1 year	Thursday October 6

Thursday 7:
30 day	Saturday November 6
60 day	Monday December 6
90 day	Wednesday January 5
180 day	Tuesday April 5
1 year	Friday October 7

8 FRIDAY	281 / 084

Friday 8:
30 day	Sunday November 7
60 day	Tuesday December 7
90 day	Thursday January 6
180 day	Wednesday April 6
1 year	Saturday October 8

OCTOBER

M	T	W	T	F	S	S
				1	2	3
4	5	6	7	8	9	10
11	12	13	14	15	16	17
18	19	20	21	22	23	24
25	26	27	28	29	30	31

NOVEMBER

M	T	W	T	F	S	S
1	2	3	4	5	6	7
8	9	10	11	12	13	14
15	16	17	18	19	20	21
22	23	24	25	26	27	28
29	30					

DECEMBER

M	T	W	T	F	S	S
		1	2	3	4	5
6	7	8	9	10	11	12
13	14	15	16	17	18	19
20	21	22	23	24	25	26
27	28	29	30	31		

* Weekly avg closing values- except Fed Funds Rate & CAN overnight tgt rate which are weekly closing values.

CONSUMER SWITCH
SELL CONSUMER STAPLES
BUY CONSUMER DISCRETIONARY
Con. Discretionary Outperforms From Oct 28 to Apr 22

☑ **2008 Performance**

The move back into the discretionary sector in October was timely as the market started to rally on the 28th. The main period of outperformance over the S&P 500 was from the March low to the end of the seasonal cycle in April.

This is the time to sell the sector of "need" and buy the sector of "want."

Companies that are classified as consumer staples sell products to the consumer that they need for their everyday life. Consumers will generally still buy products from a consumer staples company, such as a drugstore, even if the economy turns down.

On the other hand, consumer discretionary companies sell products that consumers do not necessarily need, such as furniture.

Why is this important? Consumer discretionary companies tend to outperform in the six favorable months of the market. The discretionary sector benefits from the positive market forces and positive market forecasts that tend to take place in this period.

The consumer staples and discretionary sectors average year graphs illustrate the individual trends of the sectors. The discretionary sector tends to outperform strongly from the end of December to April. Although the staples sector in the summer months has a slightly average negative performance, it still outperforms the discretionary sector. At the end of the year, both sectors do well, but the discretionary sector outperforms the staples sector.

Consumer Discretionary Avg. Year 1990 to 2008

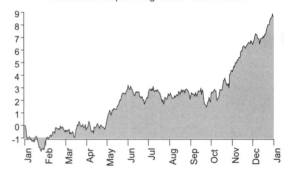

Consumer Staples Avg. Year 1990 to 2008

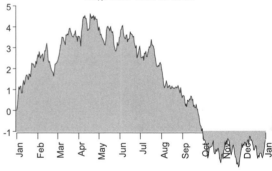

Con. Discretionary / Staples - Relative Strength Avg. Year 1990 to 2008

Alternate Strategy — The consumer discretionary stocks have dramatically outperformed the consumer staples stocks from December 27th to April 22nd. With both the discretionary and staples sectors performing well in November and December, depending on market conditions, investors can delay some or all of their allocation to the discretionary sector until the end of December.

OCTOBER

11 MONDAY	284 / 081

12 TUESDAY	285 / 080

WEEK 41

**Market Indices & Rates
Weekly Values***

Stock Markets	2007	2008
Dow	14,079	9,138
S&P 500	1,559	969
Nasdaq	2,796	1,731
TSX	14,266	9,756
FTSE	6,649	4,361
DAX	8,003	5,032
Nikkei	17,282	9,453
Hang Seng	28,508	15,744

Commodities	2007	2008
Oil (WTI)	81.47	86.22
Gold (London PM)	741.90	887.95

Bond Yields	2007	2008
USA 5 Yr Treasury	4.38	2.63
USA 10 Yr Treasury	4.67	3.69
USA 20 Yr Treasury	4.95	4.28
Moody's Aaa Corporate	5.78	6.12
Moody's Baa Corporate	6.57	8.25
CAN 5 Yr Treasury	4.40	2.81
CAN 10 Yr Treasury	4.46	3.59

Money Market	2007	2008
USA Fed Funds	4.75	1.50
USA 3 Mo T-Bill	4.11	0.58
CAN tgt overnight rate	4.50	2.50
CAN 3 Mo T-Bill	3.96	0.73

Foreign Exchange	2007	2008
USD / EUR	1.41	1.36
USD / GBP	2.04	1.73
CAN / USD	0.98	1.12
JPY / USD	117.42	100.80

Monday 11:
30 day	Wednesday November 10
60 day	Friday December 10
90 day	Sunday January 9
180 day	Saturday April 9
1 year	Tuesday October 11

Tuesday 12:
30 day	Thursday November 11
60 day	Saturday December 11
90 day	Monday January 10
180 day	Sunday April 10
1 year	Wednesday October 12

13 WEDNESDAY	286 / 079

14 THURSDAY	287 / 078

OCTOBER

M	T	W	T	F	S	S
				1	2	3
4	5	6	7	8	9	10
11	12	13	14	15	16	17
18	19	20	21	22	23	24
25	26	27	28	29	30	31

NOVEMBER

M	T	W	T	F	S	S
1	2	3	4	5	6	7
8	9	10	11	12	13	14
15	16	17	18	19	20	21
22	23	24	25	26	27	28
29	30					

Wednesday 13:
30 day	Friday November 12
60 day	Sunday December 12
90 day	Tuesday January 11
180 day	Monday April 11
1 year	Thursday October 13

Thursday 14:
30 day	Saturday November 13
60 day	Monday December 13
90 day	Wednesday January 12
180 day	Tuesday April 12
1 year	Friday October 14

15 FRIDAY	288 / 077

DECEMBER

M	T	W	T	F	S	S
		1	2	3	4	5
6	7	8	9	10	11	12
13	14	15	16	17	18	19
20	21	22	23	24	25	26
27	28	29	30	31		

Friday 15:
30 day	Sunday November 14
60 day	Tuesday December 14
90 day	Thursday January 13
180 day	Wednesday April 13
1 year	Saturday October 15

* Weekly avg closing values- except Fed Funds Rate & CAN overnight tgt rate which are weekly closing values.

✓ **2008 Performance**

In 2008, autumn was volatile to say the least – but the retail sector trade caught one of the sweet spots. As positive expectations were increasing in the economy, investors realized that the consumer was not "dead" yet and bid up retail stocks higher than the market.

Although the *Retail – Shop Early* strategy is the second retail sector strategy of the year, it occurs before the biggest shopping season of the year– the Christmas holiday season.

3.0% extra & 14 of 19 times better than S&P 500

The time to go shopping for retail stocks is at the end of October, which is about one month before Thanksgiving. It is the time when two favorable influences happen at the same time.

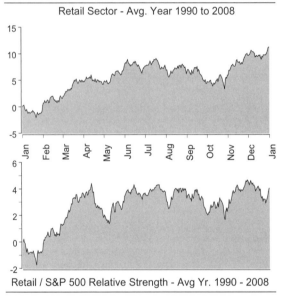

Retail Sector - Avg. Year 1990 to 2008

Retail / S&P 500 Relative Strength - Avg Yr. 1990 - 2008

First, the three best months in a row for the market have been November, December and January (see *Three Stars* strategy). The end of October usually represents an excellent buying opportunity, not only for the next three months, but the next six months.

Second, investors tend to buy retail stocks in anticipation of a strong holiday sales season. At the same time that the market tends to increase, investors are

attracted back into the retail sector. Retail sales tend to be lower in the summer and a lot of investors view investing in retail stocks at this time as dead money. They prefer to invest in another sector of the market until the retail sector comes back into favor. The end of October presents that opportunity.

The trick to investing is not to be too early, but early. If an investor gets into a sector too early they can suffer from the frustration of having dead money (having an investment that goes nowhere, while the rest of the market increases). If you move into a sector too late there is very little upside potential. In fact, this can be a dangerous strategy because if the sales or earnings numbers disappoint the analysts, the sector can severely correct.

For the Retail Shop Early strategy the time to enter is approximately one month before Black Friday. Coincidentally the end of October is also typically a good time to enter the broad market.

Retail Sector vs. S&P 500 1990 to 2008

Oct 28 to Nov 29	Positive		
	Retail	S&P500	Diff
1990	9.9 %	3.8 %	6.0 %
1991	2.7	-2.3	5.0
1992	5.5	2.8	2.8
1993	6.3	-0.6	6.9
1994	0.4	-2.3	2.7
1995	9.5	4.8	4.7
1996	0.4	8.0	-7.6
1997	16.9	8.9	7.9
1998	20.4	11.9	8.4
1999	14.1	8.6	5.5
2000	9.9	-2.7	12.6
2001	7.9	3.2	4.7
2002	-1.7	4.3	-6.0
2003	2.5	2.6	-0.1
2004	7.0	4.7	2.3
2005	9.9	6.7	3.2
2006	0.2	1.6	-1.4
2007	-7.5	-4.3	-3.2
2008	7.5	5.6	1.9
Avg.	6.4 %	3.4 %	3.0 %

18 MONDAY   291 / 074

19 TUESDAY   292 / 073

WEEK 42

Market Indices & Rates
Weekly Values*

Stock Markets	2007	2008
Dow	13,840	9,022
S&P 500	1,534	959
Nasdaq	2,772	1,736
TSX	14,188	9,528
FTSE	6,615	4,131
DAX	7,945	4,905
Nikkei	17,074	9,037
Hang Seng	29,315	15,786

Commodities	2007	2008
Oil (WTI)	87.84	75.21
Gold (London PM)	761.05	819.60

Bond Yields	2007	2008
USA 5 Yr Treasury	4.23	2.90
USA 10 Yr Treasury	4.57	4.02
USA 20 Yr Treasury	4.88	4.60
Moody's Aaa Corporate	5.68	6.47
Moody's Baa Corporate	6.49	9.09
CAN 5 Yr Treasury	4.34	2.96
CAN 10 Yr Treasury	4.41	3.77

Money Market	2007	2008
USA Fed Funds	4.75	1.50
USA 3 Mo T-Bill	4.04	0.46
CAN tgt overnight rate	4.50	2.50
CAN 3 Mo T-Bill	3.90	1.63

Foreign Exchange	2007	2008
USD / EUR	1.42	1.36
USD / GBP	2.04	1.74
CAN / USD	0.98	1.17
JPY / USD	116.61	101.13

Monday 18:
30 day — Wednesday November 17
60 day — Friday December 17
90 day — Sunday January 16
180 day — Saturday April 16
1 year — Tuesday October 18

Tuesday 19:
30 day — Thursday November 18
60 day — Saturday December 18
90 day — Monday January 17
180 day — Sunday April 17
1 year — Wednesday October 19

20 WEDNESDAY   293 / 072

21 THURSDAY   294 / 071

OCTOBER

M	T	W	T	F	S	S
				1	2	3
4	5	6	7	8	9	10
11	12	13	14	15	16	17
18	19	20	21	22	23	24
25	26	27	28	29	30	31

NOVEMBER

M	T	W	T	F	S	S
1	2	3	4	5	6	7
8	9	10	11	12	13	14
15	16	17	18	19	20	21
22	23	24	25	26	27	28
29	30					

Wednesday 20:
30 day — Friday November 19
60 day — Sunday December 19
90 day — Tuesday January 18
180 day — Monday April 18
1 year — Thursday October 20

Thursday 21:
30 day — Saturday November 20
60 day — Monday December 20
90 day — Wednesday January 19
180 day — Tuesday April 19
1 year — Friday October 21

22 FRIDAY   295 / 070

DECEMBER

M	T	W	T	F	S	S
		1	2	3	4	5
6	7	8	9	10	11	12
13	14	15	16	17	18	19
20	21	22	23	24	25	26
27	28	29	30	31		

Friday 22:
30 day — Sunday November 21
60 day — Tuesday December 21
90 day — Thursday January 20
180 day — Wednesday April 20
1 year — Saturday October 22

* Weekly avg closing values- except Fed Funds Rate & CAN overnight tgt rate which are weekly closing values.

LAST 4 MARKET DAYS IN OCTOBER
The 1% Difference

☑ 2008 Performance

In 2008 investors who entered the market four days before the end of October were rewarded handsomely. The moral of this strategy – do not wait until the beginning of November, invest earlier.

The adage "buy at the beginning of November and sell at the end of April" has been around a long time. A lot of prudent investors believe in the merits of this strategy and have profited handsomely. Nevertheless, if they entered the market four market days earlier they would have received, on average, an extra 0.9% per year (almost 1%) from 1950 to 2008.

Average Return of 1% & Positive 59% of the time

It is not just the four days gain that is attractive, the seasonal safety net that follows has been very solid. The last four days is followed by one of the best months: November. This month is also the first month of the best three months in a row (see *Three Stars* strategy) and the first month of the six favorable months.

Although October has a reputation for being a "tough month," its average return has been positive from 1950 to 2007. It is October's volatility that shakes investors up. The interesting fact is that almost all of the gains for October

can be attributed to the last four market days. The average daily gain for all days in October, except the last four, is 0.01%. This pales in comparison to the average daily gain for the last four days of the market, 0.28%.

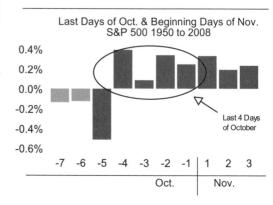

Last Days of Oct. & Beginning Days of Nov.
S&P 500 1950 to 2008

Last 4 Days of October

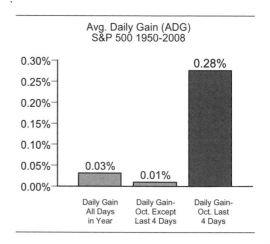

Avg. Daily Gain (ADG)
S&P 500 1950-2008

0.28%
0.03%
0.01%

Daily Gain All Days in Year | Daily Gain- Oct. Except Last 4 Days | Daily Gain- Oct. Last 4 Days

Last 4 Market Days in October % Gain 1950 to 2008 — Positive

1950	-0.4 %	1960	2.3 %	1970	-0.1 %	1980	-0.3 %	1990	-2.0 %	2000	4.7 %
1951	0.6	1961	0.4	1971	-0.9	1981	3.2	1991	2.1	2001	-3.7
1952	1.8	1962	3.3	1972	0.8	1982	0.3	1992	0.1	2002	-1.3
1953	0.9	1963	0.0	1973	-2.0	1983	-1.8	1993	0.8	2003	1.9
1954	-0.9	1964	-0.2	1974	5.4	1984	-0.1	1994	2.3	2004	3.2
1955	-0.7	1965	0.8	1975	-0.8	1985	1.2	1995	-0.2	2005	0.9
1956	-0.6	1966	1.6	1976	2.8	1986	2.2	1996	0.6	2006	-0.3
1957	1.2	1967	-1.3	1977	1.5	1987	10.6	1997	4.3	2007	2.3
1958	1.8	1968	-0.4	1978	-4.3	1988	-1.2	1998	2.5	2008	14.1
1959	1.0	1969	-0.9	1979	1.8	1989	-0.6	1999	5.4		
Average	0.5 %		0.6 %		0.4 %		1.3 %		1.6 %		2.4 %

25 MONDAY 298 / 067

26 TUESDAY 299 / 066

27 WEDNESDAY 300 / 065

28 THURSDAY 301 / 064

29 FRIDAY 302 / 063

WEEK 43

Market Indices & Rates
Weekly Values*

Stock Markets	2007	2008
Dow	13,679	8,778
S&P 500	1,518	924
Nasdaq	2,777	1,648
TSX	14,128	9,582
FTSE	6,539	4,105
DAX	7,870	4,601
Nikkei	16,407	8,619
Hang Seng	29,469	14,202

Commodities	2007	2008
Oil (WTI)	89.58	68.27
Gold (London PM)	762.73	748.70

Bond Yields	2007	2008
USA 5 Yr Treasury	4.04	2.64
USA 10 Yr Treasury	4.39	3.74
USA 20 Yr Treasury	4.72	4.46
Moody's Aaa Corporate	5.54	6.32
Moody's Baa Corporate	6.37	9.29
CAN 5 Yr Treasury	4.22	2.82
CAN 10 Yr Treasury	4.30	3.65

Money Market	2007	2008
USA Fed Funds	4.75	1.50
USA 3 Mo T-Bill	3.95	1.05
CAN tgt overnight rate	4.50	2.25
CAN 3 Mo T-Bill	3.88	1.92

Foreign Exchange	2007	2008
USD / EUR	1.43	1.30
USD / GBP	2.05	1.65
CAN / USD	0.97	1.23
JPY / USD	114.22	98.33

OCTOBER

M	T	W	T	F	S	S
				1	2	3
4	5	6	7	8	9	10
11	12	13	14	15	16	17
18	19	20	21	22	23	24
25	26	27	28	29	30	31

NOVEMBER

M	T	W	T	F	S	S
1	2	3	4	5	6	7
8	9	10	11	12	13	14
15	16	17	18	19	20	21
22	23	24	25	26	27	28
29	30					

DECEMBER

M	T	W	T	F	S	S
		1	2	3	4	5
6	7	8	9	10	11	12
13	14	15	16	17	18	19
20	21	22	23	24	25	26
27	28	29	30	31		

* Weekly avg closing values- except Fed Funds Rate & CAN overnight tgt rate which are weekly closing values.

RISK SWEET SPOT
NOT JUST FOR U.S. EQUITIES

☑ 2008 Performance

In 2008 the "best six" months substantially outperformed the "worst six" months in all four of the markets illustrated in the tables to the right. The crash in September definitely skewed the results. Historically major crashes in the market are more likely to occur in the worst six months of the market.

Earlier in the book the Six'n'Six – Take a Break – May 6th to October 27th strategy was presented. Essentially this strategy presents the merits of reducing equity positions from the beginning of May to the end of October.

Generally, the six month cycle is applicable to stock markets globally. The same phenomenon occurs in the major markets overseas. It does not matter if it is Tokyo, London or Paris, the markets tend to cycle together and perform better from the end of October to the beginning of May. There are obvious differences depending on the composition of the market and other variables, but the general trend is the same.

The best six month cycle is really a risk cycle and applies to more than the stock markets. Investors tend to increase the amount of risk in their portfolio from the end of October to the beginning of May. This can be seen in asset classes such as corporate high yield and emerging market bonds.

I often get asked, "does the cycle still work if the market goes up from May to October?" Yes, the cycle still works as the best six months have produced bigger gains more often than the worst six months, even accounting for some of the outliers, i.e., 2008. The point is that investors should consider increasing their risk in the best six months and lowering their risk in the worst six months, obviously within risk tolerances.

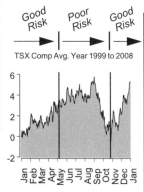

TSX Comp Avg. Year 1999 to 2008

	Avg. Year 1999 to 2008	
	Positive	
	Oct 28-May 5	May 6-Oct 27
TSX Composite		
1998/99	36.9 %	-0.2 %
1999/00	-14.4	-2.9
2000/01	9.4	-12.2
2001/02	4.0	-16.4
2002/03	10.3	15.1
2003/04	7.8	3.9
2004/05	19.8	8.1
2005/06	12.2	0.0
2006/07	-0.2	3.8
2007/08	15.7	-40.2
Avg.	10.2 %	-4.1 %

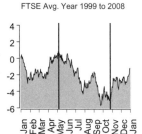

FTSE Avg. Year 1999 to 2008

	FTSE (London Stock Exchange)	
1998/99	3.2	-3.9
1999/00	-7.8	2.0
2000/01	0.3	-11.6
2001/02	-2.4	-21.4
2002/03	7.5	8.1
2003/04	5.9	1.6
2004/05	17.5	6.3
2005/06	7.2	1.1
2006/07	-6.7	0.9
2007/08	12.6	-36.8
Avg.	3.7 %	-5.4 %

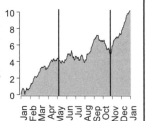

Barclays Emerging Markets (Bond USD) Total Return Avg. Year 1999 to 2008

	Barclays Emerging Markets (Bonds USD) Total Return*	
1998/99	11.8	2.6
1999/00	6.5	6.1
2000/01	5.2	-0.2
2001/02	23.4	-2.5
2002/03	2.1	6.2
2003/04	5.2	10.9
2004/05	6.3	5.5
2005/06	5.4	5.9
2006/07	2.3	1.6
2007/08	35.2	-31.0
Avg.	10.3 %	0.5 %

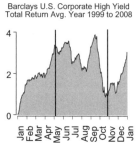

Barclays U.S. Corporate High Yield Total Return Avg. Year 1999 to 2008

	Barclays U.S. Corporate High Yield Total Return*	
1998/99	-0.1	-3.5
1999/00	2.7	-0.7
2000/01	7.5	-4.6
2001/02	24.4	-12.3
2002/03	5.2	8.6
2003/04	1.0	6.6
2004/05	5.0	3.5
2005/06	7.3	4.8
2006/07	0.0	-0.4
2007/08	20.0	-27.1
Avg.	7.3 %	-2.5 %

Source: Barclays Capital Inc. Used with permission.
For more information on Barclays Total Return Bond Indices, see www.barcap.com.

NOVEMBER

1 MONDAY	305 / 060

2 TUESDAY	306 / 059

WEEK 44

Market Indices & Rates
Weekly Values*

Stock Markets	2007	2008
Dow	13,751	8,948
S&P 500	1,528	928
Nasdaq	2,820	1,646
TSX	14,420	9,362
FTSE	6,641	4,138
DAX	7,947	4,765
Nikkei	16,695	8,121
Hang Seng	31,308	12,923

Commodities	2007	2008
Oil (WTI)	93.57	65.44
Gold (London PM)	789.60	742.20

Bond Yields	2007	2008
USA 5 Yr Treasury	4.04	2.77
USA 10 Yr Treasury	4.39	3.92
USA 20 Yr Treasury	4.71	4.59
Moody's Aaa Corporate	5.54	6.42
Moody's Baa Corporate	6.39	9.49
CAN 5 Yr Treasury	4.19	2.80
CAN 10 Yr Treasury	4.28	3.71

Money Market	2007	2008
USA Fed Funds	4.50	1.00
USA 3 Mo T-Bill	3.87	0.62
CAN tgt overnight rate	4.50	2.25
CAN 3 Mo T-Bill	3.95	1.99

Foreign Exchange	2007	2008
USD / EUR	1.44	1.27
USD / GBP	2.07	1.60
CAN / USD	0.95	1.25
JPY / USD	114.95	96.07

30 day	Wednesday December 1
60 day	Friday December 31
90 day	Sunday January 30
180 day	Saturday April 30
1 year	Tuesday November 1

30 day	Thursday December 2
60 day	Saturday January 1
90 day	Monday January 31
180 day	Sunday May 1
1 year	Wednesday November 2

3 WEDNESDAY	307 / 058

4 THURSDAY	308 / 057

NOVEMBER

M	T	W	T	F	S	S
1	2	3	4	5	6	7
8	9	10	11	12	13	14
15	16	17	18	19	20	21
22	23	24	25	26	27	28
29	30					

DECEMBER

M	T	W	T	F	S	S
		1	2	3	4	5
6	7	8	9	10	11	12
13	14	15	16	17	18	19
20	21	22	23	24	25	26
27	28	29	30	31		

30 day	Friday December 3
60 day	Sunday January 2
90 day	Tuesday February 1
180 day	Monday May 2
1 year	Thursday November 3

30 day	Saturday December 4
60 day	Monday January 3
90 day	Wednesday February 2
180 day	Tuesday May 3
1 year	Friday November 4

5 FRIDAY	309 / 056

JANUARY

M	T	W	T	F	S	S
					1	2
3	4	5	6	7	8	9
10	11	12	13	14	15	16
17	18	19	20	21	22	23
24	25	26	27	28	29	30
31						

30 day	Sunday December 5
60 day	Tuesday January 4
90 day	Thursday February 3
180 day	Wednesday May 4
1 year	Saturday November 5

* Weekly avg closing values- except Fed Funds Rate & CAN overnight tgt rate which are weekly closing values.

NOVEMBER

	MONDAY	TUESDAY	WEDNESDAY
WEEK 44	**1** 29	**2** 28	**3** 27
WEEK 45	**8** 22	**9** 21	**10** 20
WEEK 46	**15** 15	**16** 14	**17** 13
WEEK 47	**22** 8	**23** 7	**24** 6
WEEK 48	**29** 1	**30**	**1**

THURSDAY		FRIDAY	
4	26	**5**	25
11	19	**12**	18
18	12	**19**	11
25	5	**26**	4
USA Market Closed- Thanksgiving Day		USA Early Market Close Thanksgiving	
2		**3**	

DECEMBER

M	T	W	T	F	S	S
		1	2	3	4	5
6	7	8	9	10	11	12
13	14	15	16	17	18	19
20	21	22	23	24	25	26
27	28	29	30	31		

JANUARY

M	T	W	T	F	S	S
					1	2
3	4	5	6	7	8	9
10	11	12	13	14	15	16
17	18	19	20	21	22	23
24	25	26	27	28	29	30
31						

FEBRUARY

M	T	W	T	F	S	S
	1	2	3	4	5	6
7	8	9	10	11	12	13
14	15	16	17	18	19	20
21	22	23	24	25	26	27
28						

MARCH

M	T	W	T	F	S	S
	1	2	3	4	5	6
7	8	9	10	11	12	13
14	15	16	17	18	19	20
21	22	23	24	25	26	27
28	29	30	31			

NOVEMBER
S U M M A R Y

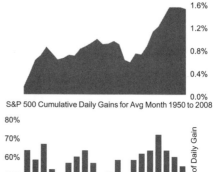

S&P 500 Cumulative Daily Gains for Avg Month 1950 to 2008

STRATEGIES	PAGE
STRATEGIES STARTING	
Metals & Mining - Don't Melt In Your Portfolio	135
Three Stars	137
Thanksgiving - Give Thanks and Take Returns	141
STRATEGIES FINISHING	
Transportation on a Roll	113
Retail – II of II Strategies for the Year	125
Thanksgiving - Give Thanks and Take Returns	141

♦ November typically performs well, but when it is negative it tends to have large losses. It lost 8.0%, 4.4% and 7.5% in 2000, 2007 and 2008 respectively. ♦ The day before and the day after Thanksgiving tend to be very good (see *Thanksgiving - Give Thanks and Take Returns* strategy). In 2008 the Thanksgiving trade produced a gain of 4.5%. ♦ The Metals and Mining sector tends to start its ascent mid-November. In 2008-2009 from November 19th to May 5th the sector gained 61.1%.

BEST / WORST NOVEMBER BROAD MKTS. 1999-2008

BEST NOVEMBER MARKETS
♦ Nasdaq (2001) 14.2%
♦ Nasdaq (1999) 12.5%
♦ Nasdaq (2002) 11.2%

WORST NOVEMBER MARKETS
♦ Nasdaq (2000) -22.9%
♦ Russell 3000 Gr (2000) -15.0%
♦ Russell 2000 (2008) -12.0%

Index Values End of Month

	1999	2000	2001	2002	2003	2004	2005	2006	2007	2008
Dow	10,878	10,415	9,852	8,896	9,782	10,428	10,806	12,222	13,372	8,829
S&P 500	1,389	1,315	1,139	936	1,058	1,174	1,249	1,401	1,481	896
Nasdaq	3,336	2,598	1,931	1,479	1,960	2,097	2,233	2,432	2,661	1,536
TSX	7,523	8,820	7,426	6,570	7,859	9,030	10,824	12,752	13,689	9,271
Russell 1000	1,394	1,331	1,152	952	1,093	1,210	1,306	1,464	1,550	925
Russell 2000	1,130	1,108	1,145	1,010	1,358	1,575	1,683	1,954	1,908	1,176
Russell 3000 Growth	2,898	2,547	1,979	1,520	1,776	1,868	2,026	2,180	2,415	1,433
Russell 3000 Value	2,073	2,095	2,018	1,795	2,072	2,429	2,601	3,057	3,046	1,834

Percent Gain for November

	1999	2000	2001	2002	2003	2004	2005	2006	2007	2008
Dow	1.4	-5.1	8.6	5.9	-0.2	4.0	3.5	1.2	-4.0	-5.3
S&P 500	1.9	-8.0	7.5	5.7	0.7	3.9	3.5	1.6	-4.4	-7.5
Nasdaq	12.5	-22.9	14.2	11.2	1.5	6.2	5.3	2.7	-6.9	-10.8
TSX	3.7	-8.5	7.8	5.1	1.1	1.8	4.2	3.3	-6.4	-5.0
Russell 1000	2.4	-9.3	7.5	5.7	1.0	4.1	3.5	1.9	-4.5	-7.9
Russell 2000	5.8	-10.4	7.6	8.8	3.5	8.6	4.7	2.5	-7.3	-12.0
Russell 3000 Growth	5.7	-15.0	9.5	5.6	1.1	3.7	4.3	1.9	-4.1	-8.5
Russell 3000 Value	-0.9	-3.8	5.7	6.1	1.3	5.1	3.0	2.0	-5.4	-7.9

November Market Avg. Performance 1999 to 2008 [1]

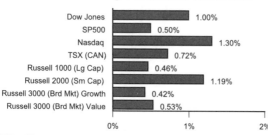

Interest Corner Nov[2]

	Fed Funds % [3]	3 Mo. T-Bill % [4]	10 Yr % [5]	20 Yr % [6]
2008	1.00	0.01	2.93	3.71
2007	4.50	3.15	3.97	4.44
2006	5.25	5.03	4.46	4.66
2005	4.00	3.95	4.49	4.81
2004	2.00	2.23	4.36	5.03

(1) Russell Data provided by Russell (2) Federal Reserve Bank of St. Louis- end of month values (3) Target rate set by FOMC (4)(5)(6) Constant yield maturities

THACKRAY SECTOR THERMOMETER

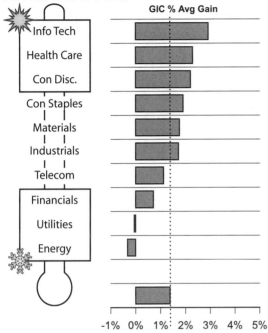

	GIC[2] % Avg Gain	Fq % Gain >S&P 500	
	SP GIC SECTOR 1990-2008[1]		
Info Tech	2.9 %	68 %	Information Technology
Health Care	2.3	58	Health Care
Con Disc.	2.2	63	Consumer Discretionary
Con Staples	1.9	47	Consumer Staples
Materials	1.8	53	Materials
Industrials	1.7	63	Industrials
Telecom	1.1	37	Telecom
Financials	0.7	37	Financials
Utilities	-0.1	37	Utilities
Energy	-0.3	26	Energy
	1.4 %	N/A %	S&P 500

-1% 0% 1% 2% 3% 4% 5%

Hot Box - 3 Best Sectors
Info Tech ♦ Health Care ♦ Con Disc.
November Portfolio

	Avg % Gain	Avg % Gain > S&P 500	Fq % Gain >S&P 500
1990-2008	2.5%	1.1%	74%
2008	-9.5%	-2.0%	

Cold Box - 3 Worst Sectors
Financials ♦ Utilities ♦ Energy
November Portfolio

	Avg % Gain	Avg % Gain > S&P 500	Fq % Gain >S&P 500
1990-2008	0.1%	-1.3%	32%
2008	-5.3%	2.2%	

Commentary

♦ November is usually a very strong month and Information Technology is a major recipient of the positive momentum. In 2008 the S&P 500 was down 7.5% for the month. Information Technology was down over 11%. The only sector that fared worse was the Financial sector. It lost a total 18.7%.

♦ In 2008, The *Cold Box 3 Worst Sectors*, which includes the Financial sector, outperformed the S&P 500. It was able to do so because of the strong performance of the other two sectors in the trio. Both the Utilities and Energy sectors were in the top three sectors for the month. In volatile times where the market goes against its trend, very often it is the underperforming sectors that do well.

(1) Sector data provided by Standard and Poors (2) GIC is short form for Global Industry Classification (3) Sub Sector data provided by Standard and Poors, except where marked by symbol.

METALS AND MINING
(M&Ms Don't Melt In Your Portfolio)
November 19th to May 5th

☑ **2008 Performance**

It does not get much better than the performance of the metals and mining sector during its seasonally strong period in 2008. Beating the market by over 50% definitely boosted the overall portfolio performance.

At the macro level, the metals and mining (M&M) sector is driven by future growth expectations of the economy. When worldwide growth expectations are increasing, there is a greater need for raw materials, when they are decreasing, the need is less.

Within the macro trend, the M&M sector has traditionally followed the overall market cycle of performing well from autumn until spring. This is the time of year that investors have a positive outlook on the economy and as a result the cyclical part of the market tends to outperform; for example, the consumer discretionary sector outperforms the consumer staples sector.

The real "sweet spot" for this sector is from November 19th until the end of the year, but it pays to hold the sector until the beginning of May.

From Nov 19 to May 5th, an extra 7.9% and better than S&P 500 58% of the time

The M&M sector continues to do well on both an absolute and relative basis until May 5th.

From a portfolio perspective, it is important to consider reducing exposure at the beginning of May. The danger of holding on too long is that the sector tends not to do well in the late summer, particularly in September. For more detail on why the metals and mining sector underperforms in late summer, see the *September Pair Strategy - Long Gold and Short Metals and Mining Strategy.*

S&P Metals & Mining Sector vs.
S&P 500 1990/01 to 2008/09

Nov 19 to May 5	M&M	SP500	Positive	Diff
1990 / 01	15.0 %	20.1 %		-5.1 %
1991 / 02	4.8	8.2		-3.4
1992 / 03	16.9	5.1		11.8
1993 / 04	-1.7	-2.6		1.0
1994 / 05	-1.1	12.7		-13.8
1995 / 06	15.3	6.9		8.4
1996 / 07	-2.7	12.7		-15.4
1997 / 08	8.4	18.9		-10.5
1998 / 09	20.3	17.7		2.6
1999 / 00	-2.4	0.5		-3.0
2000 / 01	41.9	-7.4		49.3
2001 / 02	13.2	-5.7		18.9
2002 / 03	5.4	2.9		2.5
2003 / 04	-4.6	8.4		-13.0
2004 / 05	-11.0	-0.9		-10.1
2005 / 06	45.1	6.2		38.8
2006 / 07	25.2	7.5		17.7
2007 / 08	13.7	-3.5		17.2
2008 / 09	61.1	5.2		55.9
Avg.	13.8 %	5.9 %		7.9 %

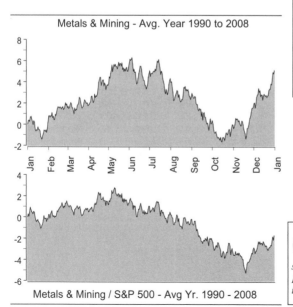

Metals & Mining - Avg. Year 1990 to 2008

Metals & Mining / S&P 500 - Avg Yr. 1990 - 2008

ⓘ *Metals & Mining*
SP GIC Sector #151040
An index designed to represent a cross section of metals and mining companies.
For more information on the metals and mining sector, see www.standardandpoors.com.

8 MONDAY	312 / 053	**9** TUESDAY	313 / 052

Stock Markets	2007	2008
Dow	13,363	9,145
S&P 500	1,485	952
Nasdaq	2,739	1,689
TSX	14,152	9,775
FTSE	6,402	4,450
DAX	7,813	5,045
Nikkei	15,994	9,029
Hang Seng	29,127	14,320

Commodities	2007	2008
Oil (WTI)	95.77	64.31
Gold (London PM)	826.87	742.85

Bond Yields	2007	2008
USA 5 Yr Treasury	3.89	2.56
USA 10 Yr Treasury	4.32	3.82
USA 20 Yr Treasury	4.68	4.58
Moody's Aaa Corporate	5.53	6.37
Moody's Baa Corporate	6.41	9.33
CAN 5 Yr Treasury	4.15	2.79
CAN 10 Yr Treasury	4.27	3.75

30 day Wednesday December 8
60 day Friday January 7
90 day Sunday February 6
180 day Saturday May 7
1 year Tuesday November 8

30 day Thursday December 9
60 day Saturday January 8
90 day Monday February 7
180 day Sunday May 8
1 year Wednesday November 9

Money Market	2007	2008
USA Fed Funds	4.50	1.00
USA 3 Mo T-Bill	3.52	0.40
CAN tgt overnight rate	4.50	2.25
CAN 3 Mo T-Bill	3.96	1.77

10 WEDNESDAY	314 / 051	**11** THURSDAY	315 / 050

Foreign Exchange	2007	2008
USD / EUR	1.46	1.28
USD / GBP	2.10	1.59
CAN / USD	0.93	1.18
JPY / USD	113.30	98.52

NOVEMBER

M	T	W	T	F	S	S
1	2	3	4	5	6	7
8	9	10	11	12	13	14
15	16	17	18	19	20	21
22	23	24	25	26	27	28
29	30					

DECEMBER

M	T	W	T	F	S	S
			1	2	3	4	5
6	7	8	9	10	11	12
13	14	15	16	17	18	19
20	21	22	23	24	25	26
27	28	29	30	31		

30 day Friday December 10
60 day Sunday January 9
90 day Tuesday February 8
180 day Monday May 9
1 year Thursday November 10

30 day Saturday December 11
60 day Monday January 10
90 day Wednesday February 9
180 day Tuesday May 10
1 year Friday November 11

12 FRIDAY	316 / 049

JANUARY

M	T	W	T	F	S	S
					1	2
3	4	5	6	7	8	9
10	11	12	13	14	15	16
17	18	19	20	21	22	23
24	25	26	27	28	29	30
31						

30 day Sunday December 12
60 day Tuesday January 11
90 day Thursday February 10
180 day Wednesday May 11
1 year Saturday November 12

* Weekly avg closing values- except Fed Funds Rate & CAN overnight tgt rate which are weekly closing values.

★★★ THREE STARS

Nov Dec Jan

☒ 2008 Performance

In 2008 the Three Stars turned out to be two duds (November and January) and one mediocre performer (December). This is the second year in a row that the three stars have produced a negative return.

Having one "star" month is good. Having three "star" months is very good. Having three "star" months in a row—who could ask for anything more!

4.3% average gain from November to December & positive 73% of the time

November is the start of the traditional six month favorable time period. It performs well by itself, but so do the two following months: December and January. Put them all together and you have a powerhouse. From 1950 to 2008 this combination has produced a return of 4.3% and has been positive 73% of the time.

Nov to Jan S&P 500- 1950/51 to 2008/09

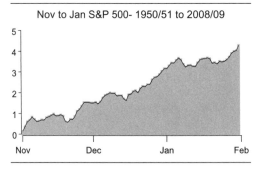

November by itself is typically an excellent month. It has an average return of 1.5% and has been positive 66% of the time.

Over the last fifty-six years, there have been only three years when November and December have both been negative (1969, 1974 and 2007). In the same fifty-six year period, only twice have all three months (Nov, Dec and Jan) been negative. The 1969/70 bear market produced a return of -12.5% and the bear market of 2007/08 produced a return of -11.0%.

S&P 500 %
Gain 1950-2008/09   Positive [   ]

	Nov	Dec	Jan	Compound Growth
50 / 51	-0.1 %	4.6	6.1 %	10.9 %
51 / 52	-0.3	3.9	1.6	5.2
52 / 53	4.6	3.5	-0.7	7.6
53 / 54	0.9	0.2	5.1	6.3
54 / 55	8.1	5.1	1.8	15.6
55 / 56	7.5	-0.1	-3.6	3.5
56 / 57	-1.1	3.5	-4.2	-1.9
57 / 58	1.6	-4.1	4.3	1.6
58 / 59	2.2	5.2	0.4	8.0
59 / 60	1.3	2.8	-7.1	-3.3
60 / 61	4.0	4.6	6.3	15.7
61 / 62	3.9	0.3	-3.8	0.3
62 / 63	10.2	1.3	4.9	17.1
63 / 64	-1.1	2.4	2.7	4.1
64 / 65	-0.5	0.4	3.3	3.2
65 / 66	-0.9	0.9	0.5	0.5
66 / 67	0.3	-0.1	7.8	8.0
67 / 68	0.8	2.6	-4.4	-1.1
68 / 69	4.8	-4.2	-0.8	-0.4
69 / 70	-3.4	-1.9	-7.6	-12.5
70 / 71	4.7	5.7	4.0	15.2
71 / 72	-0.3	8.6	1.8	10.3
72 / 73	4.6	1.2	-1.7	4.0
73 / 74	-11.4	1.7	-1.0	-10.8
74 / 75	-5.3	-2.0	12.3	4.2
75 / 76	2.5	-1.2	11.8	13.3
76 / 77	-0.8	5.2	-5.1	-0.8
77 / 78	2.7	0.3	-6.2	-3.3
78 / 79	1.7	1.5	4.0	7.3
79 / 80	4.3	1.7	5.8	12.1
80 / 81	10.2	-3.4	-4.6	1.6
81 / 82	3.7	-3.0	-1.8	-1.2
82 / 83	3.6	1.5	3.3	8.7
83 / 84	1.7	-0.9	-0.9	-0.1
84 / 85	-1.5	2.2	7.4	8.2
85 / 86	6.5	4.5	0.2	11.6
86 / 87	2.1	-2.8	13.2	12.3
87 / 88	-8.5	7.3	4.0	2.1
88 / 89	-1.9	1.5	7.1	6.6
89 / 90	1.7	2.1	-6.9	-3.3
90 / 91	6.0	2.5	4.2	13.1
91 / 92	-4.4	11.2	-2.0	4.2
92 / 93	3.0	1.0	0.7	4.8
93 / 94	-1.3	1.0	3.3	2.9
94 / 95	-4.0	1.2	2.4	-0.4
95 / 96	4.1	1.7	3.3	9.4
96 / 97	7.3	-2.2	6.1	11.5
97 / 98	4.5	1.6	1.0	7.2
98 / 99	5.9	5.6	4.1	16.5
99 / 00	1.9	5.8	-5.1	2.3
00 / 01	-8.0	0.4	3.5	-4.4
01 / 02	7.5	0.8	-1.6	6.6
02 / 03	5.7	-6.0	-2.7	-3.4
03 / 04	0.7	5.1	1.7	7.7
04 / 05	3.9	3.2	-2.5	4.5
05 / 06	3.5	-0.1	2.5	6.1
06 / 07	1.6	1.3	1.4	4.4
07 / 08	-4.4	-0.9	-6.1	-11.0
08 / 09	-7.5	0.8	-8.6	-14.7
Avg	1.5 %	1.6 %	1.1 %	4.3 %
Fq > 0	66 %	75 %	61 %	73 %

NOVEMBER

15 MONDAY 319 / 046

16 TUESDAY 320 / 045

WEEK 46

Market Indices & Rates
Weekly Values*

Stock Markets	2007	2008
Dow	13,162	8,636
S&P 500	1,460	891
Nasdaq	2,632	1,562
TSX	13,628	9,289
FTSE	6,357	4,247
DAX	7,729	4,754
Nikkei	15,275	8,657
Hang Seng	28,200	13,898

Commodities	2007	2008
Oil (WTI)	93.68	58.64
Gold (London PM)	801.00	734.50

Bond Yields	2007	2008
USA 5 Yr Treasury	3.77	2.41
USA 10 Yr Treasury	4.22	3.78
USA 20 Yr Treasury	4.61	4.49
Moody's Aaa Corporate	5.49	6.37
Moody's Baa Corporate	6.42	9.26
CAN 5 Yr Treasury	4.05	2.75
CAN 10 Yr Treasury	4.18	3.69

Money Market	2007	2008
USA Fed Funds	4.50	1.00
USA 3 Mo T-Bill	3.40	0.21
CAN tgt overnight rate	4.50	2.25
CAN 3 Mo T-Bill	3.99	1.80

Foreign Exchange	2007	2008
USD / EUR	1.46	1.27
USD / GBP	2.06	1.53
CAN / USD	0.97	1.20
JPY / USD	110.42	97.44

Monday 15:
30 day	Wednesday December 15
60 day	Friday January 14
90 day	Sunday February 13
180 day	Saturday May 14
1 year	Tuesday November 15

Tuesday 16:
30 day	Thursday December 16
60 day	Saturday January 15
90 day	Monday February 14
180 day	Sunday May 15
1 year	Wednesday November 16

17 WEDNESDAY 321 / 044

18 THURSDAY 322 / 043

Wednesday 17:
30 day	Friday December 17
60 day	Sunday January 16
90 day	Tuesday February 15
180 day	Monday May 16
1 year	Thursday November 17

Thursday 18:
30 day	Saturday December 18
60 day	Monday January 17
90 day	Wednesday February 16
180 day	Tuesday May 17
1 year	Friday November 18

19 FRIDAY 323 / 042

Friday 19:
30 day	Sunday December 19
60 day	Tuesday January 18
90 day	Thursday February 17
180 day	Wednesday May 18
1 year	Saturday November 19

Weekly avg closing values- except Fed Funds Rate & CAN overnight tgt rate which are weekly closing values.

NOVEMBER

M	T	W	T	F	S	S
1	2	3	4	5	6	7
8	9	10	11	12	13	14
15	16	17	18	19	20	21
22	23	24	25	26	27	28
29	30					

DECEMBER

M	T	W	T	F	S	S
		1	2	3	4	5
6	7	8	9	10	11	12
13	14	15	16	17	18	19
20	21	22	23	24	25	26
27	28	29	30	31		

JANUARY

M	T	W	T	F	S	S
					1	2
3	4	5	6	7	8	9
10	11	12	13	14	15	16
17	18	19	20	21	22	23
24	25	26	27	28	29	30
31						

U.S. DOLLAR
WEAK DECEMBER – STRONG JANUARY

The U.S. dollar performed very well in January 2008 with some help from a plummeting stock market. As the fear of a meltdown unfolded, investors sought the "safety" of the U.S. dollar which jumped almost 4%.

From 1973 to 2009 the U.S. dollar (USD) has had a seasonal trend of decreasing in December and increasing in January.

0.9% gain & 68% of the time better than Trade Weighted Major World Currencies in Jan.

U.S. Dollar / Trade Weighted Major World Currencies
Avg. Year 1973 to 2008

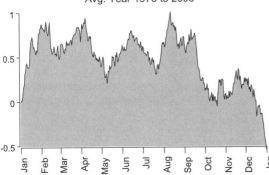

This "v" shape trend provides an opportunity for a nimble trader to sell the USD at the beginning of December and buy it back at the end of the month, in the expectation of making a profit. The second half of the opportunity is in January when the dollar tends to reverse its downward trend. An investor would have

reaped a double benefit from 1982 to 2008 with the combined strategy of going "short" the dollar in December and "long" in January. The focus of this analysis is on profiting from the rising dollar in January.

Why does the dollar, on average, produce this "v" shape pattern?

Typically, firms in other countries tend to settle their foreign exchange books at end of year in their domestic currency. The conversion to non-USD currencies tends to push the USD down.

The good news is that the reverse process takes place in January. Foreign firms increase their net dollar holdings to pay for purchases that require USD. This upward bounce has taken place on a fairly consistent basis with the dollar rising 68% of the time.

The dollar has risen in January in both up and down years for the currency. The worst streak that the trade has had since 1973 is two years of negative performance in a row and the best streak of positive performance is five years in a row.

January U.S. Dollar vs. Trade Weighted
Major World Currencies- Month of January Gain   Positive ☐

		1980	-0.2 %	1990	0.2 %	2000	2.5 %
		1981	3.0	1991	-1.6	2001	1.0
		1982	2.7	1992	2.8	2002	2.1
1973	-0.5 %	1983	2.4	1993	0.2	2003	-1.9
1974	2.7	1984	1.8	1994	-1.3	2004	0.9
1975	-1.0	1985	0.9	1995	-0.3	2005	2.7
1976	-0.3	1986	-1.3	1996	2.5	2006	-2.2
1977	0.5	1987	-3.2	1997	3.6	2007	1.3
1978	0.4	1988	3.9	1998	0.6	2008	-1.2
1979	2.5	1989	3.0	1999	0.9	2009	3.8
Avg.	0.6 %		1.3 %		0.8 %		0.9 %

⚠ CAUTION:
Most currency traders use leverage to make a profit. The use of leverage can be risky and it is important to make sure that all investments are done within risk tolerance.

ⓘ *The U.S. dollar is measured against the Trade Weighted Major World Currencies. The Euro is becoming a substantial benchmark, but at the current time there is not enough data to establish long-term trends.*

Source: Federal Reserve

22 MONDAY   326 / 039

23 TUESDAY   327 / 038

Market Indices & Rates
Weekly Values*

Stock Markets	2007	2008
Dow	12,937	8,059
S&P 500	1,433	814
Nasdaq	2,587	1,410
TSX	13,387	8,400
FTSE	6,167	4,000
DAX	7,566	4,368
Nikkei	14,995	8,148
Hang Seng	26,879	12,844

Commodities	2007	2008
Oil (WTI)	97.69	52.32
Gold (London PM)	798.17	749.30

Bond Yields	2007	2008
USA 5 Yr Treasury	3.48	2.12
USA 10 Yr Treasury	4.04	3.38
USA 20 Yr Treasury	4.49	4.14
Moody's Aaa Corporate	5.40	5.99
Moody's Baa Corporate	6.39	9.14
CAN 5 Yr Treasury	3.80	2.62
CAN 10 Yr Treasury	4.02	3.49

Money Market	2007	2008
USA Fed Funds	4.50	1.00
USA 3 Mo T-Bill	3.24	0.07
CAN tgt overnight rate	4.50	2.25
CAN 3 Mo T-Bill	3.93	1.83

Foreign Exchange	2007	2008
USD / EUR	1.48	1.26
USD / GBP	2.06	1.50
CAN / USD	0.98	1.25
JPY / USD	109.15	96.05

30 day   Wednesday December 22
60 day   Friday January 21
90 day   Sunday February 20
180 day   Saturday May 21
1 year   Tuesday November 22

30 day   Thursday December 23
60 day   Saturday January 22
90 day   Monday February 21
180 day   Sunday May 22
1 year   Wednesday November 23

24 WEDNESDAY   328 / 037

25 THURSDAY   329 / 036

NOVEMBER

M	T	W	T	F	S	S
1	2	3	4	5	6	7
8	9	10	11	12	13	14
15	16	17	18	19	20	21
22	23	24	25	26	27	28
29	30					

30 day   Friday December 24
60 day   Sunday January 23
90 day   Tuesday February 22
180 day   Monday May 23
1 year   Thursday November 24

30 day   Saturday December 25
60 day   Monday January 24
90 day   Wednesday February 23
180 day   Tuesday May 24
1 year   Friday November 25

DECEMBER

M	T	W	T	F	S	S
		1	2	3	4	5
6	7	8	9	10	11	12
13	14	15	16	17	18	19
20	21	22	23	24	25	26
27	28	29	30	31		

26 FRIDAY   330 / 035

JANUARY

M	T	W	T	F	S	S
					1	2
3	4	5	6	7	8	9
10	11	12	13	14	15	16
17	18	19	20	21	22	23
24	25	26	27	28	29	30
31						

30 day   Sunday December 26
60 day   Tuesday January 25
90 day   Thursday February 24
180 day   Wednesday May 25
1 year   Saturday November 26

Weekly avg closing values- except Fed Funds Rate & CAN overnight tgt rate which are weekly closing values.

THANKSGIVING
GIVE THANKS & TAKE RETURNS
Day Before and After – Two of the Best Days

☑ **2008 Performance**

Once again in 2008, Thanksgiving was a time to celebrate. For those investors who spent some time shopping in the markets, this trade produced a 4.5% return.

We have a lot to be thankful for on Thanksgiving Day. As a bonus, the day before and the day after Thanksgiving have been two of the best days of the year in the stock market. Each day by itself has produced spectacular results. From 1950 to 2007, the S&P 500 has had an average gain of 0.4% on the day before Thanksgiving and 0.4% on the day after.

The day before Thanksgiving and the day after have had an average cumulative return of 0.8% and have each been positive 78% of the time

To put the performance of these two days in perspective, the average daily return of the market over the same time period is 0.031%. The Thanksgiving days are almost ten times better. Also, the frequency of positive Thanksgiving days is a very high 78%.

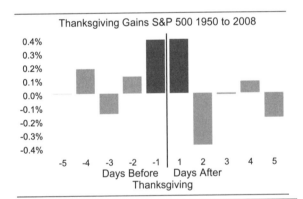

Thanksgiving Gains S&P 500 1950 to 2008

(Ⓨ) *Alternate Strategy — Although the focus has been on the performance of two specific days, the day before and the day after Thanksgiving, the holiday occurs at the end of November which tends to be a strong month. December, the next month is also strong. Investors have the good option of expanding their trade out to include the "Santa Arrives Early & Stays Late" Strategy.*

(ⓘ) *History of Thanksgiving:*
It was originally a "thanksgiving feast" by the pilgrims for surviving their first winter. Initially it was celebrated sporadically and the holiday, when it was granted, had its date changed several times. It was not until 1941 that it was proclaimed to be the 4th Thursday in November.

		Positive
	Day	Day
S&P500	Before	After
1950	1.4	0.8
1951	-0.2	-1.1
1952	0.6	0.5
1953	0.1	0.6
1954	0.6	1.0
1955	0.1	-0.1
1956	-0.5	1.1
1957	2.9	1.1
1958	1.7	1.1
1959	0.2	0.5
1960	0.1	0.6
1961	-0.1	0.2
1962	0.6	1.2
1963	-0.2	1.4
1964	-0.3	-0.3
1965	0.2	0.1
1966	0.7	0.8
1967	0.6	0.3
1968	0.5	0.6
1969	0.4	0.6
1970	0.4	1.0
1971	0.2	1.8
1972	0.6	0.3
1973	1.1	-0.3
1974	0.7	0.0
1975	0.3	0.3
1976	0.4	0.7
1977	0.4	0.2
1978	0.5	0.3
1979	0.2	0.8
1980	0.6	0.2
1981	0.4	0.8
1982	0.7	0.7
1983	0.1	0.1
1984	0.2	1.5
1985	0.9	-0.2
1986	0.2	0.2
1987	-0.9	-1.5
1988	0.7	-0.7
1989	0.7	0.6
1990	0.2	-0.3
1991	-0.4	-0.4
1992	0.4	0.2
1993	0.3	0.2
1994	0.0	0.5
1995	-0.3	0.3
1996	-0.1	0.3
1997	0.1	0.4
1998	0.3	0.5
1999	0.9	0.0
2000	-1.9	1.5
2001	-0.5	1.2
2002	2.8	-0.3
2003	0.4	0.0
2004	0.4	0.1
2005	0.3	0.2
2006	0.2	-0.4
2007	-1.6	1.7
2008	3.5	1.0
Total Avg %	0.4%	0.4%
Fq > 0 %	78%	78%

(THANKSGIVING DAY)

NOVEMBER/DECEMBER

29 MONDAY 333 / 032

30 TUESDAY 334 / 031

30 day	Wednesday December 29
60 day	Friday January 28
90 day	Sunday February 27
180 day	Saturday May 28
1 year	Tuesday November 29

30 day	Thursday December 30
60 day	Saturday January 29
90 day	Monday February 28
180 day	Sunday May 29
1 year	Wednesday November 30

1 WEDNESDAY 335 / 030

2 THURSDAY 336 / 029

30 day	Friday December 31
60 day	Sunday January 30
90 day	Tuesday March 1
180 day	Monday May 30
1 year	Thursday December 1

30 day	Saturday January 1
60 day	Monday January 31
90 day	Wednesday March 2
180 day	Tuesday May 31
1 year	Friday December 2

3 FRIDAY 337 / 028

30 day	Sunday January 2
60 day	Tuesday February 1
90 day	Thursday March 3
180 day	Wednesday June 1
1 year	Saturday December 3

Weekly avg closing values- except Fed Funds Rate & CAN overnight tgt rate which are weekly closing values.

WEEK 48

Market Indices & Rates
Weekly Values*

Stock Markets	2007	2008
Dow	13,135	8,620
S&P 500	1,451	873
Nasdaq	2,623	1,501
TSX	13,535	8,710
FTSE	6,282	4,198
DAX	7,692	4,602
Nikkei	15,341	8,356
Hang Seng	27,867	13,229

Commodities	2007	2008
Oil (WTI)	92.49	53.06
Gold (London PM)	804.10	816.80

Bond Yields	2007	2008
USA 5 Yr Treasury	3.39	2.06
USA 10 Yr Treasury	3.94	3.10
USA 20 Yr Treasury	4.40	3.84
Moody's Aaa Corporate	5.29	5.75
Moody's Baa Corporate	6.37	9.10
CAN 5 Yr Treasury	3.80	2.50
CAN 10 Yr Treasury	3.99	3.39

Money Market	2007	2008
USA Fed Funds	4.50	1.00
USA 3 Mo T-Bill	3.10	0.07
CAN tgt overnight rate	4.50	2.25
CAN 3 Mo T-Bill	3.90	1.74

Foreign Exchange	2007	2008
USD / EUR	1.48	1.29
USD / GBP	2.07	1.53
CAN / USD	0.99	1.24
JPY / USD	109.31	95.35

DECEMBER

M	T	W	T	F	S	S
			1	2	3	4	5
6	7	8	9	10	11	12
13	14	15	16	17	18	19
20	21	22	23	24	25	26
27	28	29	30	31		

JANUARY

M	T	W	T	F	S	S
					1	2
3	4	5	6	7	8	9
10	11	12	13	14	15	16
17	18	19	20	21	22	23
24	25	26	27	28	29	30
31						

FEBRUARY

M	T	W	T	F	S	S
1	2	3	4	5	6
7	8	9	10	11	12	13
14	15	16	17	18	19	20
21	22	23	24	25	26	27
28						

- 142 -

DECEMBER

	MONDAY	TUESDAY	WEDNESDAY
WEEK 48	29	30	1 30
WEEK 49	6 25	7 24	8 23
WEEK 50	13 18	14 17	15 16
WEEK 51	20 11	21 10	22 9
WEEK 52	27 4 CAN Market Closed-Christmas Day	28 3 CAN Early Market Close Boxing Day	29 2

THURSDAY	FRIDAY
2 29	**3** 28
9 22	**10** 21
16 15	**17** 14
23 8	**24** 7
	USA Market Closed- Christmas Day
30 1	**31**

JANUARY

M	T	W	T	F	S	S
					1	2
3	4	5	6	7	8	9
10	11	12	13	14	15	16
17	18	19	20	21	22	23
24	25	26	27	28	29	30
31						

FEBRUARY

M	T	W	T	F	S	S
	1	2	3	4	5	6
7	8	9	10	11	12	13
14	15	16	17	18	19	20
21	22	23	24	25	26	27
28						

MARCH

M	T	W	T	F	S	S
	1	2	3	4	5	6
7	8	9	10	11	12	13
14	15	16	17	18	19	20
21	22	23	24	25	26	27
28	29	30	31			

APRIL

M	T	W	T	F	S	S
				1	2	3
4	5	6	7	8	9	10
11	12	13	14	15	16	17
18	19	20	21	22	23	24
25	26	27	28	29	30	

DECEMBER SUMMARY

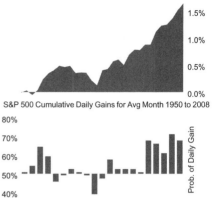

1.5%
1.0%
0.5%
0.0%

S&P 500 Cumulative Daily Gains for Avg Month 1950 to 2008

80%
70%
60%
50%
40%

Prob. of Daily Gain

♦ December is one of the best months of the year. Make sure your Christmas shopping includes stocks. ♦ The best method of participating in the Christmas rally has been to enter the stock market on December 15th (see *Santa Arrives Early & Stays Late* strategy). ♦ The Nasdaq tends to outperform the S&P 500 from December 15th to January 23rd. ♦ The US dollar has a habit of weakening in December for a rally in January. ♦ In 2008 December produced a small gain in the S&P 500, and Santa rewarded investors with the Christmas trade.

BEST / WORST DECEMBER BROAD MKTS. 1999-2008

BEST DECEMBER MARKETS
♦ Nasdaq (1999) 22.0%
♦ TSX (1999) 11.8%
♦ Russell 2000 (1999) 11.2%

WORST DECEMBER MARKETS
♦ Nasdaq (2002) -9.7%
♦ Russell 3000 Gr (2002) -7.0%
♦ Dow (2002) -6.2%

Index Values End of Month

	1999	2000	2001	2002	2003	2004	2005	2006	2007	200
Dow	11,497	10,788	10,022	8,342	10,454	10,783	10,718	12,463	13,265	8,77
S&P 500	1,469	1,320	1,148	880	1,112	1,212	1,248	1,418	1,468	90
Nasdaq	4,069	2,471	1,950	1,336	2,003	2,175	2,205	2,415	2,652	1,57
TSX	8,414	8,934	7,688	6,615	8,221	9,247	11,272	12,908	13,833	8,98
Russell 1000	1,477	1,346	1,163	896	1,143	1,251	1,306	1,480	1,538	93
Russell 2000	1,256	1,202	1,214	952	1,384	1,619	1,673	1,958	1,904	1,24
Russell 3000 Growth	3,211	2,481	1,982	1,413	1,831	1,939	2,018	2,184	2,406	1,46
Russell 3000 Value	2,083	2,204	2,068	1,713	2,191	2,502	2,610	3,116	3,009	1,86

Percent Gain for December

	1999	2000	2001	2002	2003	2004	2005	2006	2007	200
Dow	5.7	3.6	1.7	-6.2	6.9	3.4	-0.8	2.0	-0.8	-0.
S&P 500	5.8	0.4	0.8	-6.0	5.1	3.2	-0.1	1.3	-0.9	0.
Nasdaq	22.0	-4.9	1.0	-9.7	2.2	3.7	-1.2	-0.7	-0.3	2.
TSX	11.8	1.3	3.5	0.7	4.6	2.4	4.1	1.2	1.1	-3.
Russell 1000	5.9	1.1	0.9	-5.8	4.6	3.5	0.0	1.1	-0.8	1.
Russell 2000	11.2	8.4	6.0	-5.7	1.9	2.8	-0.6	0.2	-0.2	5.
Russell 3000 Growth	10.8	-2.6	0.1	-7.0	3.1	3.8	-0.4	0.2	-0.4	1.
Russell 3000 Value	0.5	5.2	2.4	-4.5	5.7	3.0	0.3	1.9	-1.2	1.

December Market Avg. Performance 1999 to 2008[1]

Dow Jones — 1.48%
SP500 — 1.03%
Nasdaq — 1.48%
TSX (CAN) — 2.77%
Russell 1000 (Lg Cap) — 1.19%
Russell 2000 (Sm Cap) — 2.95%
Russell 3000 (Brd Mkt) Growth — 0.95%
Russell 3000 (Brd Mkt) Value — 1.49%

0%   1%   2%   3%   4%

Interest Corner Dec[2]

	Fed Funds % [3]	3 Mo. T-Bill % [4]	10 Yr % [5]	20 Yr % [6]
2008	0.25	0.11	2.25	3.05
2007	4.25	3.36	4.04	4.50
2006	5.25	5.02	4.71	4.91
2005	4.25	4.08	4.39	4.61
2004	2.25	2.22	4.24	4.85

(1) Russell Data provided by Russell (2) Federal Reserve Bank of St. Louis- end of month values (3) Target rate set by FOMC (4)(5)(6) Constant yield maturities

DECEMBER SECTOR PERFORMANCE

THACKRAY SECTOR THERMOMETER

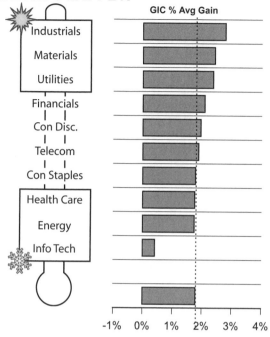

	GIC(2) % Avg Gain	Fq % Gain >S&P 500	SP GIC SECTOR 1990-2008(1)
Industrials	2.8 %	63 %	Industrials
Materials	2.4	47	Materials
Utilities	2.4	53	Utilities
Financials	2.1	58	Financials
Con Disc.	2.0	53	Consumer Discretionary
Telecom	1.9	53	Telecom
Con Staples	1.8	47	Consumer Staples
Health Care	1.8	53	Health Care
Energy	1.7	42	Energy
Info Tech	0.4	37	Information Technology
	1.8 %	N/A %	S&P 500

-1% 0% 1% 2% 3% 4%

Hot Box - 3 Best Sectors
Industrials ♦ Materials ♦ Utilities
December Portfolio

	Avg % Gain	Avg % Gain > S&P 500	Fq % Gain >S&P 500
1990-2008	2.5%	0.7%	74%
2008	-0.9%	-1.7%	

Cold Box - 3 Worst Sectors
Health Care ♦ Energy ♦ Info Tech
December Portfolio

	Avg % Gain	Avg % Gain > S&P 500	Fq % Gain >S&P 500
1990-2008	1.3%	-0.5%	37%
2008	1.4%	0.6%	

Commentary

♦ The average December poor performance of Technology stocks surprises a lot of investors. After a strong November and a few days into December, Information Technology stocks tend to underperform the broad market. This can be explained somewhat by investors selling off their more volatile holdings and generating tax losses at the end of the year (see *Small Company Effect* strategy). ♦ Santa needs a sleigh and sleigh production helps the Industrial sector. This is a sector that usually tracks the market closely, however in January the Industrial sector makes the top of the thermometer with an average gain of 2.8% and a 63% frequency of outperforming the market.

(1) Sector data provided by Standard and Poors (2) GIC is short form for Global Industry Classification (3) Sub Sector data provided by Standard and Poors, except where marked by symbol.

FINANCIALS YEAR END CLEAN UP
Outperform January 19th to April 13th

☑ **2009 Performance**

In 2008 the financial sector was in the cortex of the falling stock markets. The market waited to judge the sector until mid-January 2009 when the banks came out with their earnings. Their stronger than expected earnings were the seed for a strong March rally.

Disclaimer:

It should be noted that the strong seasonal performance of the financial sector has been adjusted from starting in the middle of December to starting approximately one month later in the middle of January (January 19th).

The financial sector often starts its strong performance in October and then steps up its performance in mid-December and then really outperforms starting in mid-January. If fundamental and technical indicators are favorable then a justification to enter the market early can exist, otherwise a mid-January date represents the start of the seasonal sweet spot.

Financials Sector vs. S&P 500 1989/90 to 2008/09			
Jan 19 to Apr 13	Positive Financials	S&P 500	Diff
1989/90	-4.3 %	1.8 %	-6.1 %
1990/91	27.7	14.5	13.2
1991/92	-2.8	-3.1	0.2
1992/93	11.3	2.8	8.5
1993/94	-2.7	-5.9	3.2
1994/95	10.4	8.4	1.9
1995/96	5.6	4.7	1.0
1996/97	-2.6	-5.0	2.4
1997/98	22.3	15.4	6.9
1998/99	13.2	8.6	4.6
1999/00	5.9	-1.0	6.9
2000/01	-6.3	-12.2	5.9
2001/02	2.6	-1.5	4.1
2002/03	-5.2	-3.7	-1.5
2003/04	0.6	-0.9	1.5
2004/05	-6.2	-1.9	-4.4
2005/06	1.1	0.9	0.2
2006/07	-3.1	1.9	-5.0
2007/08	-1.4	0.6	-2.0
2008/09	15.4	1.0	14.4
Avg.	4.1 %	1.3 %	2.8 %

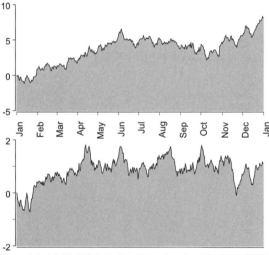

Financials Sector - Avg. Year 1990 to 2008

Financials / S&P 500 Relative Strength - Avg Yr. 1990-2008

Extra 2.8% &
14 out of 20 times better than the S&P 500

In the 1990s and early 2000s, financial stocks benefited from the tailwind of falling interest rates. During this period, with a few exceptions, this sector has participated in both the rallies and the declines. The real sweet spot on average each year, from 1989/90 to 2007/08, has been from mid-January to mid-April.

The main driver for the strong seasonal performance of the financial sector has been the year-end earnings of the banks that start to report in mid-January. A strong performance from mid-December has been the result of investors getting into the market early to take advantage of positive year-end earnings.

Interest rates are at historic lows and although they may move lower over the next few years, it is not possible for them to have the same decline that they have had since the 1980s. Given this situation investors should concentrate their financial investment during the strong seasonal period. It should be noted that Canadian banks have their year-ends at the end of October (reporting in November) and as such their seasonally strong period starts in October.

ⓘ *Financial SP GIC Sector # 40:*
An index that contains companies involved in activities such as banking, mortgage finance, consumer finance, specialized finance, investment banking and brokerage, asset management and custody, corporate lending, insurance, financial investment, and real estate, including REITs.

DECEMBER

6 MONDAY	340 / 025

7 TUESDAY	341 / 024

WEEK 49

Market Indices & Rates
Weekly Values*

Stock Markets	2007	2008
Dow	13,451	8,434
S&P 500	1,486	851
Nasdaq	2,668	1,459
TSX	13,737	8,241
FTSE	6,447	4,114
DAX	7,905	4,488
Nikkei	15,710	8,021
Hang Seng	29,057	13,692

Commodities	2007	2008
Oil (WTI)	88.73	45.50
Gold (London PM)	793.75	769.30

Bond Yields	2007	2008
USA 5 Yr Treasury	3.35	1.63
USA 10 Yr Treasury	3.97	2.66
USA 20 Yr Treasury	4.46	3.44
Moody's Aaa Corporate	5.38	5.31
Moody's Baa Corporate	6.53	8.78
CAN 5 Yr Treasury	3.74	2.25
CAN 10 Yr Treasury	3.94	3.12

Money Market	2007	2008
USA Fed Funds	4.50	1.00
USA 3 Mo T-Bill	3.08	0.04
CAN tgt overnight rate	4.25	2.25
CAN 3 Mo T-Bill	3.84	1.49

Foreign Exchange	2007	2008
USD / EUR	1.47	1.27
USD / GBP	2.05	1.47
CAN / USD	1.01	1.26
JPY / USD	110.60	92.98

---

30 day	Wednesday January 5
60 day	Friday February 4
90 day	Sunday March 6
180 day	Saturday June 4
1 year	Tuesday December 6

30 day	Thursday January 6
60 day	Saturday February 5
90 day	Monday March 7
180 day	Sunday June 5
1 year	Wednesday December 7

8 WEDNESDAY	342 / 023

9 THURSDAY	343 / 022

30 day	Friday January 7
60 day	Sunday February 6
90 day	Tuesday March 8
80 day	Monday June 6
1 year	Thursday December 8

30 day	Saturday January 8
60 day	Monday February 7
90 day	Wednesday March 9
180 day	Tuesday June 7
1 year	Friday December 9

10 FRIDAY	344 / 021

30 day	Sunday January 9
60 day	Tuesday February 8
90 day	Thursday March 10
80 day	Wednesday June 8
1 year	Saturday December 10

Weekly avg closing values- except Fed Funds Rate & CAN overnight tgt rate which are weekly closing values.

DECEMBER

M	T	W	T	F	S	S
		1	2	3	4	5
6	7	8	9	10	11	12
13	14	15	16	17	18	19
20	21	22	23	24	25	26
27	28	29	30	31		

JANUARY

M	T	W	T	F	S	S
					1	2
3	4	5	6	7	8	9
10	11	12	13	14	15	16
17	18	19	20	21	22	23
24	25	26	27	28	29	30
31						

FEBRUARY

M	T	W	T	F	S	S
1	2	3	4	5	6	
7	8	9	10	11	12	13
14	15	16	17	18	19	20
21	22	23	24	25	26	27
28						

DO THE "NAZ" WITH SANTA
Nasdaq gives more at Christmas – Dec 15th to Jan 23rd

☑ **2008 Performance**

Towards the end of 2008 the market was in a good mood and rallied. At the very end of the year and the beginning of 2009 the market started to correct. Despite the correction the Nasdaq was able to outperform the S&P 500.

One of the best times to invest in the major markets is Christmas time. What few investors know is that this seasonally strong time favors the Nasdaq market. From December 15th to January 23rd, starting in 1972 and ending in 2008, the Nasdaq has outperformed the S&P 500 by an average 2.4% per year. This rate of return is considered to be very high given that the length of favorable time is just over one month.

2.4% extra & 84% of time better than S&P 500

Looking for reasons that the Nasdaq outperforms? Interestingly, the Nasdaq starts to outperform at the same time as small companies in December (see *Small Company Effect* strategy). As investors move into the market to scoop up bargains that have been sold for tax losses, smaller companies and stocks with greater volatility tend to outperform. Compared with the S&P 500 and Dow Jones, the Nasdaq market, given its composition, tends to be a much greater recipient of the upward move created by investors picking up cheap stocks at this time of the year.

Nasdaq vs. S&P 500 Dec 15th to Jan 23rd 1971/72 To 2008/09

Dec 15 to Jan 23	Nasdaq	S&P 500	Positive Diff
1971/72	7.5 %	6.1 %	1.3 %
1972/73	-0.7	0.0	-0.7
1973/74	6.8	4.1	2.8
1974/75	8.9	7.5	1.4
1975/76	13.8	13.0	0.9
1976/77	2.8	-1.7	4.5
1977/78	-3.5	-5.1	1.6
1978/79	6.2	4.7	1.4
1979/80	5.6	4.1	1.5
1980/81	3.3	0.8	2.5
1981/82	-5.0	-6.0	1.0
1982/83	5.5	4.7	0.8
1983/84	1.4	0.9	0.4
1984/85	13.3	9.0	4.3
1985/86	0.8	-2.7	3.5
1986/87	10.2	9.2	1.0
1987/88	9.1	1.8	7.3
1988/89	4.6	3.3	1.3
1989/90	-3.8	-5.5	1.7
1990/91	4.1	1.0	3.1
1991/92	15.2	7.9	7.2
1992/93	7.2	0.8	6.4
1993/94	5.7	2.5	3.2
1994/95	4.7	2.4	2.3
1995/96	-1.0	-0.7	-0.3
1996/97	7.3	6.7	0.6
1997/98	2.6	0.4	2.1
1998/99	18.9	7.4	11.6
1999/00	18.6	2.7	15.9
2000/01	4.1	1.5	2.6
2001/02	-1.6	0.5	-2.0
2002/03	1.9	-0.2	2.1
2003/04	9.0	6.3	2.7
2004/05	-5.8	-3.0	-2.9
2005/06	-0.6	-0.7	0.1
2006/07	-0.9	0.2	-1.1
2007/08	-12.1	-8.8	-3.3
2008/09	-4.1	-5.4	1.3
Avg	4.2 %	1.8 %	2.4 %

Alternate Strategy — For those investors who favor the Nasdaq, an alternative strategy is to invest in the Nasdaq at an earlier date: October 28th. Historically, on average the Nasdaq has started its out performance at this time. The "Do the Naz with Santa" strategy focuses on the sweet spot of the Nasdaq's outperformance.

Nasdaq is a market with a number of sectors. It is more focused on technology and is typically more volatile than the S&P 500.

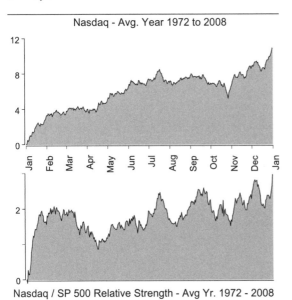

Nasdaq - Avg. Year 1972 to 2008

Nasdaq / SP 500 Relative Strength - Avg Yr. 1972 - 2008

13 MONDAY	347 / 018		**14** TUESDAY	348 / 017

Market Indices & Rates
Weekly Values*

Stock Markets	2007	2008
Dow	13,498	8,716
S&P 500	1,487	890
Nasdaq	2,669	1,547
TSX	13,779	8,501
FTSE	6,485	4,344
DAX	7,999	4,746
Nikkei	15,790	8,468
Hang Seng	28,311	15,150

Commodities	2007	2008
Oil (WTI)	91.16	44.71
Gold (London PM)	804.49	798.30

Bond Yields	2007	2008
USA 5 Yr Treasury	3.49	1.62
USA 10 Yr Treasury	4.12	2.67
USA 20 Yr Treasury	4.61	3.38
Moody's Aaa Corporate	5.55	5.35
Moody's Baa Corporate	6.72	8.72
CAN 5 Yr Treasury	3.91	2.18
CAN 10 Yr Treasury	4.06	3.08

30 day	Wednesday January 12
60 day	Friday February 11
90 day	Sunday March 13
180 day	Saturday June 11
1 year	Tuesday December 13

30 day	Thursday January 13
60 day	Saturday February 12
90 day	Monday March 14
180 day	Sunday June 12
1 year	Wednesday December 14

Money Market	2007	2008
USA Fed Funds	4.25	1.00
USA 3 Mo T-Bill	2.92	0.02
CAN tgt overnight rate	4.25	1.50
CAN 3 Mo T-Bill	3.86	1.21

15 WEDNESDAY	349 / 016		**16** THURSDAY	350 / 015

Foreign Exchange	2007	2008
USD / EUR	1.47	1.30
USD / GBP	2.04	1.49
CAN / USD	1.01	1.25
JPY / USD	111.88	92.20

DECEMBER

M	T	W	T	F	S	S
				1	2	3	4	5
6	7	8	9	10	11	12
13	14	15	16	17	18	19
20	21	22	23	24	25	26
27	28	29	30	31		

JANUARY

M	T	W	T	F	S	S
					1	2
3	4	5	6	7	8	9
10	11	12	13	14	15	16
17	18	19	20	21	22	23
24	25	26	27	28	29	30
31						

30 day	Friday January 14
60 day	Sunday February 13
90 day	Tuesday March 15
180 day	Monday June 13
1 year	Thursday December 15

30 day	Saturday January 15
60 day	Monday February 14
90 day	Wednesday March 16
180 day	Tuesday June 14
1 year	Friday December 16

17 FRIDAY	351 / 014

FEBRUARY

M	T	W	T	F	S	S
	1	2	3	4	5	6
7	8	9	10	11	12	13
14	15	16	17	18	19	20
21	22	23	24	25	26	27
28						

30 day	Sunday January 16
60 day	Tuesday February 15
90 day	Thursday March 17
180 day	Wednesday June 15
1 year	Saturday December 17

Weekly avg closing values- except Fed Funds Rate & CAN overnight tgt rate which are weekly closing values.

SANTA ARRIVES EARLY & STAYS LATE
Dec 15th to Jan 6th

☑ **2008 Performance**

Despite 2008 being a bad year in the markets, Santa came at Christmas - and left a return of over 6% in the S&P 500. The Santa Claus rally is the sweet spot of the market and a good way to start the New Year.

Every year investors wait for Santa Claus to come to town. They often get rewarded, but many leave with small returns because they focus on one or two days of outperformance. The best way to get the gift of Christmas is to get in early and stay late. The market typically makes a move up about halfway through December and continues through to the first week in January.

The first part of this move can be attributed to investors taking advantage of the *"January Effect,"* buying stocks that have been beaten down because of tax-loss selling (see *Small Company Effect* strategy). The second part of the move, the start of January, benefits from the beginning of the month effect (see *Super Seven* strategy). The first few days in January are also boosted by money managers locking in their selections for the New Year.

Dec 15th to Jan 6th Avg. Gain vs.
15 Market Day - Avg. Gain

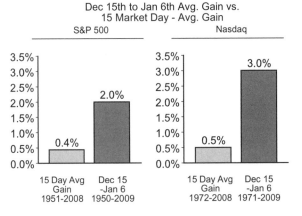

The *Santa Arrives Early & Stays Late* strategy starts on December 15th and ends January 6th. This Christmas strategy with the S&P 500 from 1950 to 2008 has on average lasted fifteen days and produced a return of 1.9%. This compares to the 0.5% return for the average fifteen day period (taken from any time period) from 1951 to 2007 (year adjustment is used to more closely align strategy with benchmark years). The net result is that this Christmas strategy has been four times better than the average fifteen day period.

Alternate Strategy—The Extended Santa Rally:
The focus of the "Santa Arrives Early Stays Late" is around the Christmas days, but on average, after January 6th, the market tends to tread water for only a few days before rallying until the beginning of February (February 3rd).

Date	% Change Dec 15th to Jan 6th	
	S&P 500 Change	Nasdaq Change
50 / 51	7.5 %	N/A %
51 / 52	2.4	"
52 / 53	1.7	"
53 / 54	1.8	"
54 / 55	2.0	"
55 / 56	0.2	"
56 / 57	0.3	"
57 / 58	-0.1	"
58 / 59	4.5	"
59 / 60	1.8	"
60 / 61	2.7	"
61 / 62	-3.2	"
62 / 63	2.5	"
63 / 64	2.2	"
64 / 65	1.7	"
65 / 66	1.3	"
66 / 67	-0.6	"
67 / 68	0.5	"
68 / 69	-4.7	"
69 / 70	2.2	"
70 / 71	2.8	"
71 / 72	6.0	6.1
72 / 73	1.4	1.9
73 / 74	6.0	5.0
74 / 75	6.0	4.3
75 / 76	6.5	7.2
76 / 77	0.0	2.8
77 / 78	-2.6	-2.2
78 / 79	3.2	3.3
79 / 80	-2.2	-1.3
80 / 81	6.9	6.7
81 / 82	-2.9	-2.3
82 / 83	5.7	2.3
83 / 84	3.6	4.2
84 / 85	0.6	3.0
85 / 86	0.3	0.6
86 / 87	2.2	2.8
87 / 88	6.9	12.1
88 / 89	1.9	3.2
89 / 90	0.4	2.4
90 / 91	-1.8	-0.4
91 / 92	8.7	10.5
92 / 93	0.4	4.1
93 / 94	0.9	3.9
94 / 95	1.3	3.3
95 / 96	0.0	-0.5
96 / 97	2.6	2.5
97 / 98	1.4	2.8
98 / 99	11.5	18.0
99 / 00	0.0	4.4
00 / 01	-3.2	-11.8
01 / 02	4.4	5.4
02 / 03	4.4	4.3
03 / 04	4.6	5.6
04 / 05	-1.3	-3.2
05 / 06	1.0	1.9
06 / 07	-1.1	-0.8
07 / 08	-3.8	-5.0
08 / 09	6.2	7.2
AVG.	2.0 %	3.0 %

20 MONDAY	354 / 011	**21** TUESDAY	355 / 010

WEEK 51

Market Indices & Rates
Weekly Values*

Stock Markets	2007	2008
Dow	13,261	8,699
S&P500	1,460	892
Nasdaq	2,621	1,559
TSX	13,428	8,541
FTSE	6,324	4,306
DAX	7,877	4,709
Nikkei	15,155	8,620
Hang Seng	27,001	15,253

Commodities	2007	2008
Oil	91.28	39.65
Gold	800.10	845.05

Bond Yields	2007	2008
USA 5 Yr Treasury	3.52	1.36
USA 10 Yr T	4.12	2.26
USA 20 Yr T	4.58	3.04
Moody's Aaa	5.51	4.95
Moody's Baa	6.65	8.30
CAN 5 Yr T	3.91	1.92
CAN 10 Yr T	4.03	2.90

Money Market	2007	2008
USA Fed Funds	4.25	0.25
USA 3 Mo T-B	2.99	0.03
CAN tgt overnight rate	4.25	1.50
CAN 3 Mo T-B	3.83	0.82

Foreign Exchange	2007	2008
USD / EUR	1.44	1.40
USD / GBP	2.00	1.52
CAN / USD	1.01	1.22
JPY / USD	113.25	89.35

Monday 20:

30 day	Wednesday January 19
60 day	Friday February 18
90 day	Sunday March 20
180 day	Saturday June 18
1 year	Tuesday December 20

Tuesday 21:

30 day	Thursday January 20
60 day	Saturday February 19
90 day	Monday March 21
180 day	Sunday June 19
1 year	Wednesday December 21

22 WEDNESDAY	356 / 009	**23** THURSDAY	357 / 008

Wednesday 22:

30 day	Friday January 21
60 day	Sunday February 20
90 day	Tuesday March 22
180 day	Monday June 20
1 year	Thursday December 22

Thursday 23:

30 day	Saturday January 22
60 day	Monday February 21
90 day	Wednesday March 23
180 day	Tuesday June 21
1 year	Friday December 23

24 FRIDAY	358 / 007

Friday 24:

30 day	Sunday January 23
60 day	Tuesday February 22
90 day	Thursday March 24
180 day	Wednesday June 22
1 year	Saturday December 24

DECEMBER

M	T	W	T	F	S	S
				1	2	3	4	5
6	7	8	9	10	11	12
13	14	15	16	17	18	19
20	21	22	23	24	25	26
27	28	29	30	31		

JANUARY

M	T	W	T	F	S	S
					1	2
3	4	5	6	7	8	9
10	11	12	13	14	15	16
17	18	19	20	21	22	23
24	25	26	27	28	29	30
31						

FEBRUARY

M	T	W	T	F	S	S
	1	2	3	4	5	6
7	8	9	10	11	12	13
14	15	16	17	18	19	20
21	22	23	24	25	26	27
28						

*Weekly avg closing values- except Fed Funds Rate & CAN overnight tgt rate which are weekly closing values.

SMALL CAP (SMALL COMPANY) EFFECT
January Effect Starts Early - Ends Late
Small Companies Outperform - Dec 19th to Mar 7th

☒ **2008-2009 Performance**

From mid-December to the end of the month the small cap strategy was looking good with a positive performance. In January (year-end for the banks), investors returned to the big question still overhanging the market - is the financial system viable? Investors were in no mood to favor higher beta sectors such as small caps. This unusual time period was not corrected until the beginning of March.

At different parts of the business cycle, small capitalization companies (small caps represented by the Russell 2000), perform better than the large capitalization companies (large caps represented by the Russell 1000). Evidence shows that the small caps relative outperformance also has a seasonal component as they typically outperform large caps from December 19th to March 7th.

3.4% extra & 21 times out of 30
better than the S&P 500

Russell 2000 vs. Russell 1000 Gains
Dec 19th to Mar 7th 1979 to 2009
Positive☐

Dec 19 - Mar7	Russell 2000	Russell 1000	Diff
79 / 80	-0.4	-1.3	0.9
80 / 81	4.0	-2.	6.8
81 / 82	-12.1	-12.4	0.3
82 / 83	19.8	11.8	8.0
83 / 84	-7.5	-6.4	-1.1
84 / 85	17.1	7.7	9.4
85 / 86	11.7	8.2	3.5
86 / 87	21.5	17.2	4.3
87 / 88	16.8	8.3	8.5
88 / 89	9.1	6.9	2.2
89 / 90	-1.8	-2.0	0.2
90 / 91	28.8	14.7	14.2
91 / 92	16.8	6.0	10.8
92 / 93	5.1	1.5	3.7
93 / 94	5.6	0.6	5.1
94 / 95	5.5	5.3	0.1
95 / 96	7.9	8.3	-0.4
96 / 97	3.5	9.5	-6.0
97 / 98	10.1	10.2	-0.2
98 / 99	0.1	7.3	-7.2
99 / 00	27.7	-1.7	29.4
00 / 01	4.7	-5.2	9.8
01 / 02	1.9	1.6	0.3
02 / 03	-7.8	-6.7	-1.0
03 / 04	9.6	6.4	3.3
04 / 05	0.3	2.8	-2.5
05 / 06	5.6	0.8	4.7
06 / 07	-0.8	-1.6	0.9
07 / 08	-12.5	-10.9	-1.5
08 / 09	-26.7	-22.2	-4.5
Avg.	5.4 %	2.1 %	3.4 %

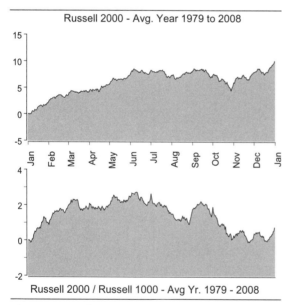

Russell 2000 - Avg. Year 1979 to 2008

Russell 2000 / Russell 1000 - Avg Yr. 1979 - 2008

vestors sell stocks in December fo tax loss reasons, artificially driving down prices, and creating a great opportunity for astute investors The January Effect is more pronounced for small caps as their prices are more volatile than large caps providing a greater opportunity to take advantage of tax loss selling Over the years as more and more investors have caught onto the idea the buy date for stocks has been pushed back to mid-December.

The core part of the small cap seasonal strategy occurs in January and includes what has been described as the January Effect (Wachtel 1942, 184). This well documented anomaly of superior performance of stocks in the month of January is based upon the tenet that in-

ⓘ *Russell 2000 (small cap index): The 2000 smallest companies in the Russell 3000 stock index (a broad market index). Russell 1000 (large cap index): The 1000 largest companies in the Russell 3000 stock index*
For more information on the Russell indexes, see www.Russell.com

Wachtel, S.B. 1942. Certain observations on seasonal movements in stock prices. The Journal of Business and Economics (Winter): 184.

27 MONDAY 361 / 004

28 TUESDAY 362 / 003

WEEK 52

Market Indices & Rates
Weekly Values*

Stock Markets	2007	2008
Dow	13,457	8,481
S&P500	1,487	869
Nasdaq	2,697	1,527
TSX	13,731	8,291
FTSE	6,485	4,241
DAX	8,053	4,634
Nikkei	15,520	8,645
Hang Seng	27,781	14,342

Commodities	2007	2008
Oil	96.20	32.41
Gold	831.38	846.25

Bond Yields	2007	2008
USA 5 Yr Treasury	3.63	1.50
USA 10 Yr T	4.21	2.18
USA 20 Yr T	4.66	2.93
Moody's Aaa	5.57	4.72
Moody's Baa	6.72	8.09
CAN 5 Yr T	3.95	1.83
CAN 10 Yr T	4.08	2.80

Money Market	2007	2008
USA Fed Funds	4.25	0.25
USA 3 Mo T-B	3.25	0.02
CAN tgt overnight rate	4.25	1.50
CAN 3 Mo T-B	3.85	0.84

Foreign Exchange	2007	2008
USD/EUR	1.45	1.40
USD/GBP	1.99	1.47
CAN/USD	0.98	1.21
JPY/USD	113.95	90.28

27 MONDAY
30 day	Wednesday January 26
60 day	Friday February 25
90 day	Sunday March 27
180 day	Saturday June 25
1 year	Tuesday December 27

28 TUESDAY
30 day	Thursday January 27
60 day	Saturday February 26
90 day	Monday March 28
180 day	Sunday June 26
1 year	Wednesday December 28

29 WEDNESDAY 363 / 002

30 THURSDAY 364 / 001

DECEMBER

M	T	W	T	F	S	S
		1	2	3	4	5
6	7	8	9	10	11	12
13	14	15	16	17	18	19
20	21	22	23	24	25	26
27	28	29	30	31		

JANUARY

M	T	W	T	F	S	S
					1	2
3	4	5	6	7	8	9
10	11	12	13	14	15	16
17	18	19	20	21	22	23
24	25	26	27	28	29	30
31						

29 WEDNESDAY
30 day	Friday January 28
60 day	Sunday February 27
90 day	Tuesday March 29
180 day	Monday June 27
1 year	Thursday December 29

30 THURSDAY
30 day	Saturday January 29
60 day	Monday February 28
90 day	Wednesday March 30
180 day	Tuesday June 28
1 year	Friday December 30

31 FRIDAY 365 / 000

FEBRUARY

M	T	W	T	F	S	S
	1	2	3	4	5	6
7	8	9	10	11	12	13
14	15	16	17	18	19	20
21	22	23	24	25	26	27
28						

31 FRIDAY
30 day	Sunday January 30
60 day	Tuesday March 1
90 day	Thursday March 31
180 day	Wednesday June 29
1 year	Saturday December 31

*Weekly avg closing values- except Fed Funds Rate & CAN overnight tgt rate which are weekly closing values.

APPENDIX

STOCK MARKET RETURNS

STOCK MKT — S&P 500 PERCENT CHANGES

	JAN	FEB	MAR	APR	MAY	JUN
1950	1.7 %	1.0 %	0.4 %	4.5 %	3.9 %	— 5.8 %
1951	6.1	0.6	— 1.8	4.8	— 4.1	— 2.6
1952	1.6	— 3.6	4.8	— 4.3	2.3	4.6
1953	— 0.7	— 1.8	— 2.4	— 2.6	— 0.3	— 1.6
1954	5.1	0.3	3.0	4.9	3.3	0.1
1955	1.8	0.4	— 0.5	3.8	— 0.1	8.2
1956	— 3.6	3.5	6.9	— 0.2	— 6.6	3.9
1957	— 4.2	— 3.3	2.0	3.7	3.7	— 0.1
1958	4.3	2.1	3.1	3.2	1.5	2.6
1959	0.4	— 0.1	0.1	3.9	1.9	— 0.4
1960	— 7.1	0.9	— 1.4	— 1.8	2.7	2.0
1961	6.3	2.7	2.6	0.4	1.9	— 2.9
1962	— 3.8	1.6	— 0.6	— 6.2	— 8.6	— 8.2
1963	4.9	— 2.9	3.5	4.9	1.4	— 2.0
1964	2.7	1.0	1.5	0.6	1.1	1.6
1965	3.3	— 0.1	— 1.5	3.4	— 0.8	— 4.9
1966	0.5	— 1.8	— 2.2	2.1	— 5.4	— 1.6
1967	7.8	0.2	3.9	4.2	— 5.2	1.8
1968	— 4.4	— 3.1	0.9	8.0	1.3	0.9
1969	— 0.8	— 4.7	3.4	2.1	— 0.2	— 5.6
1970	— 7.6	5.3	0.1	— 9.0	— 6.1	— 5.0
1971	4.0	0.9	3.7	3.6	— 4.2	— 0.9
1972	1.8	2.5	0.6	0.4	1.7	— 2.2
1973	— 1.7	— 3.7	— 0.1	— 4.1	— 1.9	— 0.7
1974	— 1.0	— 0.4	— 2.3	— 3.9	— 3.4	— 1.5
1975	12.3	6.0	2.2	4.7	4.4	4.4
1976	11.8	— 1.1	3.1	— 1.1	— 1.4	4.1
1977	— 5.1	— 2.2	— 1.4	0.0	— 2.4	4.5
1978	— 6.2	— 2.5	2.5	8.5	0.4	— 1.8
1979	4.0	— 3.7	5.5	0.2	— 2.6	3.9
1980	5.8	— 0.4	— 10.2	4.1	4.7	2.7
1981	— 4.6	1.3	3.6	— 2.3	— 0.2	— 1.0
1982	— 1.8	— 6.1	— 1.0	4.0	— 3.9	— 2.0
1983	3.3	1.9	3.3	7.5	— 1.2	3.2
1984	— 0.9	— 3.9	1.3	0.5	— 5.9	1.7
1985	7.4	0.9	— 0.3	— 0.5	5.4	1.2
1986	0.2	7.1	5.3	— 1.4	5.0	1.4
1987	13.2	3.7	2.6	— 1.1	0.6	4.8
1988	4.0	4.2	— 3.3	0.9	0.3	4.3
1989	7.1	— 2.9	2.1	5.0	3.5	— 0.8
1990	— 6.9	0.9	2.4	— 2.7	9.2	— 0.9
1991	4.2	6.7	2.2	0.0	3.9	— 4.8
1992	— 2.0	1.0	— 2.2	2.8	0.1	— 1.7
1993	0.7	1.0	1.9	— 2.5	2.3	0.1
1994	3.3	— 3.0	— 4.6	1.2	1.2	— 2.7
1995	2.4	3.6	2.7	2.8	3.6	2.1
1996	3.3	0.7	0.8	1.3	2.3	0.2
1997	6.1	0.6	— 4.3	5.8	5.9	4.3
1998	1.0	7.0	5.0	0.9	— 1.9	3.9
1999	4.1	— 3.2	3.9	3.8	— 2.5	5.4
2000	— 5.1	— 2.0	9.7	— 3.1	— 2.2	2.4
2001	3.5	— 9.2	— 6.4	7.7	0.5	— 2.5
2002	— 1.6	— 2.1	3.7	— 6.1	— 0.9	— 7.2
2003	— 2.7	— 1.7	0.8	8.1	5.1	1.1
2004	1.7	1.2	— 1.6	— 1.7	1.2	1.8
2005	— 2.5	1.9	— 1.9	— 2.0	3.0	0.0
2006	2.5	0.0	1.1	1.2	— 3.1	0.0
2007	1.4	— 2.2	1.0	4.3	3.3	— 1.8
2008	— 6.1	— 3.5	— 0.6	4.8	1.1	— 8.6
FQ POS*	37 / 59	31 / 59	38 / 59	40 / 59	34 / 59	30 / 59
% FQ POS*	63 %	53 %	64 %	68 %	58 %	51 %
AVG GAIN*	1.3 %	-0.1 %	1.0 %	1.4 %	0.3 %	0.0 %
RANK GAIN*	4	11	5	3	8	10

S&P 500 PERCENT CHANGES — STOCK MKT

JUL	AUG	SEP	OCT	NOV	DEC		YEAR
0.8 %	3.3 %	5.6 %	0.4 %	— 0.1 %	4.6 %	1950	21.8 %
6.9	3.9	— 0.1	— 1.4	— 0.3	3.9	1951	16.5
1.8	— 1.5	— 2.0	— 0.1	4.6	3.5	1952	11.8
2.5	— 5.8	0.1	5.1	0.9	0.2	1953	— 6.6
5.7	— 3.4	8.3	— 1.9	8.1	5.1	1954	45.0
6.1	— 0.8	1.1	— 3.0	7.5	— 0.1	1955	26.4
5.2	— 3.8	— 4.5	0.5	— 1.1	3.5	1956	2.6
1.1	— 5.6	— 6.2	— 3.2	1.6	— 4.1	1957	— 14.3
4.3	1.2	4.8	2.5	2.2	5.2	1958	38.1
3.5	— 1.5	— 4.6	1.1	1.3	2.8	1959	8.5
— 2.5	2.6	— 6.0	— 0.2	4.0	4.6	1960	— 3.0
3.3	2.0	— 2.0	2.8	3.9	0.3	1961	23.1
6.4	1.5	— 4.8	0.4	10.2	1.3	1962	— 11.8
— 0.3	4.9	— 1.1	3.2	— 1.1	2.4	1963	18.9
1.8	— 1.6	2.9	0.8	— 0.5	0.4	1964	13.0
1.3	2.3	3.2	2.7	— 0.9	0.9	1965	9.1
— 1.3	— 7.8	— 0.7	4.8	0.3	— 0.1	1966	— 13.1
4.5	— 1.2	3.3	— 3.5	0.8	2.6	1967	20.1
— 1.8	1.1	3.9	0.7	4.8	— 4.2	1968	7.7
— 6.0	4.0	— 2.5	4.3	— 3.4	— 1.9	1969	— 11.4
7.3	4.4	3.4	— 1.2	4.7	5.7	1970	0.1
— 3.2	3.6	— 0.7	— 4.2	— 0.3	8.6	1971	10.8
0.2	3.4	— 0.5	0.9	4.6	1.2	1972	15.6
3.8	— 3.7	4.0	— 0.1	— 11.4	1.7	1973	— 17.4
— 7.8	— 9.0	— 11.9	16.3	— 5.3	— 2.0	1974	— 29.7
— 6.8	— 2.1	— 3.5	6.2	2.5	— 1.2	1975	31.5
— 0.8	— 0.5	2.3	— 2.2	— 0.8	5.2	1976	19.1
— 1.6	— 2.1	— 0.2	— 4.3	2.7	0.3	1977	— 11.5
5.4	2.6	— 0.7	— 9.2	1.7	1.5	1978	1.1
0.9	5.3	0.0	— 6.9	4.3	1.7	1979	12.3
6.5	0.6	2.5	1.6	10.2	— 3.4	1980	25.8
— 0.2	— 6.2	— 5.4	4.9	3.7	— 3.0	1981	— 9.7
— 2.3	11.6	0.8	11.0	3.6	1.5	1982	14.8
— 3.0	1.1	1.0	— 1.5	1.7	— 0.9	1983	17.3
— 1.6	10.6	— 0.3	0.0	— 1.5	2.2	1984	1.4
— 0.5	— 1.2	— 3.5	4.3	6.5	4.5	1985	26.3
— 5.9	7.1	— 8.5	5.5	2.1	— 2.8	1986	14.6
4.8	3.5	— 2.4	— 21.8	— 8.5	7.3	1987	2.0
— 0.5	— 3.9	4.0	2.6	— 1.9	1.5	1988	12.4
8.8	1.6	— 0.7	— 2.5	1.7	2.1	1989	27.3
— 0.5	— 9.4	— 5.1	— 0.7	6.0	2.5	1990	— 6.6
4.5	2.0	— 1.9	1.2	— 4.4	11.2	1991	26.3
3.9	— 2.4	0.9	0.2	3.0	1.0	1992	4.5
— 0.5	3.4	— 1.0	1.9	— 1.3	1.0	1993	7.1
3.1	3.8	— 2.7	2.1	— 4.0	1.2	1994	— 1.5
3.2	0.0	4.0	— 0.5	4.1	1.7	1995	34.1
— 4.6	1.9	5.4	2.6	7.3	— 2.2	1996	20.3
7.8	— 5.7	5.3	— 3.4	4.5	1.6	1997	31.0
— 1.2	— 14.6	6.2	8.0	5.9	5.6	1998	26.7
— 3.2	— 0.6	— 2.9	6.3	1.9	5.8	1999	19.5
— 1.6	6.1	— 5.3	— 0.5	— 8.0	0.4	2000	— 10.1
— 1.1	— 6.4	— 8.2	1.8	7.5	0.8	2001	— 13.0
— 7.9	0.5	— 11.0	8.6	5.7	— 6.0	2002	— 23.4
1.6	1.8	— 1.2	5.5	0.7	5.1	2003	26.4
-3.4	0.2	0.9	1.4	3.9	3.2	2004	9.0
3.6	— 1.1	0.7	— 1.8	3.5	— 0.1	2005	3.0
0.5	2.1	2.5	3.2	1.6	1.3	2006	13.6
— 3.2	1.3	3.6	1.5	— 4.4	— 0.9	2007	3.5
— 1.0	1.2	— 9.2	— 16.8	— 7.5	0.8	2008	-38.5
31 / 59	33 / 59	25 / 59	35 / 59	39 / 59	45 / 59		43 / 59
53 %	56 %	42 %	59 %	66 %	76 %		73 %
0.8 %	0.1 %	— 0.7 %	0.6 %	1.5 %	1.7 %		8.4 %
6	9	12	7	2	1		

S&P 500 MONTH CLOSING VALUES

	JAN	FEB	MAR	APR	MAY	JUN
1950	17	17	17	18	19	18
1951	22	22	21	22	22	21
1952	24	23	24	23	24	25
1953	26	26	25	25	25	24
1954	26	26	27	28	29	29
1955	37	37	37	38	38	41
1956	44	45	48	48	45	47
1957	45	43	44	46	47	47
1958	42	41	42	43	44	45
1959	55	55	55	58	59	58
1960	56	56	55	54	56	57
1961	62	63	65	65	67	65
1962	69	70	70	65	60	55
1963	66	64	67	70	71	69
1964	77	78	79	79	80	82
1965	88	87	86	89	88	84
1966	93	91	89	91	86	85
1967	87	87	90	94	89	91
1968	92	89	90	97	99	100
1969	103	98	102	104	103	98
1970	85	90	90	82	77	73
1971	96	97	100	104	100	99
1972	104	107	107	108	110	107
1973	116	112	112	107	105	104
1974	97	96	94	90	87	86
1975	77	82	83	87	91	95
1976	101	100	103	102	100	104
1977	102	100	98	98	96	100
1978	89	87	89	97	97	96
1979	100	96	102	102	99	103
1980	114	114	102	106	111	114
1981	130	131	136	133	133	131
1982	120	113	112	116	112	110
1983	145	148	153	164	162	168
1984	163	157	159	160	151	153
1985	180	181	181	180	190	192
1986	212	227	239	236	247	251
1987	274	284	292	288	290	304
1988	257	268	259	261	262	274
1989	297	289	295	310	321	318
1990	329	332	340	331	361	358
1991	344	367	375	375	390	371
1992	409	413	404	415	415	408
1993	439	443	452	440	450	451
1994	482	467	446	451	457	444
1995	470	487	501	515	533	545
1996	636	640	646	654	669	671
1997	786	791	757	801	848	885
1998	980	1049	1102	1112	1091	1134
1999	1280	1238	1286	1335	1302	1373
2000	1394	1366	1499	1452	1421	1455
2001	1366	1240	1160	1249	1256	1224
2002	1130	1107	1147	1077	1067	990
2003	856	841	848	917	964	975
2004	1131	1145	1126	1107	1121	1141
2005	1181	1204	1181	1157	1192	1191
2006	1280	1281	1295	1311	1270	1270
2007	1438	1407	1421	1482	1531	1503
2008	1379	1331	1323	1386	1400	1280

S&P 500 MONTH CLOSING VALUES

JUL	AUG	SEP	OCT	NOV	DEC	
18	18	19	20	20	20	1950
22	23	23	23	23	24	1951
25	25	25	25	26	27	1952
25	23	23	25	25	25	1953
31	30	32	32	34	36	1954
44	43	44	42	46	45	1955
49	48	45	46	45	47	1956
48	45	42	41	42	40	1957
47	48	50	51	52	55	1958
61	60	57	58	58	60	1959
56	57	54	53	56	58	1960
67	68	67	69	71	72	1961
58	59	56	57	62	63	1962
69	73	72	74	73	75	1963
83	82	84	85	84	85	1964
85	87	90	92	92	92	1965
84	77	77	80	80	80	1966
95	94	97	93	94	96	1967
98	99	103	103	108	104	1968
92	96	93	97	94	92	1969
78	82	84	83	87	92	1970
96	99	98	94	94	102	1971
107	111	111	112	117	118	1972
108	104	108	108	96	98	1973
79	72	64	74	70	69	1974
89	87	84	89	91	90	1975
103	103	105	103	102	107	1976
99	97	97	92	95	95	1977
101	103	103	93	95	96	1978
104	109	109	102	106	108	1979
122	122	125	127	141	136	1980
131	123	116	122	126	123	1981
107	120	120	134	139	141	1982
163	164	166	164	166	165	1983
151	167	166	166	164	167	1984
191	189	182	190	202	211	1985
236	253	231	244	249	242	1986
319	330	322	252	230	247	1987
272	262	272	279	274	278	1988
346	351	349	340	346	353	1989
356	323	306	304	322	330	1990
388	395	388	392	375	417	1991
424	414	418	419	431	436	1992
448	464	459	468	462	466	1993
458	475	463	472	454	459	1994
562	562	584	582	605	616	1995
640	652	687	705	757	741	1996
954	899	947	915	955	970	1997
1121	957	1017	1099	1164	1229	1998
1329	1320	1283	1363	1389	1469	1999
1431	1518	1437	1429	1315	1320	2000
1211	1134	1041	1060	1139	1148	2001
912	916	815	886	936	880	2002
990	1008	996	1051	1058	1112	2003
1102	1104	1115	1130	1174	1212	2004
1234	1220	1229	1207	1249	1248	2005
1277	1304	1336	1378	1401	1418	2006
1455	1474	1527	1549	1481	1468	2007
1267	1283	1165	969	896	903	2008

DOW JONES PERCENT MONTH CHANGES

	JAN	FEB	MAR	APR	MAY	JUN
1950	0.8 %	0.8 %	1.3 %	4.0 %	4.2 %	− 6.4 %
1951	5.7	1.3	− 1.7	4.5	− 3.6	− 2.8
1952	0.6	− 3.9	3.6	− 4.4	2.1	4.3
1953	− 0.7	− 2.0	− 1.5	− 1.8	− 0.9	− 1.5
1954	4.1	0.7	3.1	5.2	2.6	1.8
1955	1.1	0.8	− 0.5	3.9	− 0.2	6.2
1956	− 3.6	2.8	5.8	0.8	− 7.4	3.1
1957	− 4.1	− 3.0	2.2	4.1	2.1	− 0.3
1958	3.3	− 2.2	1.6	2.0	1.5	3.3
1959	1.8	1.6	− 0.3	3.7	3.2	0.0
1960	− 8.4	1.2	− 2.1	− 2.4	4.0	2.4
1961	5.2	2.1	2.2	0.3	2.7	− 1.8
1962	− 4.3	1.2	− 0.2	− 5.9	− 7.8	− 8.5
1963	4.7	− 2.9	3.0	5.2	1.3	− 2.8
1964	2.9	1.9	1.6	− 0.3	1.2	1.3
1965	3.3	0.1	− 1.6	3.7	− 0.5	− 5.4
1966	1.5	− 3.2	− 2.8	1.0	− 5.3	− 1.6
1967	8.2	− 1.2	3.2	3.6	− 5.0	0.9
1968	− 5.5	− 1.8	0.0	8.5	− 1.4	− 0.1
1969	0.2	− 4.3	3.3	1.6	− 1.3	− 6.9
1970	− 7.0	4.5	1.0	− 6.3	− 4.8	− 2.4
1971	3.5	1.2	2.9	4.1	− 3.6	− 1.8
1972	1.3	2.9	1.4	1.4	0.7	− 3.3
1973	− 2.1	− 4.4	− 0.4	− 3.1	− 2.2	− 1.1
1974	0.6	0.6	− 1.6	− 1.2	− 4.1	0.0
1975	14.2	5.0	3.9	6.9	1.3	5.6
1976	14.4	− 0.3	2.8	− 0.3	− 2.2	2.8
1977	− 5.0	− 1.9	− 1.8	0.8	− 3.0	2.0
1978	− 7.4	− 3.6	2.1	10.5	0.4	− 2.6
1979	4.2	− 3.6	6.6	− 0.8	− 3.8	2.4
1980	4.4	− 1.5	− 9.0	4.0	4.1	2.0
1981	− 1.7	2.9	3.0	− 0.6	− 0.6	− 1.5
1982	− 0.4	− 5.4	− 0.2	3.1	− 3.4	− 0.9
1983	2.8	3.4	1.6	8.5	− 2.1	1.8
1984	− 3.0	− 5.4	0.9	0.5	− 5.6	2.5
1985	6.2	− 0.2	− 1.3	− 0.7	4.6	1.5
1986	1.6	8.8	6.4	− 1.9	5.2	0.9
1987	13.8	3.1	3.6	− 0.8	0.2	5.5
1988	1.0	5.8	− 4.0	2.2	− 0.1	5.4
1989	8.0	− 3.6	1.6	5.5	2.5	− 1.6
1990	− 5.9	1.4	3.0	− 1.9	8.3	0.1
1991	3.9	5.3	1.1	− 0.9	4.8	− 4.0
1992	1.7	1.4	− 1.0	3.8	1.1	− 2.3
1993	0.3	1.8	1.9	− 0.2	2.9	− 0.3
1994	6.0	− 3.7	− 5.1	1.3	2.1	− 3.5
1995	0.2	4.3	3.7	3.9	3.3	2.0
1996	5.4	1.7	1.9	− 0.3	1.3	0.2
1997	5.7	0.9	− 4.3	6.5	4.6	4.7
1998	0.0	8.1	3.0	3.0	− 1.8	0.6
1999	1.9	− 0.6	5.2	10.2	− 2.1	3.9
2000	− 4.5	− 7.4	7.8	− 1.7	− 2.0	− 0.7
2001	0.9	− 3.6	− 5.9	8.7	1.6	− 3.8
2002	− 1.0	1.9	2.9	− 4.4	− 0.2	− 6.9
2003	− 3.5	− 2.0	1.3	6.1	4.4	1.5
2004	0.3	0.9	− 2.1	− 1.3	− 0.4	2.4
2005	− 2.7	2.6	− 2.4	− 3.0	2.7	− 1.8
2006	1.4	1.2	1.1	2.3	− 1.7	− 0.2
2007	1.3	− 2.8	0.7	5.7	4.3	− 1.6
2008	− 4.6	− 3.0	0.0	4.5	− 1.4	− 10.2
FQ POS	39 / 59	33 / 59	37 / 59	37 / 59	30 / 59	28 / 59
% FQ POS	66 %	56 %	63 %	63 %	51 %	47 %
AVG GAIN	1.2 %	0.1 %	0.9 %	1.9 %	0.1 %	− 0.3 %
RANK GAIN	4	9	6	1	8	11

DOW JONES PERCENT MONTH CHANGES — STOCK MKT

JUL	AUG	SEP	OCT	NOV	DEC		YEAR
0.1 %	3.6 %	4.4 %	− 0.6 %	1.2 %	3.4 %	1950	17.6 %
6.3	4.8	0.3	− 3.2	− 0.4	3.0	1951	14.4
1.9	− 1.6	− 1.6	− 0.5	5.4	2.9	1952	8.4
2.6	− 5.2	1.1	4.5	2.0	− 0.2	1953	− 3.8
4.3	− 3.5	7.4	− 2.3	9.9	4.6	1954	44.0
3.2	0.5	− 0.3	− 2.5	6.2	1.1	1955	20.8
5.1	− 3.1	− 5.3	1.0	− 1.5	5.6	1956	2.3
1.0	− 4.7	− 5.8	− 3.4	2.0	− 3.2	1957	− 12.8
5.2	1.1	4.6	2.1	2.6	4.7	1958	34.0
4.9	− 1.6	− 4.9	2.4	1.9	3.1	1959	16.4
− 3.7	1.5	− 7.3	0.1	2.9	3.1	1960	− 9.3
3.1	2.1	− 2.6	0.4	2.5	1.3	1961	18.7
6.5	1.9	− 5.0	1.9	10.1	0.4	1962	− 10.8
− 1.6	4.9	0.5	3.1	− 0.6	1.7	1963	17.0
1.2	− 0.3	4.4	− 0.3	0.3	− 0.1	1964	14.6
1.6	1.3	4.2	3.2	− 1.5	2.4	1965	10.9
− 2.6	− 7.0	− 1.8	4.2	− 1.9	− 0.7	1966	− 18.9
5.1	− 0.3	2.8	− 5.1	− 0.4	3.3	1967	15.2
− 1.6	1.5	4.4	1.8	3.4	− 4.2	1968	4.3
− 6.6	2.6	− 2.8	5.3	− 5.1	− 1.5	1969	− 15.2
7.4	4.2	− 0.5	− 0.7	5.1	5.6	1970	4.8
− 3.7	4.6	− 1.2	− 5.4	− 0.9	7.1	1971	6.1
− 0.5	4.2	− 1.1	0.2	6.6	0.2	1972	14.6
3.9	− 4.2	6.7	1.0	− 14.0	3.5	1973	− 16.6
− 5.6	− 10.4	− 10.4	9.5	− 7.0	− 0.4	1974	− 27.6
− 5.4	0.5	− 5.0	5.3	3.0	− 1.0	1975	38.3
1.8	− 1.1	1.7	− 2.6	− 1.8	6.1	1976	17.9
− 2.9	− 3.2	− 1.7	− 3.4	1.4	0.2	1977	− 17.3
5.3	1.7	− 1.3	− 8.5	0.8	0.8	1978	− 3.2
0.5	4.9	− 1.0	− 7.2	0.8	2.0	1979	4.2
7.8	− 0.3	0.0	− 0.8	7.4	− 2.9	1980	14.9
− 2.5	− 7.4	− 3.6	0.3	4.3	− 1.6	1981	− 9.2
− 0.4	11.5	− 0.6	10.6	4.8	0.7	1982	19.6
− 1.9	1.4	1.4	− 0.6	4.1	− 1.4	1983	20.3
− 1.5	9.8	− 1.4	0.1	− 1.5	1.9	1984	− 3.7
0.9	− 1.0	− 0.4	3.4	7.1	5.1	1985	27.7
− 6.2	6.9	− 6.9	6.2	1.9	− 1.0	1986	22.6
6.4	3.5	− 2.5	− 23.2	− 8.0	5.7	1987	2.3
− 0.6	− 4.6	4.0	1.7	− 1.6	2.6	1988	11.9
9.0	2.9	− 1.6	− 1.8	2.3	1.7	1989	27.0
0.9	− 10.0	− 6.2	− 0.4	4.8	2.9	1990	− 4.3
4.1	0.6	− 0.9	1.7	− 5.7	9.5	1991	20.3
2.3	− 4.0	0.4	− 1.4	2.4	− 0.1	1992	4.2
0.7	3.2	− 2.6	3.5	0.1	1.9	1993	13.7
3.8	4.0	− 1.8	1.7	− 4.3	2.5	1994	2.1
3.3	− 2.1	3.9	− 0.7	6.7	0.8	1995	33.5
− 2.2	1.6	4.7	2.5	8.2	− 1.1	1996	26.0
7.2	− 7.3	4.2	− 6.3	5.1	1.1	1997	22.6
− 0.8	− 15.1	4.0	9.6	6.1	0.7	1998	16.1
− 2.9	1.6	− 4.5	3.8	1.4	5.3	1999	24.7
0.7	6.6	− 5.0	3.0	− 5.1	3.6	2000	− 5.8
0.2	− 5.4	− 11.1	2.6	8.6	1.7	2001	− 7.1
− 5.5	− 0.8	− 12.4	10.6	5.9	− 6.2	2002	− 16.8
2.8	2.0	− 1.5	5.7	− 0.2	6.9	2003	25.3
− 2.8	0.3	− 0.9	− 0.5	4.0	3.4	2004	3.1
3.6	− 1.5	0.8	− 1.2	3.5	− 0.8	2005	− 0.6
0.3	1.7	2.6	3.4	1.2	2.0	2006	16.3
− 1.5	1.1	4.0	0.2	− 4.0	− 0.8	2007	6.4
0.2	1.5	− 6.0	− 14.1	− 5.3	− 0.6	2008	− 33.8
36 / 59	34 / 59	22 / 59	34 / 59	39 / 59	41 / 59		41 / 59
61 %	58 %	37 %	58 %	66 %	69 %		69 %
1.0 %	0.0 %	− 1.0 %	0.3 %	1.5 %	1.7 %		7.9 %
5	10	12	7	3	2		

DOW JONES
MONTH CLOSING VALUES

	JAN	FEB	MAR	APR	MAY	JUN
1950	202	203	206	214	223	209
1951	249	252	248	259	250	243
1952	271	260	270	258	263	274
1953	290	284	280	275	272	268
1954	292	295	304	319	328	334
1955	409	412	410	426	425	451
1956	471	484	512	516	478	493
1957	479	465	475	494	505	503
1958	450	440	447	456	463	478
1959	594	604	602	624	644	644
1960	623	630	617	602	626	641
1961	648	662	677	679	697	684
1962	700	708	707	665	613	561
1963	683	663	683	718	727	707
1964	785	800	813	811	821	832
1965	903	904	889	922	918	868
1966	984	952	925	934	884	870
1967	850	839	866	897	853	860
1968	856	841	841	912	899	898
1969	946	905	936	950	938	873
1970	744	778	786	736	700	684
1971	869	879	904	942	908	891
1972	902	928	941	954	961	929
1973	999	955	951	921	901	892
1974	856	861	847	837	802	802
1975	704	739	768	821	832	879
1976	975	973	1000	997	975	1003
1977	954	936	919	927	899	916
1978	770	742	757	837	841	819
1979	839	809	862	855	822	842
1980	876	863	786	817	851	868
1981	947	975	1004	998	992	977
1982	871	824	823	848	820	812
1983	1076	1113	1130	1226	1200	1222
1984	1221	1155	1165	1171	1105	1132
1985	1287	1284	1267	1258	1315	1336
1986	1571	1709	1819	1784	1877	1893
1987	2158	2224	2305	2286	2292	2419
1988	1958	2072	1988	2032	2031	2142
1989	2342	2258	2294	2419	2480	2440
1990	2591	2627	2707	2657	2877	2881
1991	2736	2882	2914	2888	3028	2907
1992	3223	3268	3236	3359	3397	3319
1993	3310	3371	3435	3428	3527	3516
1994	3978	3832	3636	3682	3758	3625
1995	3844	4011	4158	4321	4465	4556
1996	5395	5486	5587	5569	5643	5655
1997	6813	6878	6584	7009	7331	7673
1998	7907	8546	8800	9063	8900	8952
1999	9359	9307	9786	10789	10560	10971
2000	10941	10128	10922	10734	10522	10448
2001	10887	10495	9879	10735	10912	10502
2002	9920	10106	10404	9946	9925	9243
2003	8054	7891	7992	8480	8850	8985
2004	10488	10584	10358	10226	10188	10435
2005	10490	10766	10504	10193	10467	10275
2006	10865	10993	11109	11367	11168	11150
2007	12622	12269	12354	13063	13628	13409
2008	12650	12266	12263	12820	12638	11350

DOW JONES
MONTH CLOSING VALUES

STOCK MKT

JUL	AUG	SEP	OCT	NOV	DEC	
209	217	226	225	228	235	**1950**
258	270	271	262	261	269	**1951**
280	275	271	269	284	292	**1952**
275	261	264	276	281	281	**1953**
348	336	361	352	387	404	**1954**
466	468	467	455	483	488	**1955**
518	502	475	480	473	500	**1956**
509	484	456	441	450	436	**1957**
503	509	532	543	558	584	**1958**
675	664	632	647	659	679	**1959**
617	626	580	580	597	616	**1960**
705	720	701	704	722	731	**1961**
598	609	579	590	649	652	**1962**
695	729	733	755	751	763	**1963**
841	839	875	873	875	874	**1964**
882	893	931	961	947	969	**1965**
847	788	774	807	792	786	**1966**
904	901	927	880	876	905	**1967**
883	896	936	952	985	944	**1968**
816	837	813	856	812	800	**1969**
734	765	761	756	794	839	**1970**
858	898	887	839	831	890	**1971**
925	964	953	956	1018	1020	**1972**
926	888	947	957	822	851	**1973**
757	679	608	666	619	616	**1974**
832	835	794	836	861	852	**1975**
985	974	990	965	947	1005	**1976**
890	862	847	818	830	831	**1977**
862	877	866	793	799	805	**1978**
846	888	879	816	822	839	**1979**
935	933	932	925	993	964	**1980**
952	882	850	853	889	875	**1981**
809	901	896	992	1039	1047	**1982**
1199	1216	1233	1225	1276	1259	**1983**
1115	1224	1207	1207	1189	1212	**1984**
1348	1334	1329	1374	1472	1547	**1985**
1775	1898	1768	1878	1914	1896	**1986**
2572	2663	2596	1994	1834	1939	**1987**
2129	2032	2113	2149	2115	2169	**1988**
2661	2737	2693	2645	2706	2753	**1989**
2905	2614	2453	2442	2560	2634	**1990**
3025	3044	3017	3069	2895	3169	**1991**
3394	3257	3272	3226	3305	3301	**1992**
3540	3651	3555	3681	3684	3754	**1993**
3765	3913	3843	3908	3739	3834	**1994**
4709	4611	4789	4756	5075	5117	**1995**
5529	5616	5882	6029	6522	6448	**1996**
8223	7622	7945	7442	7823	7908	**1997**
8883	7539	7843	8592	9117	9181	**1998**
10655	10829	10337	10730	10878	11453	**1999**
10522	11215	10651	10971	10415	10788	**2000**
10523	9950	8848	9075	9852	10022	**2001**
8737	8664	7592	8397	8896	8342	**2002**
9234	9416	9275	9801	9782	10454	**2003**
10140	10174	10080	10027	10428	10783	**2004**
10641	10482	10569	10440	10806	10718	**2005**
11186	11381	11679	12801	12222	12463	**2006**
13212	13358	13896	13930	13372	13265	**2007**
11378	11544	10851	9325	8829	8776	**2008**

NASDAQ PERCENT MONTH CHANGES

	JAN	FEB	MAR	APR	MAY	JUN
1972	4.2	5.5	2.2	2.5	0.9	— 1.8
1973	— 4.0	— 6.2	— 2.4	— 8.2	— 4.8	— 1.6
1974	3.0	— 0.6	— 2.2	— 5.9	— 7.7	— 5.3
1975	16.6	4.6	3.6	3.8	5.8	4.7
1976	12.1	3.7	0.4	— 0.6	— 2.3	2.6
1977	— 2.4	— 1.0	— 0.5	1.4	0.1	4.3
1978	— 4.0	0.6	4.7	8.5	4.4	0.0
1979	6.6	— 2.6	7.5	1.6	— 1.8	5.1
1980	7.0	— 2.3	— 17.1	6.9	7.5	4.9
1981	— 2.2	0.1	6.1	3.1	3.1	— 3.5
1982	— 3.8	— 4.8	— 2.1	5.2	— 3.3	— 4.1
1983	6.9	5.0	3.9	8.2	5.3	3.2
1984	— 3.7	— 5.9	— 0.7	— 1.3	— 5.9	2.9
1985	12.8	2.0	— 1.8	0.5	3.6	1.9
1986	3.4	7.1	4.2	2.3	4.4	1.3
1987	12.4	8.4	1.2	— 2.9	— 0.3	2.0
1988	4.3	6.5	2.1	1.2	— 2.3	6.6
1989	5.2	— 0.4	1.8	5.1	4.3	— 2.4
1990	— 8.6	2.4	2.3	— 3.5	9.3	0.7
1991	10.8	9.4	6.4	0.5	4.4	— 6.0
1992	5.8	2.1	— 4.7	— 4.2	1.1	— 3.7
1993	2.9	— 3.7	2.9	— 4.2	5.9	0.5
1994	3.0	— 1.0	— 6.2	— 1.3	0.2	— 4.0
1995	0.4	5.1	3.0	3.3	2.4	8.0
1996	0.7	3.8	0.1	8.1	4.4	— 4.7
1997	6.9	— 5.1	— 6.7	3.2	11.1	3.0
1998	3.1	9.3	3.7	1.8	— 4.8	6.5
1999	14.3	— 8.7	7.6	3.3	— 2.8	8.7
2000	— 3.2	19.2	— 2.6	— 15.6	— 11.9	16.6
2001	12.2	— 22.4	— 14.5	15.0	— 0.3	2.4
2002	— 0.8	— 10.5	6.6	— 8.5	— 4.3	— 9.4
2003	— 1.1	1.3	0.3	9.2	9.0	1.7
2004	3.1	— 1.8	— 1.8	— 3.7	3.5	3.1
2005	— 5.2	— 0.5	— 2.6	— 3.9	7.6	— 0.5
2006	4.6	— 1.1	2.6	— 0.7	— 6.2	— 0.3
2007	2.0	— 1.9	0.2	4.3	3.1	0.0
2008	— 9.9	— 5.0	0.3	5.9	4.6	— 9.1
FQ POS	25/37	18/37	23/37	23/37	23/37	22/37
% FQ POS	68 %	49 %	62 %	62 %	62 %	59 %
AVG GAIN	3.1 %	0.3 %	0.2 %	1.1 %	1.3 %	0.9 %
RANK GAIN	1	9	10	5	4	6

NASDAQ PERCENT MONTH CHANGES

STOCK MKT

JUL	AUG	SEP	OCT	NOV	DEC		YEAR
— 1.8	1.7	— 0.3	0.5	2.1	0.6	1972	17.2
7.6	— 3.5	6.0	— 0.9	— 15.1	— 1.4	1973	— 31.1
— 7.9	— 10.9	— 10.7	17.2	— 3.5	— 5.0	1974	— 35.1
— 4.4	— 5.0	— 5.9	3.6	2.4	— 1.5	1975	29.8
1.1	— 1.7	1.7	— 1.0	0.9	7.4	1976	26.1
0.9	— 0.5	0.7	— 3.3	5.8	1.8	1977	7.3
5.0	6.9	— 1.6	— 16.4	3.2	2.9	1978	12.3
2.3	6.4	— 0.3	— 9.6	6.4	4.8	1979	28.1
8.9	5.7	3.4	2.7	8.0	— 2.8	1980	33.9
— 1.9	— 7.5	— 8.0	8.4	3.1	— 2.7	1981	— 3.2
— 2.3	6.2	5.6	13.3	9.3	0.0	1982	18.7
— 4.6	— 3.8	1.4	— 7.4	4.1	— 2.5	1983	19.9
— 4.2	10.9	— 1.8	— 1.2	— 1.9	1.9	1984	— 11.3
1.7	— 1.2	— 5.8	4.4	7.4	3.5	1985	31.5
— 8.4	3.1	— 8.4	2.9	— 0.3	— 3.0	1986	7.4
2.4	4.6	— 2.4	— 27.2	— 5.6	8.3	1987	— 5.2
— 1.9	— 2.8	2.9	— 1.3	— 2.9	2.7	1988	15.4
4.2	3.4	0.8	— 3.7	0.1	— 0.3	1989	19.2
— 5.2	— 13.0	— 9.6	— 4.3	8.9	4.1	1990	— 17.8
5.5	4.7	0.2	3.1	— 3.5	11.9	1991	56.9
3.1	— 3.0	3.6	3.8	7.9	3.7	1992	15.5
0.1	5.4	2.7	2.2	— 3.2	3.0	1993	14.7
2.3	6.0	— 0.2	1.7	— 3.5	0.2	1994	— 3.2
7.3	1.9	2.3	— 0.7	2.2	— 0.7	1995	39.9
— 8.8	5.6	7.5	— 0.4	5.8	— 0.1	1996	22.7
10.5	— 0.4	6.2	— -5.5	0.4	— 1.9	1997	21.6
— 1.2	— 19.9	13.0	4.6	10.1	12.5	1998	39.6
— 1.8	3.8	0.2	8.0	12.5	22.0	1999	85.6
— 5.0	11.7	— 12.7	— 8.3	— 22.9	— 4.9	2000	— 39.3
— 6.2	— 10.9	— 17.0	12.8	14.2	1.0	2001	— 21.1
— 9.2	— 1.0	— 10.9	13.5	11.2	— 9.7	2002	— 31.5
6.9	4.3	— 1.3	8.1	1.5	2.2	2003	50.0
— 7.8	— 2.6	3.2	4.1	6.2	3.7	2004	8.6
6.2	— 1.5	0.0	— 1.5	5.3	— 1.2	2005	1.4
— 3.7	4.4	3.4	4.8	2.7	— 0.7	2006	9.5
— 2.2	2.0	4.0	5.8	— 6.9	— 0.3	2007	9.8
1.4	1.8	— 11.6	— 17.7	— 10.8	2.7	2008	— 40.5
18/37	20/37	19/37	20/37	25/37	21/37		26/37
49 %	54 %	51 %	54 %	68 %	57 %		70 %
— 0.3 %	0.3 %	— 1.1 %	0.4 %	1.7 %	1.7 %		10.9 %
11	8	12	7	3	2		

NASDAQ MONTH CLOSING VALUES

	JAN	FEB	MAR	APR	MAY	JUN
1972	119	125	128	131	133	130
1973	128	120	117	108	103	101
1974	95	94	92	87	80	76
1975	70	73	76	79	83	87
1976	87	90	91	90	88	90
1977	96	95	94	95	96	100
1978	101	101	106	115	120	120
1979	126	123	132	134	131	138
1980	162	158	131	140	150	158
1981	198	198	210	217	223	216
1982	188	179	176	185	179	171
1983	248	261	271	293	309	319
1984	268	253	251	247	233	240
1985	279	284	279	281	291	296
1986	336	360	375	383	400	406
1987	392	425	430	418	417	425
1988	345	367	375	379	370	395
1989	401	400	407	428	446	435
1990	416	426	436	420	459	462
1991	414	453	482	485	506	476
1992	620	633	604	579	585	564
1993	696	671	690	661	701	704
1994	800	793	743	734	735	706
1995	755	794	817	844	865	933
1996	1060	1100	1101	1191	1243	1185
1997	1380	1309	1222	1261	1400	1442
1998	1619	1771	1836	1868	1779	1895
1999	2506	2288	2461	2543	2471	2686
2000	3940	4697	4573	3861	3401	3966
2001	2773	2152	1840	2116	2110	2161
2002	1934	1731	1845	1688	1616	1463
2003	1321	1338	1341	1464	1596	1623
2004	2066	2030	1994	1920	1987	2048
2005	2062	2052	1999	1922	2068	2057
2006	2306	2281	2340	2323	2179	2172
2007	2464	2416	2422	2525	2605	2603
2008	2390	2271	2279	2413	2523	2293

NASDAQ MONTH CLOSING VALUES
STOCK MKT

JUL	AUG	SEP	OCT	NOV	DEC	
128	130	130	130	133	134	1972
109	105	111	110	94	92	1973
70	62	56	65	63	60	1974
83	79	74	77	79	78	1975
91	90	91	90	91	98	1976
101	100	101	98	103	105	1977
126	135	133	111	115	118	1978
141	150	150	136	144	151	1979
172	182	188	193	208	202	1980
212	196	180	195	201	196	1981
167	178	188	213	232	232	1982
304	292	297	275	286	279	1983
230	255	250	247	242	247	1984
301	298	280	293	314	325	1985
371	383	351	361	360	349	1986
435	455	444	323	305	331	1987
387	377	388	383	372	381	1988
454	469	473	456	456	455	1989
438	381	345	330	359	374	1990
502	526	527	543	524	586	1991
581	563	583	605	653	677	1992
705	743	763	779	754	777	1993
722	766	764	777	750	752	1994
1001	1020	1044	1036	1059	1052	1995
1081	1142	1227	1222	1293	1291	1996
1594	1587	1686	1594	1601	1570	1997
1872	1499	1694	1771	1950	2193	1998
2638	2739	2746	2966	3336	4069	1999
3767	4206	3673	3370	2598	2471	2000
2027	1805	1499	1690	1931	1950	2001
1328	1315	1172	1330	1479	1336	2002
1735	1810	1787	1932	1960	2003	2003
1887	1838	1897	1975	2097	2175	2004
2185	2152	2152	2120	2233	2205	2005
2091	2184	2258	2367	2432	2415	2006
2546	2596	2702	2859	2661	2652	2007
2326	2368	2092	1721	1536	1577	2008

S&P/TSX MONTH PERCENT CHANGES

	JAN	FEB	MAR	APR	MAY	JUN
1985	8.1	0.0	0.7	0.8	3.8	— 0.8
1986	— 1.7	0.5	6.7	1.1	1.4	— 1.2
1987	9.2	4.5	6.9	— 0.6	— 0.9	1.5
1988	— 3.3	4.8	3.4	0.8	— 2.7	5.9
1989	6.7	— 1.2	0.2	1.4	2.2	1.5
1990	— 6.7	— 0.5	— 1.3	— 8.2	6.7	— 0.6
1991	0.5	5.8	1.0	-0.8	2.2	— 2.3
1992	2.4	— 0.4	— 4.7	— 1.7	1.0	0.0
1993	— 1.3	4.4	4.4	5.2	2.5	2.2
1994	5.4	— 2.9	— 2.1	— 1.4	1.4	— 7.0
1995	— 4.7	2.7	4.6	— -0.8	4.0	1.8
1996	5.4	— 0.7	0.8	3.5	1.9	— 3.9
1997	3.1	0.8	— 5.0	2.2	6.8	0.9
1998	0.0	5.9	6.6	1.4	— 1.0	— 2.9
1999	3.8	— 6.2	4.5	6.3	— 2.5	2.5
2000	0.8	7.6	3.7	— 1.2	— 1.0	10.2
2001	4.3	— 13.3	— 5.8	4.5	2.7	— 5.2
2002	— 0.5	— 0.1	2.8	— 2.4	— 0.1	— 6.7
2003	— 0.7	— 0.2	— 3.2	3.8	4.2	1.8
2004	3.7	3.1	— 2.3	— 4.0	2.1	1.5
2005	— 0.5	5.0	— 0.6	— 3.5	3.6	3.1
2006	6.0	— 2.2	3.6	0.8	— 3.8	— 1.1
2007	1.0	0.1	0.9	1.9	4.8	— 1.1
2008	— 4.9	3.3	— 1.7	4.4	5.6	— 1.7
FQ POS	15/24	13/24	15/24	14/24	17/24	11/24
% FQ POS	63 %	54 %	63 %	58 %	71 %	46 %
AVG GAIN	1.5 %	0.9 %	1.0 %	0.6 %	1.9 %	-0.1 %
RANK GAIN	3	5	4	7	2	9

S&P/TSX MONTH PERCENT CHANGES
STOCK MKT

JUL	AUG	SEP	OCT	NOV	DEC	YEAR	
2.4	1.5	— 6.7	1.6	6.8	1.3	**1985**	20.5
— 4.9	3.2	— 1.6	1.6	0.7	0.6	**1986**	6.0
7.8	— 0.9	— 2.3	— 22.6	— 1.4	6.1	**1987**	3.1
— 1.9	— 2.7	— 0.1	3.4	— 3.0	2.9	**1988**	7.3
5.6	1.0	— 1.7	— 0.6	0.6	0.7	**1989**	17.1
0.5	— 6.0	— 5.6	— 2.5	2.3	3.4	**1990**	— 18.0
2.1	— 0.6	— 3.7	3.8	— 1.9	1.9	**1991**	7.8
1.6	— 1.2	— 3.1	1.2	— 1.6	2.1	**1992**	— 4.6
0.0	4.3	— 3.6	6.6	— 1.8	3.4	**1993**	29.0
3.8	4.1	0.1	— 1.4	— 4.6	2.9	**1994**	— 2.5
1.9	— 2.1	0.3	— 1.6	4.5	1.1	**1995**	11.9
— 2.3	4.3	2.9	5.8	7.5	— 1.5	**1996**	25.7
6.8	— 3.9	6.5	— 2.8	— 4.8	2.9	**1997**	13.0
— 5.9	— 20.2	1.5	10.6	2.2	2.2	**1998**	— 3.2
1.0	— 1.6	— 0.2	4.3	3.6	11.9	**1999**	29.7
2.1	8.1	— 7.7	— 7.1	— 8.5	1.3	**2000**	6.2
— 0.6	— 3.8	— 7.6	0.7	7.8	3.5	**2001**	— 13.9
— 7.6	0.1	— 6.5	1.1	5.1	0.7	**2002**	— 14.0
3.9	3.6	— 1.3	4.7	1.1	4.6	**2003**	24.3
— 1.0	— 1.0	3.5	2.3	1.8	2.4	**2004**	12.5
5.3	2.4	3.2	— 5.7	4.2	4.1	**2005**	21.9
1.9	2.1	— 2.6	5.0	3.3	1.2	**2006**	14.5
— 0.3	— 1.5	3.2	3.7	— 6.4	1.1	**2007**	7.2
— 6.0	1.3	— 14.7	— 16.9	— 5.0	— 3.1	**2008**	— 35.0
15/24	12/24	8/24	15/24	14/24	22/24		17/24
63 %	50 %	33 %	63 %	58 %	92 %		71 %
0.7 %	— 0.4 %	— 2.0 %	— 0.2 %	0.5 %	2.4 %		6.9 %
6	11	12	10	8	1		

S&P/TSX MONTH CLOSING VALUES

	JAN	FEB	MAR	APR	MAY	JUN
1985	2595	2595	2613	2635	2736	2713
1986	2843	2856	3047	3079	3122	3086
1987	3349	3499	3739	3717	3685	3740
1988	3057	3205	3314	3340	3249	3441
1989	3617	3572	3578	3628	3707	3761
1990	3704	3687	3640	3341	3565	3544
1991	3273	3462	3496	3469	3546	3466
1992	3596	3582	3412	3356	3388	3388
1993	3305	3452	3602	3789	3883	3966
1994	4555	4424	4330	4267	4327	4025
1995	4018	4125	4314	4280	4449	4527
1996	4968	4934	4971	5147	5246	5044
1997	6110	6158	5850	5977	6382	6438
1998	6700	7093	7559	7665	7590	7367
1999	6730	6313	6598	7015	6842	7010
2000	8481	9129	9462	9348	9252	10196
2001	9322	8079	7608	7947	8162	7736
2002	7649	7638	7852	7663	7656	7146
2003	6570	6555	6343	6586	6860	6983
2004	8521	8789	8586	8244	8417	8546
2005	9204	9668	9612	9275	9607	9903
2006	11946	11688	12111	12204	11745	11613
2007	13034	13045	13166	13417	14057	13907
2008	13155	13583	13350	13937	14715	14467

JUL	AUG	SEP	OCT	NOV	DEC	
2779	2820	2632	2675	2857	2893	1985
2935	3028	2979	3027	3047	3066	1986
4030	3994	3902	3019	2978	3160	1987
3377	3286	3284	3396	3295	3390	1988
3971	4010	3943	3919	3943	3970	1989
3561	3346	3159	3081	3151	3257	1990
3540	3518	3388	3516	3449	3512	1991
3443	3403	3298	3336	3283	3350	1992
3967	4138	3991	4256	4180	4321	1993
4179	4350	4354	4292	4093	4214	1994
4615	4517	4530	4459	4661	4714	1995
4929	5143	5291	5599	6017	5927	1996
6878	6612	7040	6842	6513	6699	1997
6931	5531	5614	6208	6344	6486	1998
7081	6971	6958	7256	7520	8414	1999
10406	11248	10378	9640	8820	8934	2000
7690	7399	6839	6886	7426	7688	2001
6605	6612	6180	6249	6570	6615	2002
7258	7517	7421	7773	7859	8221	2003
8458	8377	8668	8871	9030	9247	2004
10423	10669	11012	10383	10824	11272	2005
11831	12074	11761	12345	12752	12908	2006
13869	13660	14099	14625	13689	13833	2007
13593	13771	11753	9763	9271	8988	2008

S&P 500 1950 - 2008
BEST - WORST

10 BEST | 10 WORST

YEARS

	Close	Change	Change		Close	Change	Change
1954	36	11 pt	45.0 %	2008	903	− 566 pt	− 38.5 %
1958	55	15	38.1	1974	69	− 29	− 29.7
1995	616	157	34.1	2002	880	− 268	− 23.4
1975	90	22	31.5	1973	98	− 21	− 17.4
1997	970	230	31.0	1957	40	− 7	− 14.3
1989	353	76	27.3	1966	80	− 12	− 13.1
1998	1229	259	26.7	2001	1148	− 172	− 13.0
1955	45	10	26.4	1962	63	− 8	− 11.8
2003	1112	232	26.4	1977	95	− 12	− 11.5
1985	211	44	26.3	1969	92	− 12	− 11.4

MONTHS

	Close	Change	Change		Close	Change	Change
Oct 1974	74	10 pt	16.3 %	Oct 1987	252	− 70 pt	− 21.8 %
Aug 1982	120	12	11.6	Oct 2008	969	− 196	− 16.8
Dec 1991	417	42	11.2	Aug 1998	957	− 163	− 14.6
Oct 1982	134	13	11.0	Sep 1974	64	− 9	− 11.9
Aug 1984	167	16	10.6	Nov 1973	96	− 12	− 11.4
Nov 1980	141	13	10.2	Sep 2002	815	− 101	− 11.0
Nov 1962	62	6	10.2	Mar 1980	102	− 12	− 10.2
Mar 2000	1499	132	9.7	Aug 1990	323	− 34	− 9.4
May 1990	361	30	9.2	Feb 2001	1240	− 126	− 9.2
Jul 1989	346	28	8.8	Sep 2008	1165	− 118	− 9.2

DAYS

		Close	Change	Change			Close	Change	Change
Mon	2008 Oct 13	1003	104 pt	11.6 %	Mon	1987 Oct 19	225	− 58 pt	− 20.5 %
Tue	2008 Oct 28	941	92	10.8	Wed	2008 Oct 15	908	− 90	− 9.0
Wed	1987 Oct 21	258	22	9.1	Mon	2008 Dec 01	816	− 80	− 8.9
Thu	2008 Nov 13	911	59	6.9	Mon	2008 Sep 29	1106	− 107	− 8.8
Mon	2008 Nov 24	852	52	6.5	Mon	1987 Oct 26	228	− 21	− 8.3
Fri	2008 Nov 21	800	48	6.3	Thu	2008 Oct 09	910	− 75	− 7.6
Wed	2002 Jul 24	843	46	5.7	Mon	1997 Oct 27	877	− 65	− 6.9
Mon	2002 Jul 29	899	46	5.4	Mon	1998 Aug 31	957	− 70	− 6.8
Tue	1987 Oct 20	237	12	5.3	Fri	1988 Jan 8	243	− 18	− 6.8
Tue	2008 Sep 30	1166	58	5.3	Thu	2008 Nov 20	752	− 54	− 6.7

DOW JONES 1950 - 2008
BEST - WORST

STOCK MKT

10 BEST

10 WORST

YEARS

	Close	Change	Change
1954	404	124 pt	44 %
1975	852	236	38.3
1958	584	148	34.0
1995	5117	1283	33.5
1985	1547	335	27.7
1989	2753	585	27.0
1996	6448	1331	26.0
2003	10454	2112	25.3
1999	11453	2272	25.2
1997	7908	1460	22.6

YEARS

	Close	Change	Change
2008	8776	− 4488 pt	− 33.8 %
1974	616	− 235	− 27.6
1966	786	− 184	− 18.9
1977	831	− 174	− 17.3
2002	8342	− 1680	− 16.8
1973	851	− 169	− 16.6
1969	800	− 143	− 15.2
1957	436	− 64	− 12.8
1962	652	− 79	− 10.8
1960	616	− 64	− 9.3

MONTHS

	Close	Change	Change
Aug 1982	901	93 pt	11.5 %
Oct 1982	992	95	10.6
Oct 2002	8397	805	10.6
Apr 1978	837	80	10.5
Apr 1999	10789	1003	10.2
Nov 1962	649	60	10.1
Nov 1954	387	35	9.9
Aug 1984	1224	109	9.8
Oct 1998	8592	750	9.6
Oct 1974	666	58	9.5

MONTHS

	Close	Change	Change
Oct 1987	1994	− 603 pt	− 23.2 %
Aug 1998	7539	− 1344	− 15.1
Oct 2008	9325	− 1526	− 14.1
Nov 1973	822	− 134	− 14.0
Sep 2002	7592	− 1072	− 12.4
Sep 2001	8848	− 1102	− 11.1
Sep 1974	608	− 71	− 10.4
Aug 1974	679	− 79	− 10.4
Jun 2008	11350	− 1288	− 10.2
Aug 1990	2614	− 291	− 10.0

DAYS

		Close	Change	Change
Mon	2008 Oct 13	9388	936 pt	11.1 %
Tue	2008 Oct 28	9065	889	10.9
Wed	1987 Oct 21	2028	187	10.2
Thu	2008 Nov 13	8835	553	6.7
Fri	2008 Nov 21	8046	494	6.5
Wed	2002 Jul 24	8191	489	6.3
Tue	1987 Oct 20	1841	102	5.9
Mon	2002 Jul 29	8712	448	5.4
Wed	1970 May 27	663	32	5.1
Tue	1998 Sep 8	8021	381	5.0

DAYS

		Close	Change	Change
Mon	1987 Oct 19	1739	− 508 pt	− 22.6 %
Mon	1987 Oct 26	1794	− 157	− 8.0
Wed	2008 Oct 15	8578	− 733	− 7.9
Mon	2008 Dec 01	8149	− 680	− 7.7
Thu	2008 Oct 09	8579	− 679	− 7.3
Mon	1997 Oct 27	8366	− 554	− 7.2
Mon	2001 Sep 17	8921	− 685	− 7.1
Mon	2008 Sep 29	10365	− 778	− 7.0
Fri	1989 Oct 13	2569	− 191	− 6.9
Fri	1988 Jan 8	1911	− 141	− 6.9

10 BEST   10 WORST

YEARS

	Close	Change	Change
1999	4069	1877 pt	85.6 %
1991	586	213	56.9
2003	2003	668	50.0
1995	1052	300	39.9
1998	2193	622	39.6
1980	202	51	33.9
1985	325	78	31.5
1975	78	18	29.8
1979	151	33	28.1
1976	98	20	26.1

YEARS

	Close	Change	Change
2008	1577	– 1075 pt	– 40.5 %
2000	2471	– 1599	– 39.3
1974	60	– 32	– 35.1
2002	1336	– 615	– 31.5
1973	92	– 42	– 31.1
2001	1950	– 520	– 21.1
1990	374	– 81	– 17.8
1984	247	– 32	– 11.3
1987	331	– 18	– 5.2
1981	196	– 7	– 3.2

MONTHS

	Close	Change	Change
Dec 1999	4069	733 pt	22.0 %
Feb 2000	4697	756	19.2
Oct 1974	65	10	17.2
Jun 2000	3966	565	16.6
Apr 2001	2116	276	15.0
Nov 2001	1931	240	14.2
Oct 2002	1330	158	13.5
Oct 1982	1771	25	13.3
Sep 1998	1694	195	13.0
Oct 2001	1690	191	12.8

MONTHS

	Close	Change	Change
Oct 1987	323	– 121 pt	– 27.2 %
Nov 2000	2598	– 772	– 22.9
Feb 2001	2152	– 621	– 22.4
Aug 1998	1499	– 373	– 19.9
Oct 2008	1721	– 371	– 17.7
Mar 1980	131	– 27	– 17.1
Sep 2001	1499	– 307	– 17.0
Oct 1978	111	– 22	– 16.4
Apr 2000	3861	– 712	– 15.6
Nov 1973	94	– 17	– 15.1

DAYS

		Close	Change	Change
Wed	2001 Jan 3	2617	325 pt	14.2 %
Mon	2008 Oct 13	1844	195	11.8
Tue	2000 Dec 5	2890	274	10.5
Tue	2008 Oct 28	1649	144	9.5
Thu	2001 Apr 5	1785	146	8.9
Wed	2001 Apr 18	2079	156	8.1
Tue	2000 May 30	3459	254	7.9
Fri	2000 Oct 13	3317	242	7.9
Thu	2000 Oct 19	3419	247	7.8
Wed	2002 May 8	1696	122	7.8

DAYS

		Close	Change	Change
Mon	1987 Oct 19	360	– 46 pt	– 11.3 %
Fri	2000 Apr 14	3321	– 355	– 9.7
Mon	2008 Sep 29	1984	– 200	– 9.1
Mon	1987 Oct 26	299	– 30	– 9.0
Tue	1987 Oct 20	328	– 32	– 9.0
Mon	2008 Dec 01	1398	– 138	– 9.0
Mon	1998 Aug 31	1499	– 140	– 8.6
Wed	2008 Oct 15	1628	– 151	– 8.5
Mon	2000 Apr 03	4224	– 349	– 7.6
Tue	2001 Jan 02	2292	– 179	– 7.2

10 BEST

10 WORST

YEARS

	Close	Change	Change
1999	8414	1928 pt	29.7 %
1993	4321	971	29.0
1996	5927	1214	25.7
2003	8221	1606	24.3
2005	11272	2026	21.9
1985	2893	493	20.5
1989	3970	580	17.1
2006	12908	1636	14.5
1997	6699	772	13.0
2004	9247	1026	12.5

YEARS

	Close	Change	Change
2008	8988	– 4845 pt	35.0 %
1990	3257	– 713	– 18.0
2002	6615	– 1074	– 14.0
2001	7688	– 1245	– 13.9
1992	3350	– 162	– 4.6
1998	6486	– 214	– 3.2
1994	4214	– 108	– 2.5
1987	3160	94	3.1
1986	3066	173	6.0
2000	8934	520	6.2

MONTHS

	Close	Change	Change
Dec 1999	8414	894 pt	11.9 %
Oct 1998	6208	594	10.6
Jun 2000	10196	944	10.2
Jan 1985	2595	195	8.1
Aug 2000	11248	842	8.1
Nov 2001	7426	540	7.8
Jul 1987	4030	290	7.8
Feb 2000	9129	648	7.6
Nov 1996	6017	418	7.5
Mar 1987	3739	240	6.9

MONTHS

	Close	Change	Change
Oct 1987	3019	– 883 pt	– 22.6 %
Aug 1998	5531	– 1401	– 20.2
Oct 2008	9763	– 1990	– 16.9
Sep 2008	11753	– 2018	– 14.7
Feb 2001	8079	– 1243	– 13.3
Nov 2000	8820	– 820	– 8.5
Apr 1990	3341	– 299	– 8.2
Sep 2000	10378	– 870	– 7.7
Sep 2001	6839	– 561	– 7.6
Jul 2002	6605	– 540	– 7.6

DAYS

		Close	Change	Change
Tue	2008 Oct 14	9956	891 pt	9.8 %
Wed	1987 Oct 21	3246	269	9.0
Mon	2008 Oct 20	10251	689	7.2
Tue	2008 Oct 28	9152	614	7.2
Fri	2008 Sep 19	12913	848	7.0
Fri	2008 Nov 28	9271	517	5.9
Fri	2008 Nov 21	8155	431	5.6
Mon	2008 Dec 08	8567	450	5.5
Fri	1987 Oct 30	3019	147	5.1
Thu	2008 Nov 13	9353	430	4.8

DAYS

		Close	Change	Change
Mon	1987 Oct 19	3192	– 407 pt	– 11.3 %
Mon	2008 Dec 01	8406	– 864	– 9.3
Thu	2008 Nov 20	7725	– 766	– 9.0
Mon	2008 Oct 27	8537	– 757	– 8.1
Wed	2000 Oct 25	9512	– 840	– 8.1
Mon	1987 Oct 26	2846	– 233	– 7.6
Thu	2008 Oct 02	10901	– 814	– 6.9
Mon	2008 Sep 29	11285	– 841	– 6.9
Tue	1987 Oct 20	2977	– 215	– 6.7
Fri	2001 Feb 16	8393	– 574	– 6.4

BOND YIELDS

BOND YIELDS 🇺🇸 10 YEAR TREASURY*

	JAN	FEB	MAR	APR	MAY	JUN
1954	2.48	2.47	2.37	2.29	2.37	2.38
1955	2.61	2.65	2.68	2.75	2.76	2.78
1956	2.9	2.84	2.96	3.18	3.07	3
1957	3.46	3.34	3.41	3.48	3.6	3.8
1958	3.09	3.05	2.98	2.88	2.92	2.97
1959	4.02	3.96	3.99	4.12	4.31	4.34
1960	4.72	4.49	4.25	4.28	4.35	4.15
1961	3.84	3.78	3.74	3.78	3.71	3.88
1962	4.08	4.04	3.93	3.84	3.87	3.91
1963	3.83	3.92	3.93	3.97	3.93	3.99
1964	4.17	4.15	4.22	4.23	4.2	4.17
1965	4.19	4.21	4.21	4.2	4.21	4.21
1966	4.61	4.83	4.87	4.75	4.78	4.81
1967	4.58	4.63	4.54	4.59	4.85	5.02
1968	5.53	5.56	5.74	5.64	5.87	5.72
1969	6.04	6.19	6.3	6.17	6.32	6.57
1970	7.79	7.24	7.07	7.39	7.91	7.84
1971	6.24	6.11	5.7	5.83	6.39	6.52
1972	5.95	6.08	6.07	6.19	6.13	6.11
1973	6.46	6.64	6.71	6.67	6.85	6.9
1974	6.99	6.96	7.21	7.51	7.58	7.54
1975	7.5	7.39	7.73	8.23	8.06	7.86
1976	7.74	7.79	7.73	7.56	7.9	7.86
1977	7.21	7.39	7.46	7.37	7.46	7.28
1978	7.96	8.03	8.04	8.15	8.35	8.46
1979	9.1	9.1	9.12	9.18	9.25	8.91
1980	10.8	12.41	12.75	11.47	10.18	9.78
1981	12.57	13.19	13.12	13.68	14.1	13.47
1982	14.59	14.43	13.86	13.87	13.62	14.3
1983	10.46	10.72	10.51	10.4	10.38	10.85
1984	11.67	11.84	12.32	12.63	13.41	13.56
1985	11.38	11.51	11.86	11.43	10.85	10.16
1986	9.19	8.7	7.78	7.3	7.71	7.8
1987	7.08	7.25	7.25	8.02	8.61	8.4
1988	8.67	8.21	8.37	8.72	9.09	8.92
1989	9.09	9.17	9.36	9.18	8.86	8.28
1990	8.21	8.47	8.59	8.79	8.76	8.48
1991	8.09	7.85	8.11	8.04	8.07	8.28
1992	7.03	7.34	7.54	7.48	7.39	7.26
1993	6.6	6.26	5.98	5.97	6.04	5.96
1994	5.75	5.97	6.48	6.97	7.18	7.1
1995	7.78	7.47	7.2	7.06	6.63	6.17
1996	5.65	5.81	6.27	6.51	6.74	6.91
1997	6.58	6.42	6.69	6.89	6.71	6.49
1998	5.54	5.57	5.65	5.64	5.65	5.5
1999	4.72	5	5.23	5.18	5.54	5.9
2000	6.66	6.52	6.26	5.99	6.44	6.1
2001	5.16	5.1	4.89	5.14	5.39	5.28
2002	5.04	4.91	5.28	5.21	5.16	4.93
2003	4.05	3.9	3.81	3.96	3.57	3.33
2004	4.15	4.08	3.83	4.35	4.72	4.73
2005	4.22	4.17	4.5	4.34	4.14	4.00
2006	4.42	4.57	4.72	4.99	5.11	5.11
2007	4.76	4.72	4.56	4.69	4.75	5.10
2008	3.74	3.74	3.51	3.68	3.88	4.10

* Source: Federal Reserve Bank of St. Louis, monthly data calculated as average of business days

10 YEAR TREASURY BOND YIELDS

JUL	AUG	SEP	OCT	NOV	DEC	
2.3	2.36	2.38	2.43	2.48	2.51	1954
2.9	2.97	2.97	2.88	2.89	2.96	1955
3.11	3.33	3.38	3.34	3.49	3.59	1956
3.93	3.93	3.92	3.97	3.72	3.21	1957
3.2	3.54	3.76	3.8	3.74	3.86	1958
4.4	4.43	4.68	4.53	4.53	4.69	1959
3.9	3.8	3.8	3.89	3.93	3.84	1960
3.92	4.04	3.98	3.92	3.94	4.06	1961
4.01	3.98	3.98	3.93	3.92	3.86	1962
4.02	4	4.08	4.11	4.12	4.13	1963
4.19	4.19	4.2	4.19	4.15	4.18	1964
4.2	4.25	4.29	4.35	4.45	4.62	1965
5.02	5.22	5.18	5.01	5.16	4.84	1966
5.16	5.28	5.3	5.48	5.75	5.7	1967
5.5	5.42	5.46	5.58	5.7	6.03	1968
6.72	6.69	7.16	7.1	7.14	7.65	1969
7.46	7.53	7.39	7.33	6.84	6.39	1970
6.73	6.58	6.14	5.93	5.81	5.93	1971
6.11	6.21	6.55	6.48	6.28	6.36	1972
7.13	7.4	7.09	6.79	6.73	6.74	1973
7.81	8.04	8.04	7.9	7.68	7.43	1974
8.06	8.4	8.43	8.14	8.05	8	1975
7.83	7.77	7.59	7.41	7.29	6.87	1976
7.33	7.4	7.34	7.52	7.58	7.69	1977
8.64	8.41	8.42	8.64	8.81	9.01	1978
8.95	9.03	9.33	10.3	10.65	10.39	1979
10.25	11.1	11.51	11.75	12.68	12.84	1980
14.28	14.94	15.32	15.15	13.39	13.72	1981
13.95	13.06	12.34	10.91	10.55	10.54	1982
11.38	11.85	11.65	11.54	11.69	11.83	1983
13.36	12.72	12.52	12.16	11.57	11.5	1984
10.31	10.33	10.37	10.24	9.78	9.26	1985
7.3	7.17	7.45	7.43	7.25	7.11	1986
8.45	8.76	9.42	9.52	8.86	8.99	1987
9.06	9.26	8.98	8.8	8.96	9.11	1988
8.02	8.11	8.19	8.01	7.87	7.84	1989
8.47	8.75	8.89	8.72	8.39	8.08	1990
8.27	7.9	7.65	7.53	7.42	7.09	1991
6.84	6.59	6.42	6.59	6.87	6.77	1992
5.81	5.68	5.36	5.33	5.72	5.77	1993
7.3	7.24	7.46	7.74	7.96	7.81	1994
6.28	6.49	6.2	6.04	5.93	5.71	1995
6.87	6.64	6.83	6.53	6.2	6.3	1996
6.22	6.3	6.21	6.03	5.88	5.81	1997
5.46	5.34	4.81	4.53	4.83	4.65	1998
5.79	5.94	5.92	6.11	6.03	6.28	1999
6.05	5.83	5.8	5.74	5.72	5.24	2000
5.24	4.97	4.73	4.57	4.65	5.09	2001
4.65	4.26	3.87	3.94	4.05	4.03	2002
3.98	4.45	4.27	4.29	4.3	4.27	2003
4.5	4.28	4.13	4.1	4.19	4.23	2004
4.18	4.26	4.20	4.46	4.54	4.47	2005
5.09	4.88	4.72	4.73	4.60	4.56	2006
5.00	4.67	4.52	4.53	4.15	4.10	2007
4.01	3.89	3.69	3.81	3.53	2.42	2008

BOND YIELDS — 5 YEAR TREASURY*

	JAN	FEB	MAR	APR	MAY	JUN
1954	2.17	2.04	1.93	1.87	1.92	1.92
1955	2.32	2.38	2.48	2.55	2.56	2.59
1956	2.84	2.74	2.93	3.20	3.08	2.97
1957	3.47	3.39	3.46	3.53	3.64	3.83
1958	2.88	2.78	2.64	2.46	2.41	2.46
1959	4.01	3.96	3.99	4.12	4.35	4.50
1960	4.92	4.69	4.31	4.29	4.49	4.12
1961	3.67	3.66	3.60	3.57	3.47	3.81
1962	3.94	3.89	3.68	3.60	3.66	3.64
1963	3.58	3.66	3.68	3.74	3.72	3.81
1964	4.07	4.03	4.14	4.15	4.05	4.02
1965	4.10	4.15	4.15	4.15	4.15	4.15
1966	4.86	4.98	4.92	4.83	4.89	4.97
1967	4.70	4.74	4.54	4.51	4.75	5.01
1968	5.54	5.59	5.76	5.69	6.04	5.85
1969	6.25	6.34	6.41	6.30	6.54	6.75
1970	8.17	7.82	7.21	7.50	7.97	7.85
1971	5.89	5.56	5.00	5.65	6.28	6.53
1972	5.59	5.69	5.87	6.17	5.85	5.91
1973	6.34	6.60	6.80	6.67	6.80	6.69
1974	6.95	6.82	7.31	7.92	8.18	8.10
1975	7.41	7.11	7.30	7.99	7.72	7.51
1976	7.46	7.45	7.49	7.25	7.59	7.61
1977	6.58	6.83	6.93	6.79	6.94	6.76
1978	7.77	7.83	7.86	7.98	8.18	8.36
1979	9.20	9.13	9.20	9.25	9.24	8.85
1980	10.74	12.60	13.47	11.84	9.95	9.21
1981	12.77	13.41	13.41	13.99	14.63	13.95
1982	14.65	14.54	13.98	14.00	13.75	14.43
1983	10.03	10.26	10.08	10.02	10.03	10.63
1984	11.37	11.54	12.02	12.37	13.17	13.48
1985	10.93	11.13	11.52	11.01	10.34	9.60
1986	8.68	8.34	7.46	7.05	7.52	7.64
1987	6.64	6.79	6.79	7.57	8.26	8.02
1988	8.18	7.71	7.83	8.19	8.58	8.49
1989	9.15	9.27	9.51	9.30	8.91	8.29
1990	8.12	8.42	8.60	8.77	8.74	8.43
1991	7.70	7.47	7.77	7.70	7.70	7.94
1992	6.24	6.58	6.95	6.78	6.69	6.48
1993	5.83	5.43	5.19	5.13	5.20	5.22
1994	5.09	5.40	5.94	6.52	6.78	6.70
1995	7.76	7.37	7.05	6.86	6.41	5.93
1996	5.36	5.38	5.97	6.30	6.48	6.69
1997	6.33	6.20	6.54	6.76	6.57	6.38
1998	5.42	5.49	5.61	5.61	5.63	5.52
1999	4.60	4.91	5.14	5.08	5.44	5.81
2000	6.58	6.68	6.50	6.26	6.69	6.30
2001	4.86	4.89	4.64	4.76	4.93	4.81
2002	4.34	4.30	4.74	4.65	4.49	4.19
2003	3.05	2.90	2.78	2.93	2.52	2.27
2004	3.12	3.07	2.79	3.39	3.85	3.93
2005	3.71	3.77	4.17	4.00	3.85	3.77
2006	4.35	4.57	4.72	4.90	5.00	5.07
2007	4.75	4.71	4.48	4.59	4.67	5.03
2008	2.98	2.78	2.48	2.84	3.15	3.49

* Source: Federal Reserve Bank of St. Louis, monthly data calculated as average of business days

5 YEAR TREASURY  BOND YIELDS

JUL	AUG	SEP	OCT	NOV	DEC	
1.85	1.90	1.96	2.02	2.09	2.16	**1954**
2.72	2.86	2.85	2.76	2.81	2.93	**1955**
3.12	3.41	3.47	3.40	3.56	3.70	**1956**
4.00	4.00	4.03	4.08	3.72	3.08	**1957**
2.77	3.29	3.69	3.78	3.70	3.82	**1958**
4.58	4.57	4.90	4.72	4.75	5.01	**1959**
3.79	3.62	3.61	3.76	3.81	3.67	**1960**
3.84	3.96	3.90	3.80	3.82	3.91	**1961**
3.80	3.71	3.70	3.64	3.60	3.56	**1962**
3.89	3.89	3.96	3.97	4.01	4.04	**1963**
4.03	4.05	4.08	4.07	4.04	4.09	**1964**
4.15	4.20	4.25	4.34	4.46	4.72	**1965**
5.17	5.50	5.50	5.27	5.36	5.00	**1966**
5.23	5.31	5.40	5.57	5.78	5.75	**1967**
5.60	5.50	5.48	5.55	5.66	6.12	**1968**
7.01	7.03	7.57	7.51	7.53	7.96	**1969**
7.59	7.57	7.29	7.12	6.47	5.95	**1970**
6.85	6.55	6.14	5.93	5.78	5.69	**1971**
5.97	6.02	6.25	6.18	6.12	6.16	**1972**
7.33	7.63	7.05	6.77	6.92	6.80	**1973**
8.38	8.63	8.37	7.97	7.68	7.31	**1974**
7.92	8.33	8.37	7.97	7.80	7.76	**1975**
7.49	7.31	7.13	6.75	6.52	6.10	**1976**
6.84	7.03	7.04	7.32	7.34	7.48	**1977**
8.54	8.33	8.43	8.61	8.84	9.08	**1978**
8.90	9.06	9.41	10.63	10.93	10.42	**1979**
9.53	10.84	11.62	11.86	12.83	13.25	**1980**
14.79	15.56	15.93	15.41	13.38	13.60	**1981**
14.07	13.00	12.25	10.80	10.38	10.22	**1982**
11.21	11.63	11.43	11.28	11.41	11.54	**1983**
13.27	12.68	12.53	12.06	11.33	11.07	**1984**
9.70	9.81	9.81	9.69	9.28	8.73	**1985**
7.06	6.80	6.92	6.83	6.76	6.67	**1986**
8.01	8.32	8.94	9.08	8.35	8.45	**1987**
8.66	8.94	8.69	8.51	8.79	9.09	**1988**
7.83	8.09	8.17	7.97	7.81	7.75	**1989**
8.33	8.44	8.51	8.33	8.02	7.73	**1990**
7.91	7.43	7.14	6.87	6.62	6.19	**1991**
5.84	5.60	5.38	5.60	6.04	6.08	**1992**
5.09	5.03	4.73	4.71	5.06	5.15	**1993**
6.91	6.88	7.08	7.40	7.72	7.78	**1994**
6.01	6.24	6.00	5.86	5.69	5.51	**1995**
6.64	6.39	6.60	6.27	5.97	6.07	**1996**
6.12	6.16	6.11	5.93	5.80	5.77	**1997**
5.46	5.27	4.62	4.18	4.54	4.45	**1998**
5.68	5.84	5.80	6.03	5.97	6.19	**1999**
6.18	6.06	5.93	5.78	5.70	5.17	**2000**
4.76	4.57	4.12	3.91	3.97	4.39	**2001**
3.81	3.29	2.94	2.95	3.05	3.03	**2002**
2.87	3.37	3.18	3.19	3.29	3.27	**2003**
3.69	3.47	3.36	3.35	3.53	3.60	**2004**
3.98	4.12	4.01	4.33	4.45	4.39	**2005**
5.04	4.82	4.67	4.69	4.58	4.53	**2006**
4.88	4.43	4.20	4.20	3.67	3.49	**2007**
3.30	3.14	2.88	2.73	2.29	1.52	**2008**

3 MONTH TREASURY

	JAN	FEB	MAR	APR	MAY	JUN
1982	12.92	14.28	13.31	13.34	12.71	13.08
1983	8.12	8.39	8.66	8.51	8.50	9.14
1984	9.26	9.46	9.89	10.07	10.22	10.26
1985	8.02	8.56	8.83	8.22	7.73	7.18
1986	7.30	7.29	6.76	6.24	6.33	6.40
1987	5.58	5.75	5.77	5.82	5.85	5.85
1988	6.00	5.84	5.87	6.08	6.45	6.66
1999	8.56	8.84	9.14	8.96	8.74	8.43
1990	7.90	8.00	8.17	8.04	8.01	7.99
1991	6.41	6.12	6.09	5.83	5.63	5.75
1992	3.91	3.95	4.14	3.84	3.72	3.75
1993	3.07	2.99	3.01	2.93	3.03	3.14
1994	3.04	3.33	3.59	3.78	4.27	4.25
1995	5.90	5.94	5.91	5.84	5.85	5.64
1996	5.15	4.96	5.10	5.09	5.15	5.23
1997	5.17	5.14	5.28	5.30	5.20	5.07
1998	5.18	5.23	5.16	5.08	5.14	5.12
1999	4.45	4.56	4.57	4.41	4.63	4.72
2000	5.50	5.73	5.86	5.82	5.99	5.86
2001	5.29	5.01	4.54	3.97	3.70	3.57
2002	1.68	1.76	1.83	1.75	1.76	1.73
2003	1.19	1.19	1.15	1.15	1.09	0.94
2004	0.90	0.94	0.95	0.96	1.04	1.29
2005	2.37	2.58	2.80	2.84	2.90	3.04
2006	4.34	4.54	4.63	4.72	4.84	4.92
2007	5.11	5.16	5.08	5.01	4.87	4.74
2008	2.82	2.17	1.28	1.31	1.76	1.89

* Source: Federal Reserve Bank of St. Louis, monthly data calculated as average of business days

3 MONTH TREASURY ≣ BOND YIELDS

JUL	AUG	SEP	OCT	NOV	DEC	
11.86	9.00	8.19	7.97	8.35	8.20	**1982**
9.45	9.74	9.36	8.99	9.11	9.36	**1983**
10.53	10.90	10.80	10.12	8.92	8.34	**1984**
7.32	7.37	7.33	7.40	7.48	7.33	**1985**
6.00	5.69	5.35	5.32	5.50	5.68	**1986**
5.88	6.23	6.62	6.35	5.89	5.96	**1987**
6.95	7.30	7.48	7.60	8.03	8.35	**1988**
8.15	8.17	8.01	7.90	7.94	7.88	**1999**
7.87	7.69	7.60	7.40	7.29	6.95	**1990**
5.75	5.50	5.37	5.14	4.69	4.18	**1991**
3.28	3.20	2.97	2.93	3.21	3.29	**1992**
3.11	3.09	3.01	3.09	3.18	3.13	**1993**
4.46	4.61	4.75	5.10	5.45	5.76	**1994**
5.59	5.57	5.43	5.44	5.52	5.29	**1995**
5.30	5.19	5.24	5.12	5.17	5.04	**1996**
5.19	5.28	5.08	5.11	5.28	5.30	**1997**
5.09	5.04	4.74	4.07	4.53	4.50	**1998**
4.69	4.87	4.82	5.02	5.23	5.36	**1999**
6.14	6.28	6.18	6.29	6.36	5.94	**2000**
3.59	3.44	2.69	2.20	1.91	1.72	**2001**
1.71	1.65	1.66	1.61	1.25	1.21	**2002**
0.92	0.97	0.96	0.94	0.95	0.91	**2003**
1.36	1.50	1.68	1.79	2.11	2.22	**2004**
3.29	3.52	3.49	3.79	3.97	3.97	**2005**
5.08	5.09	4.93	5.05	5.07	4.97	**2006**
4.96	4.32	3.99	4.00	3.35	3.07	**2007**
1.66	1.75	1.15	0.69	0.19	0.03	**2008**

BOND YIELDS 🇺🇸 MOODY'S SEASONED CORPORATE Aaa*

	JAN	FEB	MAR	APR	MAY	JUN
1950	2.57	2.58	2.58	2.60	2.61	2.62
1951	2.66	2.66	2.78	2.87	2.89	2.94
1952	2.98	2.93	2.96	2.93	2.93	2.94
1953	3.02	3.07	3.12	3.23	3.34	3.40
1954	3.06	2.95	2.86	2.85	2.88	2.90
1955	2.93	2.93	3.02	3.01	3.04	3.05
1956	3.11	3.08	3.10	3.24	3.28	3.26
1957	3.77	3.67	3.66	3.67	3.74	3.91
1958	3.60	3.59	3.63	3.60	3.57	3.57
1959	4.12	4.14	4.13	4.23	4.37	4.46
1960	4.61	4.56	4.49	4.45	4.46	4.45
1961	4.32	4.27	4.22	4.25	4.27	4.33
1962	4.42	4.42	4.39	4.33	4.28	4.28
1963	4.21	4.19	4.19	4.21	4.22	4.23
1964	4.39	4.36	4.38	4.40	4.41	4.41
1965	4.43	4.41	4.42	4.43	4.44	4.46
1966	4.74	4.78	4.92	4.96	4.98	5.07
1967	5.20	5.03	5.13	5.11	5.24	5.44
1968	6.17	6.10	6.11	6.21	6.27	6.28
1969	6.59	6.66	6.85	6.89	6.79	6.98
1970	7.91	7.93	7.84	7.83	8.11	8.48
1971	7.36	7.08	7.21	7.25	7.53	7.64
1972	7.19	7.27	7.24	7.30	7.30	7.23
1973	7.15	7.22	7.29	7.26	7.29	7.37
1974	7.83	7.85	8.01	8.25	8.37	8.47
1975	8.83	8.62	8.67	8.95	8.90	8.77
1976	8.60	8.55	8.52	8.40	8.58	8.62
1977	7.96	8.04	8.10	8.04	8.05	7.95
1978	8.41	8.47	8.47	8.56	8.69	8.76
1979	9.25	9.26	9.37	9.38	9.50	9.29
1980	11.09	12.38	12.96	12.04	10.99	10.58
1981	12.81	13.35	13.33	13.88	14.32	13.75
1982	15.18	15.27	14.58	14.46	14.26	14.81
1983	11.79	12.01	11.73	11.51	11.46	11.74
1984	12.20	12.08	12.57	12.81	13.28	13.55
1985	12.08	12.13	12.56	12.23	11.72	10.94
1986	10.05	9.67	9.00	8.79	9.09	9.13
1987	8.36	8.38	8.36	8.85	9.33	9.32
1988	9.88	9.40	9.39	9.67	9.90	9.86
1989	9.62	9.64	9.80	9.79	9.57	9.10
1990	8.99	9.22	9.37	9.46	9.47	9.26
1991	9.04	8.83	8.93	8.86	8.86	9.01
1992	8.20	8.29	8.35	8.33	8.28	8.22
1993	7.91	7.71	7.58	7.46	7.43	7.33
1994	6.92	7.08	7.48	7.88	7.99	7.97
1995	8.46	8.26	8.12	8.03	7.65	7.30
1996	6.81	6.99	7.35	7.50	7.62	7.71
1997	7.42	7.31	7.55	7.73	7.58	7.41
1998	6.61	6.67	6.72	6.69	6.69	6.53
1999	6.24	6.40	6.62	6.64	6.93	7.23
2000	7.78	7.68	7.68	7.64	7.99	7.67
2001	7.15	7.10	6.98	7.20	7.29	7.18
2002	6.55	6.51	6.81	6.76	6.75	6.63
2003	6.17	5.95	5.89	5.74	5.22	4.97
2004	5.54	5.50	5.33	5.73	6.04	6.01
2005	5.36	5.20	5.40	5.33	5.15	4.96
2006	5.29	5.35	5.53	5.84	5.95	5.89
2007	5.40	5.39	5.30	5.47	5.47	5.79
2008	5.33	5.53	5.51	5.55	5.57	5.68

* Source: Federal Reserve Bank of St. Louis, monthly data calculated as average of business days

MOODY'S SEASONED CORPORATE Aaa 🇺🇸 BOND YIELDS

JUL	AUG	SEP	OCT	NOV	DEC	
2.65	2.61	2.64	2.67	2.67	2.67	1950
2.94	2.88	2.84	2.89	2.96	3.01	1951
2.95	2.94	2.95	3.01	2.98	2.97	1952
3.28	3.24	3.29	3.16	3.11	3.13	1953
2.89	2.87	2.89	2.87	2.89	2.90	1954
3.06	3.11	3.13	3.10	3.10	3.15	1955
3.28	3.43	3.56	3.59	3.69	3.75	1956
3.99	4.10	4.12	4.10	4.08	3.81	1957
3.67	3.85	4.09	4.11	4.09	4.08	1958
4.47	4.43	4.52	4.57	4.56	4.58	1959
4.41	4.28	4.25	4.30	4.31	4.35	1960
4.41	4.45	4.45	4.42	4.39	4.42	1961
4.34	4.35	4.32	4.28	4.25	4.24	1962
4.26	4.29	4.31	4.32	4.33	4.35	1963
4.40	4.41	4.42	4.42	4.43	4.44	1964
4.48	4.49	4.52	4.56	4.60	4.68	1965
5.16	5.31	5.49	5.41	5.35	5.39	1966
5.58	5.62	5.65	5.82	6.07	6.19	1967
6.24	6.02	5.97	6.09	6.19	6.45	1968
7.08	6.97	7.14	7.33	7.35	7.72	1969
8.44	8.13	8.09	8.03	8.05	7.64	1970
7.64	7.59	7.44	7.39	7.26	7.25	1971
7.21	7.19	7.22	7.21	7.12	7.08	1972
7.45	7.68	7.63	7.60	7.67	7.68	1973
8.72	9.00	9.24	9.27	8.89	8.89	1974
8.84	8.95	8.95	8.86	8.78	8.79	1975
8.56	8.45	8.38	8.32	8.25	7.98	1976
7.94	7.98	7.92	8.04	8.08	8.19	1977
8.88	8.69	8.69	8.89	9.03	9.16	1978
9.20	9.23	9.44	10.13	10.76	10.74	1979
11.07	11.64	12.02	12.31	12.97	13.21	1980
14.38	14.89	15.49	15.40	14.22	14.23	1981
14.61	13.71	12.94	12.12	11.68	11.83	1982
12.15	12.51	12.37	12.25	12.41	12.57	1983
13.44	12.87	12.66	12.63	12.29	12.13	1984
10.97	11.05	11.07	11.02	10.55	10.16	1985
8.88	8.72	8.89	8.86	8.68	8.49	1986
9.42	9.67	10.18	10.52	10.01	10.11	1987
9.96	10.11	9.82	9.51	9.45	9.57	1988
8.93	8.96	9.01	8.92	8.89	8.86	1989
9.24	9.41	9.56	9.53	9.30	9.05	1990
9.00	8.75	8.61	8.55	8.48	8.31	1991
8.07	7.95	7.92	7.99	8.10	7.98	1992
7.17	6.85	6.66	6.67	6.93	6.93	1993
8.11	8.07	8.34	8.57	8.68	8.46	1994
7.41	7.57	7.32	7.12	7.02	6.82	1995
7.65	7.46	7.66	7.39	7.10	7.20	1996
7.14	7.22	7.15	7.00	6.87	6.76	1997
6.55	6.52	6.40	6.37	6.41	6.22	1998
7.19	7.40	7.39	7.55	7.36	7.55	1999
7.65	7.55	7.62	7.55	7.45	7.21	2000
7.13	7.02	7.17	7.03	6.97	6.77	2001
6.53	6.37	6.15	6.32	6.31	6.21	2002
5.49	5.88	5.72	5.70	5.65	5.62	2003
5.82	5.65	5.46	5.47	5.52	5.47	2004
5.06	5.09	5.13	5.35	5.42	5.37	2005
5.85	5.68	5.51	5.51	5.33	5.32	2006
5.73	5.79	5.74	5.66	5.44	5.49	2007
5.67	5.64	5.65	6.28	6.12	5.05	2008

BOND YIELDS — MOODY'S SEASONED CORPORATE Baa*

	JAN	FEB	MAR	APR	MAY	JUN
1950	3.24	3.24	3.24	3.23	3.25	3.28
1951	3.17	3.16	3.23	3.35	3.40	3.49
1952	3.59	3.53	3.51	3.50	3.49	3.50
1953	3.51	3.53	3.57	3.65	3.78	3.86
1954	3.71	3.61	3.51	3.47	3.47	3.49
1955	3.45	3.47	3.48	3.49	3.50	3.51
1956	3.60	3.58	3.60	3.68	3.73	3.76
1957	4.49	4.47	4.43	4.44	4.52	4.63
1958	4.83	4.66	4.68	4.67	4.62	4.55
1959	4.87	4.89	4.85	4.86	4.96	5.04
1960	5.34	5.34	5.25	5.20	5.28	5.26
1961	5.10	5.07	5.02	5.01	5.01	5.03
1962	5.08	5.07	5.04	5.02	5.00	5.02
1963	4.91	4.89	4.88	4.87	4.85	4.84
1964	4.83	4.83	4.83	4.85	4.85	4.85
1965	4.80	4.78	4.78	4.80	4.81	4.85
1966	5.06	5.12	5.32	5.41	5.48	5.58
1967	5.97	5.82	5.85	5.83	5.96	6.15
1968	6.84	6.80	6.85	6.97	7.03	7.07
1969	7.32	7.30	7.51	7.54	7.52	7.70
1970	8.86	8.78	8.63	8.70	8.98	9.25
1971	8.74	8.39	8.46	8.45	8.62	8.75
1972	8.23	8.23	8.24	8.24	8.23	8.20
1973	7.90	7.97	8.03	8.09	8.06	8.13
1974	8.48	8.53	8.62	8.87	9.05	9.27
1975	10.81	10.65	10.48	10.58	10.69	10.62
1976	10.41	10.24	10.12	9.94	9.86	9.89
1977	9.08	9.12	9.12	9.07	9.01	8.91
1978	9.17	9.20	9.22	9.32	9.49	9.60
1979	10.13	10.08	10.26	10.33	10.47	10.38
1980	12.42	13.57	14.45	14.19	13.17	12.71
1981	15.03	15.37	15.34	15.56	15.95	15.80
1982	17.10	17.18	16.82	16.78	16.64	16.92
1983	13.94	13.95	13.61	13.29	13.09	13.37
1984	13.65	13.59	13.99	14.31	14.74	15.05
1985	13.26	13.23	13.69	13.51	13.15	12.40
1986	11.44	11.11	10.50	10.19	10.29	10.34
1987	9.72	9.65	9.61	10.04	10.51	10.52
1988	11.07	10.62	10.57	10.90	11.04	11.00
1989	10.65	10.61	10.67	10.61	10.46	10.03
1990	9.94	10.14	10.21	10.30	10.41	10.22
1991	10.45	10.07	10.09	9.94	9.86	9.96
1992	9.13	9.23	9.25	9.21	9.13	9.05
1993	8.67	8.39	8.15	8.14	8.21	8.07
1994	7.65	7.76	8.13	8.52	8.62	8.65
1995	9.08	8.85	8.70	8.60	8.20	7.90
1996	7.47	7.63	8.03	8.19	8.30	8.40
1997	8.09	7.94	8.18	8.34	8.20	8.02
1998	7.19	7.25	7.32	7.33	7.30	7.13
1999	7.29	7.39	7.53	7.48	7.72	8.02
2000	8.33	8.29	8.37	8.40	8.90	8.48
2001	7.93	7.87	7.84	8.07	8.07	7.97
2002	7.87	7.89	8.11	8.03	8.09	7.95
2003	7.35	7.06	6.95	6.85	6.38	6.19
2004	6.44	6.27	6.11	6.46	6.75	6.78
2005	6.02	5.82	6.06	6.05	6.01	5.86
2006	6.24	6.27	6.41	6.68	6.75	6.78
2007	6.34	6.28	6.27	6.39	6.39	6.70
2008	6.54	6.82	6.89	6.97	6.93	7.07

* Source: Federal Reserve Bank of St. Louis, monthly data calculated as average of business days

MOODY'S SEASONED CORPORATE Baa* BOND YIELDS

JUL	AUG	SEP	OCT	NOV	DEC	
3.32	3.23	3.21	3.22	3.22	3.20	1950
3.53	3.50	3.46	3.50	3.56	3.61	1951
3.50	3.51	3.52	3.54	3.53	3.51	1952
3.86	3.85	3.88	3.82	3.75	3.74	1953
3.50	3.49	3.47	3.46	3.45	3.45	1954
3.52	3.56	3.59	3.59	3.58	3.62	1955
3.80	3.93	4.07	4.17	4.24	4.37	1956
4.73	4.82	4.93	4.99	5.09	5.03	1957
4.53	4.67	4.87	4.92	4.87	4.85	1958
5.08	5.09	5.18	5.28	5.26	5.28	1959
5.22	5.08	5.01	5.11	5.08	5.10	1960
5.09	5.11	5.12	5.13	5.11	5.10	1961
5.05	5.06	5.03	4.99	4.96	4.92	1962
4.84	4.83	4.84	4.83	4.84	4.85	1963
4.83	4.82	4.82	4.81	4.81	4.81	1964
4.88	4.88	4.91	4.93	4.95	5.02	1965
5.68	5.83	6.09	6.10	6.13	6.18	1966
6.26	6.33	6.40	6.52	6.72	6.93	1967
6.98	6.82	6.79	6.84	7.01	7.23	1968
7.84	7.86	8.05	8.22	8.25	8.65	1969
9.40	9.44	9.39	9.33	9.38	9.12	1970
8.76	8.76	8.59	8.48	8.38	8.38	1971
8.23	8.19	8.09	8.06	7.99	7.93	1972
8.24	8.53	8.63	8.41	8.42	8.48	1973
9.48	9.77	10.18	10.48	10.60	10.63	1974
10.55	10.59	10.61	10.62	10.56	10.56	1975
9.82	9.64	9.40	9.29	9.23	9.12	1976
8.87	8.82	8.80	8.89	8.95	8.99	1977
9.60	9.48	9.42	9.59	9.83	9.94	1978
10.29	10.35	10.54	11.40	11.99	12.06	1979
12.65	13.15	13.70	14.23	14.64	15.14	1980
16.17	16.34	16.92	17.11	16.39	16.55	1981
16.80	16.32	15.63	14.73	14.30	14.14	1982
13.39	13.64	13.55	13.46	13.61	13.75	1983
15.15	14.63	14.35	13.94	13.48	13.40	1984
12.43	12.50	12.48	12.36	11.99	11.58	1985
10.16	10.18	10.20	10.24	10.07	9.97	1986
10.61	10.80	11.31	11.62	11.23	11.29	1987
11.11	11.21	10.90	10.41	10.48	10.65	1988
9.87	9.88	9.91	9.81	9.81	9.82	1989
10.20	10.41	10.64	10.74	10.62	10.43	1990
9.89	9.65	9.51	9.49	9.45	9.26	1991
8.84	8.65	8.62	8.84	8.96	8.81	1992
7.93	7.60	7.34	7.31	7.66	7.69	1993
8.80	8.74	8.98	9.20	9.32	9.10	1994
8.04	8.19	7.93	7.75	7.68	7.49	1995
8.35	8.18	8.35	8.07	7.79	7.89	1996
7.75	7.82	7.70	7.57	7.42	7.32	1997
7.15	7.14	7.09	7.18	7.34	7.23	1998
7.95	8.15	8.20	8.38	8.15	8.19	1999
8.35	8.26	8.35	8.34	8.28	8.02	2000
7.97	7.85	8.03	7.91	7.81	8.05	2001
7.90	7.58	7.40	7.73	7.62	7.45	2002
6.62	7.01	6.79	6.73	6.66	6.60	2003
6.62	6.46	6.27	6.21	6.20	6.15	2004
5.95	5.96	6.03	6.30	6.39	6.32	2005
6.76	6.59	6.43	6.42	6.20	6.22	2006
6.65	6.65	6.59	6.48	6.40	6.65	2007
7.16	7.15	7.31	8.88	9.21	8.43	2008

FEDERAL FUNDS

FEDERAL RESERVE FEDERAL FUNDS TARGET RATE

	JAN	FEB	MAR	APR	MAY	JUN
1990						
1991	6.75	6.25	6.00	5.75	5.75	5.75
1992	4.00	4.00	4.00	3.75	3.75	3.75
1993	3.00	3.00	3.00	3.00	3.00	3.00
1994	3.00	3.25	3.50	3.75	4.25	4.25
1995	5.50	6.00	6.00	6.00	6.00	6.00
1996	5.25	5.25	5.25	5.25	5.25	5.25
1997	5.25	5.25	5.50	5.50	5.50	5.50
1998	5.50	5.50	5.50	5.50	5.50	5.50
1999	4.75	4.75	4.75	4.75	4.75	5.00
2000	5.50	5.75	6.00	6.00	6.50	6.50
2001	5.50	5.50	5.00	4.50	4.00	3.75
2002	1.75	1.75	1.75	1.75	1.75	1.75
2003	1.25	1.25	1.25	1.25	1.25	1.00
2004	1.00	1.00	1.00	1.00	1.00	1.25
2005	2.25	2.50	2.75	2.75	3.00	3.25
2006	4.50	4.50	4.75	4.75	5.00	5.25
2007	5.25	5.25	5.25	5.25	5.25	5.25
2008	3.00	3.00	2.25	2.00	2.00	2.00

Change(s) in overnight rate

Source: Federal Reserve Bank of New York

FEDERAL FUNDS TARGET RATE

FEDERAL RESERVE

JUL	AUG	SEP	OCT	NOV	DEC	
8.00	8.00	8.00	7.75	7.50	7.00	1990
5.75	5.50	5.25	5.00	4.75	4.00	1991
3.25	3.25	3.00	3.00	3.00	3.00	1992
3.00	3.00	3.00	3.00	3.00	3.00	1993
4.25	4.75	4.75	4.75	5.50	5.50	1994
5.75	5.75	5.75	5.75	5.75	5.50	1995
5.25	5.25	5.25	5.25	5.25	5.25	1996
5.50	5.50	5.50	5.50	5.50	5.50	1997
5.50	5.50	5.25	5.00	4.75	4.75	1998
5.00	5.25	5.25	5.25	5.50	5.50	1999
6.50	6.50	6.50	6.50	6.50	6.50	2000
3.75	3.50	3.00	2.50	2.00	1.75	2001
1.75	1.75	1.75	1.75	1.25	1.25	2002
1.00	1.00	1.00	1.00	1.00	1.00	2003
1.25	1.59	1.75	1.75	2.00	2.25	2004
3.25	3.50	3.75	3.75	4.00	4.25	2005
5.25	5.25	5.25	5.25	5.25	5.25	2006
5.25	5.25	4.75	4.50	4.50	4.25	2007
2.00	2.00	2.00	1.00	1.00	0 - 0.25	2008

COMMODITIES

OIL - WEST TEXAS INTERMEDIATE
CLOSING VALUES $ / bbl

	JAN	FEB	MAR	APR	MAY	JUN
1950	2.6	2.6	2.6	2.6	2.6	2.6
1951	2.6	2.6	2.6	2.6	2.6	2.6
1952	2.6	2.6	2.6	2.6	2.6	2.6
1953	2.6	2.6	2.6	2.6	2.6	2.8
1954	2.8	2.8	2.8	2.8	2.8	2.8
1955	2.8	2.8	2.8	2.8	2.8	2.8
1956	2.8	2.8	2.8	2.8	2.8	2.8
1957	2.8	3.1	3.1	3.1	3.1	3.1
1958	3.1	3.1	3.1	3.1	3.1	3.1
1959	3.0	3.0	3.0	3.0	3.0	3.0
1960	3.0	3.0	3.0	3.0	3.0	3.0
1961	3.0	3.0	3.0	3.0	3.0	3.0
1962	3.0	3.0	3.0	3.0	3.0	3.0
1963	3.0	3.0	3.0	3.0	3.0	3.0
1964	3.0	3.0	3.0	3.0	3.0	3.0
1965	2.9	2.9	2.9	2.9	2.9	2.9
1966	2.9	2.9	2.9	2.9	2.9	2.9
1967	3.0	3.0	3.0	3.0	3.0	3.0
1968	3.1	3.1	3.1	3.1	3.1	3.1
1969	3.1	3.1	3.3	3.4	3.4	3.4
1970	3.4	3.4	3.4	3.4	3.4	3.4
1971	3.6	3.6	3.6	3.6	3.6	3.6
1972	3.6	3.6	3.6	3.6	3.6	3.6
1973	3.6	3.6	3.6	3.6	3.6	3.6
1974	10.1	10.1	10.1	10.1	10.1	10.1
1975	11.2	11.2	11.2	11.2	11.2	11.2
1976	11.2	12.0	12.1	12.2	12.2	12.2
1977	13.9	13.9	13.9	13.9	13.9	13.9
1978	14.9	14.9	14.9	14.9	14.9	14.9
1979	14.9	15.9	15.9	15.9	18.1	19.1
1980	32.5	37.0	38.0	39.5	39.5	39.5
1981	38.0	38.0	38.0	38.0	38.0	36.0
1982	33.9	31.6	28.5	33.5	35.9	35.1
1983	31.2	29.0	28.8	30.6	30.0	31.0
1984	29.7	30.1	30.8	30.6	30.5	30.0
1985	25.6	27.3	28.2	28.8	27.6	27.1
1986	22.9	15.4	12.6	12.8	15.4	13.5
1987	18.7	17.7	18.3	18.6	19.4	20.0
1988	17.2	16.8	16.2	17.9	17.4	16.5
1989	18.0	17.8	19.4	21.0	20.0	20.0
1990	22.6	22.1	20.4	18.6	18.2	16.9
1991	25.0	20.5	19.9	20.8	21.2	20.2
1992	18.8	19.0	18.9	20.2	20.9	22.4
1993	19.1	20.1	20.3	20.3	19.9	19.1
1994	15.0	14.8	14.7	16.4	17.9	19.1
1995	18.0	18.5	18.6	19.9	19.7	18.4
1996	18.9	19.1	21.4	23.6	21.3	20.5
1997	25.2	22.2	21.0	19.7	20.8	19.2
1998	16.7	16.1	15.0	15.4	14.9	13.7
1999	12.5	12.0	14.7	17.3	17.8	17.9
2000	27.2	29.4	29.9	25.7	28.8	31.8
2001	29.6	29.6	27.2	27.4	28.6	27.6
2002	19.7	20.7	24.4	26.3	27.0	25.5
2003	32.9	35.9	33.6	28.3	28.1	30.7
2004	34.3	34.7	36.8	36.7	40.3	38.0
2005	46.8	48.0	54.3	53.0	49.8	56.3
2006	65.5	61.6	62.9	69.7	70.9	71.0
2007	54.6	59.3	60.6	64.0	63.5	67.5
2008	93.0	95.4	105.6	112.6	125.4	133.9

* Source: Federal Reserve

OIL - WEST TEXAS INTERMEDIATE
CLOSING VALUES $ / bbl

COMMODITIES

JUL	AUG	SEP	OCT	NOV	DEC	
2.6	2.6	2.6	2.6	2.6	2.6	1950
2.6	2.6	2.6	2.6	2.6	2.6	1951
2.6	2.6	2.6	2.6	2.6	2.6	1952
2.8	2.8	2.8	2.8	2.8	2.8	1953
2.8	2.8	2.8	2.8	2.8	2.8	1954
2.8	2.8	2.8	2.8	2.8	2.8	1955
2.8	2.8	2.8	2.8	2.8	2.8	1956
3.1	3.1	3.1	3.1	3.1	3.0	1957
3.1	3.1	3.1	3.1	3.0	3.0	1958
3.0	3.0	3.0	3.0	3.0	3.0	1959
3.0	3.0	3.0	3.0	3.0	3.0	1960
3.0	3.0	3.0	3.0	3.0	3.0	1961
3.0	3.0	3.0	3.0	3.0	3.0	1962
3.0	3.0	3.0	3.0	3.0	3.0	1963
2.9	2.9	2.9	2.9	2.9	2.9	1964
2.9	2.9	2.9	2.9	2.9	2.9	1965
2.9	2.9	3.0	3.0	3.0	3.0	1966
3.0	3.1	3.1	3.1	3.1	3.1	1967
3.1	3.1	3.1	3.1	3.1	3.1	1968
3.4	3.4	3.4	3.4	3.4	3.4	1969
3.3	3.3	3.3	3.3	3.3	3.6	1970
3.6	3.6	3.6	3.6	3.6	3.6	1971
3.6	3.6	3.6	3.6	3.6	3.6	1972
3.6	4.3	4.3	4.3	4.3	4.3	1973
10.1	10.1	10.1	11.2	11.2	11.2	1974
11.2	11.2	11.2	11.2	11.2	11.2	1975
12.2	12.2	13.9	13.9	13.9	13.9	1976
13.9	14.9	14.9	14.9	14.9	14.9	1977
14.9	14.9	14.9	14.9	14.9	14.9	1978
21.8	26.5	28.5	29.0	31.0	32.5	1979
39.5	38.0	36.0	36.0	36.0	37.0	1980
36.0	36.0	36.0	35.0	36.0	35.0	1981
34.2	34.0	35.6	35.7	34.2	31.7	1982
31.7	31.9	31.1	30.4	29.8	29.2	1983
28.8	29.3	29.3	28.8	28.1	25.4	1984
27.3	27.8	28.3	29.5	30.8	27.2	1985
11.6	15.1	14.9	14.9	15.2	16.1	1986
21.4	20.3	19.5	19.8	18.9	17.2	1987
15.5	15.5	14.5	13.8	14.0	16.3	1988
19.6	18.5	19.6	20.1	19.8	21.1	1989
18.6	27.2	33.7	35.9	32.3	27.3	1990
21.4	21.7	21.9	23.2	22.5	19.5	1991
21.8	21.4	21.9	21.7	20.3	19.4	1992
17.9	18.0	17.5	18.1	16.7	14.5	1993
19.7	18.4	17.5	17.7	18.1	17.2	1994
17.3	18.0	18.2	17.4	18.0	19.0	1995
21.3	22.0	24.0	24.9	23.7	25.4	1996
19.6	19.9	19.8	21.3	20.2	18.3	1997
14.1	13.4	15.0	14.4	12.9	11.3	1998
20.1	21.3	23.9	22.6	25.0	26.1	1999
29.8	31.2	33.9	33.1	34.4	28.5	2000
26.5	27.5	25.9	22.2	19.7	19.3	2001
26.9	28.4	29.7	28.9	26.3	29.4	2002
30.8	31.6	28.3	30.3	31.1	32.2	2003
40.7	44.9	46.0	53.1	48.5	43.3	2004
58.7	65.0	65.6	62.4	58.3	59.4	2005
74.4	73.1	63.9	58.9	59.4	62.0	2006
74.2	72.4	79.9	86.2	94.6	91.7	2007
133.4	116.6	103.9	76.7	57.4	41.0	2008

COMMODITIES 🇺🇸 GOLD $US/OZ LONDON PM MONTH CLOSE

	JAN	FEB	MAR	APR	MAY	JUN
1970	34.9	35.0	35.1	35.6	36.0	35.4
1971	37.9	38.7	38.9	39.0	40.5	40.1
1972	45.8	48.3	48.3	49.0	54.6	62.1
1973	65.1	74.2	84.4	90.5	102.0	120.1
1974	129.2	150.2	168.4	172.2	163.3	154.1
1975	175.8	181.8	178.2	167.0	167.0	166.3
1976	128.2	132.3	129.6	128.4	125.5	123.8
1977	132.3	142.8	148.9	147.3	143.0	143.0
1978	175.8	182.3	181.6	170.9	184.2	183.1
1979	233.7	251.3	240.1	245.3	274.6	277.5
1980	653.0	637.0	494.5	518.0	535.5	653.5
1981	506.5	489.0	513.8	482.8	479.3	426.0
1982	387.0	362.6	320.0	361.3	325.3	317.5
1983	499.5	408.5	414.8	429.3	437.5	416.0
1984	373.8	394.3	388.5	375.8	384.3	373.1
1985	306.7	287.8	329.3	321.4	314.0	317.8
1986	350.5	338.2	344.0	345.8	343.2	345.5
1987	400.5	405.9	405.9	453.3	451.0	447.3
1988	458.0	426.2	457.0	449.0	455.5	436.6
1989	394.0	387.0	383.2	377.6	361.8	373.0
1990	415.1	407.7	368.5	367.8	363.1	352.2
1991	366.0	362.7	355.7	357.8	360.4	368.4
1992	354.1	353.1	341.7	336.4	337.5	343.4
1993	330.5	327.6	337.8	354.3	374.8	378.5
1994	377.9	381.6	389.2	376.5	387.6	388.3
1995	374.9	376.4	392.0	389.8	384.3	387.1
1996	405.6	400.7	396.4	391.3	390.6	382.0
1997	345.5	358.6	348.2	340.2	345.6	334.6
1998	304.9	297.4	301.0	310.7	293.6	296.3
1999	285.4	287.1	279.5	286.6	268.6	261.0
2000	283.3	293.7	276.8	275.1	272.3	288.2
2001	264.5	266.7	257.7	263.2	267.5	270.6
2002	282.3	296.9	301.4	308.2	326.6	318.5
2003	367.5	347.5	334.9	336.8	361.4	346.0
2004	399.8	395.9	423.7	388.5	393.3	395.8
2005	422.2	435.5	427.5	435.7	414.5	437.1
2006	568.8	556.0	582.0	644.0	653.0	613.5
2007	650.5	664.2	661.8	677.0	659.1	650.5
2008	923.3	971.5	933.5	871.0	885.8	930.3

* Source: Bank of England

GOLD $US/OZ LONDON PM MONTH CLOSE COMMODITIES

JUL	AUG	SEP	OCT	NOV	DEC	
35.3	35.4	36.2	37.5	37.4	37.4	**1970**
41.0	42.7	42.0	42.5	42.9	43.5	**1971**
65.7	67.0	65.5	64.9	62.9	63.9	**1972**
120.2	106.8	103.0	100.1	94.8	106.7	**1973**
143.0	154.6	151.8	158.8	181.7	183.9	**1974**
166.7	159.8	141.3	142.9	138.2	140.3	**1975**
112.5	104.0	116.0	123.2	130.3	134.5	**1976**
144.1	146.0	154.1	161.5	160.1	165.0	**1977**
200.3	208.7	217.1	242.6	193.4	226.0	**1978**
296.5	315.1	397.3	382.0	415.7	512.0	**1979**
614.3	631.3	666.8	629.0	619.8	589.8	**1980**
406.0	425.5	428.8	427.0	414.5	397.5	**1981**
342.9	411.5	397.0	423.3	436.0	456.9	**1982**
422.0	414.3	405.0	382.0	405.0	382.4	**1983**
342.4	348.3	343.8	333.5	329.0	309.0	**1984**
327.5	333.3	326.5	325.1	325.3	326.8	**1985**
357.5	384.7	423.2	401.0	383.5	388.8	**1986**
462.5	453.4	459.5	468.8	492.5	484.1	**1987**
436.8	427.8	397.7	412.4	422.6	410.3	**1988**
368.3	359.8	366.5	375.3	408.2	398.6	**1989**
372.3	387.8	408.4	379.5	384.9	386.2	**1990**
362.9	347.4	354.9	357.5	366.3	353.2	**1991**
357.9	340.0	349.0	339.3	334.2	332.9	**1992**
401.8	371.6	355.5	369.6	370.9	391.8	**1993**
384.0	385.8	394.9	383.9	383.1	383.3	**1994**
383.4	382.4	384.0	382.7	387.8	387.0	**1995**
385.3	386.5	379.0	379.5	371.3	369.3	**1996**
326.4	325.4	332.1	311.4	296.8	290.2	**1997**
288.9	273.4	293.9	292.3	294.7	287.8	**1998**
255.6	254.8	299.0	299.1	291.4	290.3	**1999**
276.8	277.0	273.7	264.5	269.1	274.5	**2000**
265.9	273.0	293.1	278.8	275.5	276.5	**2001**
304.7	312.8	323.7	316.9	319.1	347.2	**2002**
354.8	375.6	388.0	386.3	398.4	416.3	**2003**
391.4	407.3	415.7	425.6	453.4	435.6	**2004**
429.0	433.3	473.3	470.8	495.7	513.0	**2005**
632.5	623.5	599.3	603.8	646.7	632.0	**2006**
665.5	672.0	743.0	789.5	783.5	833.8	**2007**
918.0	833.0	884.5	730.8	814.5	869.8	**2008**

FOREIGN EXCHANGE

FOREIGN EXCHANGE — US DOLLAR vs CDN DOLLAR MONTHLY AVG. VALUES*

	JAN		FEB		MAR		APR		MAY		JUN	
	US / CDN	CDN / US	US / CDN	CDN / US	US / CDN	CDN /US	US / CDN	CDN / US	US / CDN	CDN / US	US / CDN	CDN / US
1971	1.01	0.99	1.01	0.99	1.01	0.99	1.01	0.99	1.01	0.99	1.02	0.98
1972	1.01	0.99	1.00	1.00	1.00	1.00	0.99	1.01	0.98	1.02	0.99	1.01
1973	1.00	1.00	0.99	1.01	1.00	1.00	1.00	1.00	1.00	1.00	1.00	1.00
1974	0.99	1.01	0.97	1.03	0.97	1.03	0.96	1.04	0.96	1.04	0.97	1.03
1975	1.00	1.00	1.00	1.00	1.00	1.00	1.02	0.98	1.02	0.98	1.03	0.97
1976	1.00	1.00	0.98	1.02	0.98	1.02	0.98	1.02	0.98	1.02	0.97	1.03
1977	1.02	0.98	1.05	0.96	1.06	0.95	1.05	0.95	1.05	0.95	1.06	0.94
1978	1.11	0.90	1.12	0.90	1.13	0.88	1.13	0.88	1.12	0.89	1.12	0.89
1979	1.20	0.83	1.19	0.84	1.16	0.86	1.14	0.88	1.16	0.86	1.17	0.86
1980	1.16	0.86	1.15	0.87	1.19	0.84	1.19	0.84	1.16	0.86	1.15	0.87
1981	1.19	0.84	1.20	0.83	1.19	0.84	1.20	0.84	1.20	0.83	1.20	0.83
1982	1.20	0.84	1.23	0.81	1.23	0.81	1.22	0.82	1.24	0.80	1.29	0.77
1983	1.24	0.81	1.23	0.81	1.23	0.81	1.23	0.82	1.23	0.81	1.23	0.81
1984	1.25	0.80	1.25	0.80	1.28	0.78	1.28	0.78	1.29	0.77	1.32	0.76
1985	1.33	0.75	1.38	0.72	1.37	0.73	1.37	0.73	1.37	0.73	1.36	0.74
1986	1.42	0.70	1.42	0.70	1.40	0.72	1.37	0.73	1.38	0.72	1.39	0.72
1987	1.34	0.75	1.33	0.75	1.31	0.77	1.34	0.75	1.34	0.75	1.33	0.75
1988	1.28	0.78	1.26	0.79	1.23	0.81	1.23	0.81	1.23	0.81	1.21	0.82
1989	1.18	0.84	1.20	0.83	1.19	0.84	1.19	0.84	1.21	0.83	1.20	0.83
1990	1.19	0.84	1.19	0.84	1.17	0.85	1.17	0.86	1.17	0.85	1.17	0.86
1991	1.16	0.86	1.15	0.87	1.16	0.86	1.15	0.87	1.15	0.87	1.14	0.88
1992	1.18	0.85	1.18	0.85	1.19	0.84	1.20	0.84	1.20	0.83	1.20	0.84
1993	1.27	0.79	1.25	0.80	1.26	0.79	1.27	0.79	1.27	0.79	1.28	0.78
1994	1.33	0.75	1.35	0.74	1.38	0.72	1.38	0.72	1.38	0.72	1.38	0.72
1995	1.42	0.70	1.39	0.72	1.40	0.71	1.36	0.74	1.37	0.73	1.37	0.73
1996	1.38	0.72	1.37	0.73	1.36	0.73	1.36	0.73	1.37	0.73	1.37	0.73
1997	1.35	0.74	1.37	0.73	1.38	0.72	1.40	0.72	1.38	0.72	1.38	0.73
1998	1.46	0.68	1.42	0.70	1.42	0.70	1.43	0.70	1.45	0.69	1.47	0.68
1999	1.51	0.66	1.51	0.66	1.51	0.66	1.46	0.68	1.47	0.68	1.48	0.68
2000	1.45	0.69	1.45	0.69	1.45	0.69	1.47	0.68	1.50	0.67	1.48	0.67
2001	1.50	0.67	1.53	0.65	1.57	0.64	1.54	0.65	1.55	0.65	1.52	0.66
2002	1.59	0.63	1.60	0.62	1.59	0.63	1.57	0.64	1.53	0.65	1.51	0.66
2003	1.53	0.65	1.49	0.67	1.47	0.68	1.44	0.69	1.37	0.73	1.35	0.74
2004	1.33	0.75	1.35	0.74	1.31	0.77	1.37	0.73	1.36	0.73	1.35	0.74
2005	1.24	0.80	1.23	0.81	1.21	0.83	1.25	0.80	1.26	0.79	1.23	0.81
2006	1.15	0.87	1.14	0.88	1.16	0.86	1.12	0.89	1.09	0.91	1.11	0.90
2007	1.18	0.85	1.17	0.86	1.15	0.87	1.12	0.90	1.07	0.93	1.05	0.95
2008	1.00	1.00	0.98	1.02	1.02	0.98	1.01	0.99	0.99	1.01	1.01	0.99

Source: Federal Reserve: Avg of daily rates, noon buying rates in New York City for cable transfers payable in foreign currencies

US DOLLAR vs CDN DOLLAR
MONTHLY AVG. VALUES

FOREIGN EXCHANGE

JUL		AUG		SEP		OCT		NOV		DEC		
US / CDN	CDN / US	US / CDN	CDN / US	US / CDN	CDN / US	US / CDN	CDN / US	US / CDN	CDN / US	US / CDN	CDN / US	
1.02	0.98	1.01	0.99	1.01	0.99	1.00	1.00	1.00	1.00	1.00	1.00	1971
0.98	1.02	0.98	1.02	0.98	1.02	0.98	1.02	0.99	1.01	1.00	1.00	1972
1.00	1.00	1.01	0.99	1.01	0.99	1.00	1.00	1.00	1.00	1.00	1.00	1973
0.98	1.02	0.99	1.01	0.99	1.01	0.98	1.02	0.99	1.01	0.99	1.01	1974
1.03	0.97	1.03	0.97	1.03	0.98	1.02	0.98	1.01	0.99	1.02	0.98	1975
0.98	1.03	0.98	1.02	0.97	1.03	0.97	1.03	1.00	1.00	1.01	0.99	1976
1.07	0.94	1.07	0.93	1.07	0.93	1.11	0.90	1.11	0.90	1.09	0.91	1977
1.13	0.88	1.15	0.87	1.18	0.84	1.17	0.86	1.17	0.85	1.19	0.84	1978
1.17	0.85	1.17	0.86	1.16	0.86	1.18	0.84	1.17	0.85	1.17	0.86	1979
1.16	0.86	1.16	0.86	1.17	0.85	1.18	0.85	1.19	0.84	1.19	0.84	1980
1.23	0.81	1.20	0.83	1.21	0.83	1.20	0.83	1.18	0.85	1.19	0.84	1981
1.26	0.80	1.24	0.81	1.24	0.81	1.23	0.82	1.24	0.81	1.23	0.81	1982
1.23	0.81	1.23	0.81	1.23	0.81	1.23	0.81	1.24	0.81	1.24	0.80	1983
1.31	0.76	1.30	0.77	1.32	0.76	1.32	0.76	1.32	0.76	1.32	0.76	1984
1.35	0.74	1.37	0.73	1.37	0.73	1.37	0.73	1.38	0.72	1.40	0.72	1985
1.38	0.72	1.39	0.72	1.39	0.72	1.39	0.72	1.38	0.72	1.38	0.72	1986
1.33	0.75	1.32	0.76	1.31	0.76	1.32	0.76	1.31	0.76	1.30	0.77	1987
1.21	0.83	1.24	0.81	1.22	0.82	1.22	0.82	1.19	0.84	1.19	0.84	1988
1.18	0.85	1.18	0.85	1.18	0.85	1.17	0.85	1.16	0.86	1.16	0.86	1989
1.15	0.87	1.15	0.87	1.16	0.86	1.17	0.86	1.17	0.86	1.16	0.86	1990
1.15	0.87	1.14	0.88	1.13	0.88	1.12	0.89	1.14	0.88	1.16	0.87	1991
1.18	0.84	1.19	0.84	1.25	0.80	1.24	0.81	1.29	0.78	1.27	0.79	1992
1.29	0.78	1.32	0.76	1.33	0.75	1.32	0.76	1.34	0.75	1.33	0.75	1993
1.39	0.72	1.37	0.73	1.34	0.74	1.35	0.74	1.38	0.73	1.40	0.71	1994
1.37	0.73	1.34	0.75	1.34	0.75	1.34	0.75	1.36	0.74	1.36	0.73	1995
1.38	0.73	1.37	0.73	1.36	0.73	1.34	0.75	1.35	0.74	1.37	0.73	1996
1.38	0.72	1.39	0.72	1.38	0.72	1.41	0.71	1.43	0.70	1.43	0.70	1997
1.50	0.67	1.55	0.64	1.52	0.66	1.55	0.65	1.54	0.65	1.55	0.65	1998
1.50	0.66	1.49	0.67	1.47	0.68	1.47	0.68	1.47	0.68	1.45	0.69	1999
1.48	0.67	1.47	0.68	1.50	0.67	1.53	0.65	1.54	0.65	1.50	0.67	2000
1.53	0.65	1.54	0.65	1.58	0.63	1.58	0.63	1.58	0.63	1.59	0.63	2001
1.58	0.63	1.56	0.64	1.58	0.63	1.57	0.64	1.57	0.64	1.58	0.63	2002
1.41	0.71	1.40	0.72	1.35	0.74	1.32	0.76	1.30	0.77	1.29	0.77	2003
1.32	0.76	1.32	0.76	1.27	0.79	1.22	0.82	1.19	0.84	1.21	0.83	2004
1.23	0.81	1.19	0.84	1.17	0.86	1.17	0.85	1.17	0.86	1.16	0.86	2005
1.12	0.89	1.11	0.90	1.11	0.90	1.13	0.89	1.14	0.88	1.16	0.86	2006
1.06	0.94	1.05	0.95	1.00	1.00	0.95	1.05	0.99	1.01	0.98	1.02	2007
1.03	.97	1.06	0.94	1.06	0.94	1.22	0.82	1.24	0.81	1.22	0.82	2008

FOREIGN EXCHANGE — U.S. DOLLAR vs EURO MONTHLY AVG. VALUES

	JAN		FEB		MAR		APR		MAY		JUN	
	EUR /US	US/ EUR	EUR /US	US/ EUR	EUR /US	US/ EUR	EUR /US	US/ EUR	EUR /US	US/ EUR	EUR /US	US/ EUR
1999	1.14	0.88	1.10	0.91	1.08	0.93	1.06	0.95	1.04	0.96	1.03	0.97
2000	0.98	1.02	0.96	1.04	0.96	1.04	0.91	1.10	0.93	1.07	0.95	1.05
2001	0.93	1.07	0.92	1.09	0.88	1.14	0.89	1.13	0.85	1.18	0.85	1.18
2002	0.86	1.16	0.87	1.16	0.87	1.15	0.90	1.11	0.93	1.07	0.99	1.01
2003	1.07	0.93	1.08	0.93	1.09	0.92	1.12	0.89	1.18	0.85	1.15	0.87
2004	1.25	0.80	1.24	0.80	1.23	0.81	1.20	0.84	1.22	0.82	1.22	0.82
2005	1.30	0.77	1.33	0.75	1.30	0.77	1.29	0.77	1.23	0.81	1.21	0.83
2006	1.22	0.82	1.19	0.84	1.21	0.82	1.26	0.79	1.28	0.78	1.28	0.78
2007	1.30	0.77	1.32	0.76	1.34	0.75	1.37	0.73	1.35	0.74	1.35	0.74
2008	1.48	0.67	1.52	0.66	1.58	0.63	1.56	0.64	1.56	0.64	1.57	0.64

Source: Federal Reserve: Avg of daily rates, noon buying rates in New York City for cable transfers payable in foreign currencies

US DOLLAR vs EURO
MONTHLY AVG. VALUES

JUL EUR / US	JUL US / EUR	AUG EUR / US	AUG US / EUR	SEP EUR / US	SEP US / EUR	OCT EUR / US	OCT US / EUR	NOV EUR / US	NOV US / EUR	DEC EUR / US	DEC US / EUR	
1.07	0.94	1.06	0.95	1.06	0.94	1.05	0.95	1.01	0.99	1.01	0.99	**1999**
0.93	1.08	0.89	1.13	0.88	1.13	0.85	1.18	0.87	1.15	0.94	1.07	**2000**
0.88	1.14	0.91	1.10	0.91	1.10	0.90	1.11	0.90	1.12	0.89	1.12	**2001**
0.98	1.02	0.98	1.02	0.99	1.01	0.99	1.01	0.99	1.01	1.05	0.95	**2002**
1.12	0.89	1.10	0.91	1.17	0.86	1.16	0.86	1.20	0.83	1.26	0.79	**2003**
1.20	0.83	1.22	0.82	1.24	0.81	1.27	0.78	1.33	0.75	1.35	0.74	**2004**
1.21	0.82	1.23	0.81	1.21	0.83	1.20	0.83	1.18	0.85	1.18	0.84	**2005**
1.28	0.78	1.28	0.78	1.27	0.79	1.28	0.78	1.33	0.75	1.32	0.76	**2006**
1.37	0.73	1.36	0.73	1.42	0.70	1.45	0.69	1.47	0.68	1.46	0.68	**2007**
1.56	0.64	1.47	0.68	1.43	0.70	1.27	0.78	1.29	0.78	1.41	0.71	**2008**